Automation and Utopia

Automation and Utopia

Human Flourishing
in a World without Work

John Danaher

Harvard University Press

Cambridge, Massachusetts, and London, England   2019

First printing

Library of Congress Cataloging-in-Publication Data

Names: Danaher, John, author.
Title: Automation and utopia : human flourishing in a world without
    work / John Danaher.
Description: Cambridge, Massachusetts : Harvard University Press, 2019. |
    Includes bibliographical references and index.
Identifiers: LCCN 2019010210 | ISBN 9780674984240 (hardcover : alk. paper)
Subjects: LCSH: Utopias. | Technological unemployment. | Quality of life. |
    Human security. | Forecasting. | Human-robot interaction.
Classification: LCC HX806 .D35 2019 | DDC 335 / .02—dc23
    LC record available at https://lccn.loc.gov/2019010210

This book is dedicated to the memory of my sister Sarah (1974–2018)—someone who was not afraid to dream of a better world, and who worked every day to make it a reality

Contents

Automation and Utopia

The Autumn of Humanity

It is the autumn of humanity
and we are moments
between raindrops.

(Kaj Sotala)

HUMAN OBSOLESCENCE IS IMMINENT. We are living through an era in which our activity is becoming less and less relevant to our well-being and to the fate of our planet. This trend toward increased obsolescence is likely to continue in the future, and we must do our best to prepare ourselves and our societies for this reality. Far from being a cause for despair, this is in fact an opportunity for optimism. Harnessed in the right way, the technology that hastens our obsolescence can open us up to new utopian possibilities and enable heightened forms of human flourishing.

That, in a nutshell, is the argument of this book. But you might question its starting presumption. Is human obsolescence really imminent? Surely humans have never been more relevant than they are right now? As I write these words, there are approximately 7.6 billion people living on earth. By the time you read these words, there will be even more. Human influence and control over the planet is unprecedented. According to one estimate, a mere 10,000 years ago, the total human population, and their livestock and pets, accounted for less than 0.1 percent of the terrestrial vertebrate bio-mass. By the late twentieth century, the figure was 98 percent.[1] Humans now dominate the planet, wielding enormous technological power to shape (and despoil) its resources to their own advantage. People now refer to this era as the anthropocene in order to capture this sense that human influence is unprecedented. To suggest that humans are growing obsolete seems obtuse.

And yet that's the view that motivates this book. The meaning of "obsolescence" is crucial here. Obsolescence is the process or condition of being no longer useful or used; it is not a state of nonexistence or death. I am not suggesting, nor assuming, that humans are on the cusp of extinction, though there are some who worry that might be the case.[2] What I am suggesting is that humans are on the cusp of becoming no longer useful—that we will no longer control the fate of the planet and the fate of our species as we have done in the recent past.

The technological forces that have made our planet-wide dominance possible are the very same forces that are hastening our obsolescence. We have created complex techno-social systems to govern our lives, manufacture our goods, and supply our services. Within these systems, we increasingly outsource and automate our decision-making through the use of robotics, artificial intelligence, and other smart machines. The trend toward automation is growing. Machines are being created to anticipate our wants and needs and provide us with all the entertainment, food, and distraction we could ever desire. Soon, there will be little left for us to do except sit back and enjoy the ride. We are moving from the anthropocene to what might be called the robocene.

To some, this sounds like a profoundly depressing prognosis.[3] The purpose of this book is to challenge that attitude. Is the automated future something to be welcomed or feared? The book will defend four main propositions by way of responding to that question.

Proposition 1: The automation of work is both possible and desirable: work is bad for most people most of the time, in ways that they don't always appreciate. We should do what we can to hasten the obsolescence of humans in the arena of work.

Proposition 2: The automation of life more generally (outside of work) is a less positive thing: there are important threats to human well-being, meaning, and flourishing that are posed by the use of automating technologies in everyday life. We need to carefully manage our relationship with technology to limit those threats.

Proposition 3: One way to manage our relationship with technology would be to build a Cyborg Utopia, but it's not clear how practical or utopian this would really be: integrating ourselves with technology, so that we become cyborgs, might regress the march toward human obsolescence outside of work. Doing so may have many advantages but will also carry practical and ethical risks that make it less desirable than it first appears.

Proposition 4: Another way to manage our relationship with technology would be to build a Virtual Utopia, and this is both more practical and utopian than is commonly assumed: instead of integrating ourselves with machines in an effort to maintain our relevance in the "real" world, we could retreat to "virtual" worlds that are created and sustained by the technological infrastructure that we have built. At first glance, this seems tantamount to giving up, but there are compelling philosophical and practical reasons for favoring this approach.

These propositions will be defended in the two main parts of the book (two per part). Each of them is contentious. Objections may be bubbling to the surface of your mind already. I can only ask for your patience. We will be spending several hundred pages together, teasing out the implications of each of these four propositions, and subjecting them to scrutiny and critique.

The picture that emerges is complicated and qualified in various ways. I will not argue that our technological future is an unalloyed good or that it is a disaster-in-waiting.[4] I will instead play the role of an *axiological imagineer*. I will imagine different possible futures and explore their consequences for human value, meaning, and flourishing ("axiology" is the philosophical term for the study of value; "imagineer" is a term sometimes used to describe a creative engineer—one who imagines and develops some unusual concept or idea). This doesn't mean that I will take a disinterested and neutral perspective. On the contrary, I will argue that some futures are more desirable than others. But it does mean that I endeavor to exercise a degree of humility and balance in how I explore and defend my particular utopian vision. This is because I don't just want to convince you of particular conclusions; I want to demonstrate and develop a way of thinking about the automated future, one that will allow you to understand why I think about it in the way that I do, and to reach your own conclusions about whether I am right or wrong.

That's all before us. I want to start our journey to the automated future by providing more support for my opening contention: that human obsolescence is imminent. This is crucial to the project that lies ahead. To a large extent this book is a thought experiment. It asks the reader to suppose that human obsolescence is inevitable and to consider the consequences that might flow from this. But the book cannot be completely on the fence about the likelihood of obsolescence. Based on previous conversations I have had about this topic, I know that people will not be convinced about the need to prepare for human obsolescence unless they are given a full and vivid picture of how automating technologies are undermining (and already have undermined) the need for human activity across virtually all sectors of society. The remainder of this chapter provides the reader with this full and vivid picture by giving a brief tour of the past, present, and future of human obsolescence. Some of this may be familiar to certain readers, but I recommend reading it even if you are already fully convinced of the imminence of human obsolescence, because the examples discussed will be used again in the arguments in future chapters.

Human Obsolescence in Agriculture

Until approximately 10,000 years ago, most humans lived in small, hunter-gatherer tribes. They moved about frequently, taking what food resources they could from the animals and plants that populated the world in which they roamed.[5] They did not engage in the intentional manipulation of the gene pools of those animals and plants; they did not settle down and form complex cities, states, and governments.

That all changed with agriculture. Through a combination of ingenuity and luck, humans learned how to actively intervene in the reproductive processes of certain animals and plants. Wheat, rice, corn, potatoes, cattle, sheep, chickens, and pigs (to name but a few) all came to depend on humans for their survival. This enabled significant increases in energy capture per person and a correlated boom in population.[6] Complex, settled societies emerged, with large government officialdoms, laws, and institutions. Many of our social values around violence, equality, and sexual propriety emerged as a result of this shift from hunting and gathering to agriculture.[7]

The agricultural revolution was important in the development of human civilization, and agriculture remains central to how we feed our ever-growing populations.[8] Initially, the shift to agriculture was made possible through the use of vast quantities of human and animal labor. For a long time, the human labor was premised on the institution of slavery, and until quite recently many economies in the Western world were, in effect, agricultural in nature, with the majority of the population employed in tilling fields, harvesting crops, and tending to livestock.

All that began to change a little over two hundred years ago. According to data collected by Max Roser, in Western European countries 30–70 percent of the population was employed in agriculture in the year 1800. The lowest figure was in the United Kingdom, where the Industrial Revolution had already taken hold. By the year 2012, the figures had declined to below 5 percent. The decline has been more striking and precipitous in some countries than in others. In the United States, for example, approximately 40 percent of the population was employed in agriculture as recently as the year 1900. By the year 2000, the figure had declined to 2 percent. None of this has come at the expense of productivity. Agricultural productivity has increased throughout this period, and there has been a fairly consistent correlation between societal wealth and the decline in agricultural employment.[9]

What happened? The answer lies in technology and the rise of machine labor. Instead of requiring armies of humans and animals to do the work, farmers could rely on a handful of powerful machines. These machines could harvest crops, plant seeds, and till fields faster than any combination of human and animal ever could. They also could assist and take over in the milking, feeding, and slaughtering of livestock. A handful of humans are still required, of course, to manage the increasingly large farm enterprises and to supplement the machine labor where needed, but the masses of seasonal laborers and small-holding farmers, who made up the bulk of farm laborers in the past, have been rendered obsolete by the rise of agricultural machinery.

That's not to say that the obsolescence of humans in agriculture is complete. Certain tasks have been stubbornly resistant to automation. The most familiar example is fruit picking. Fruits are a delicate crop, easily bruised and damaged. The brute force of a harvesting machine is ill-fitted for the task of plucking them from the branches upon which they grow. Fruit picking has, consequently, remained a source of employment for many human beings, often seasonal or migrant workers, who work under dubious conditions of employment. But this too is now changing. In the United States, fruit growers are "eager for automation" due to an ongoing decline in the availability of seasonal labor, and some companies, Abundant Robotics and FFRobotics being the best known, are racing to satisfy the demand. Early trials of Abundant's apple-picking robots have been impressive and have led companies such as Google to invest in the future of the technology. The Abundant robot has been made possible by a remarkable convergence of technological advances. These include improvements to the visual processing, pattern recognition, and physical dexterity of robots, and also changes in the genetic manipulation of apple trees and the physical design of orchards. We have bred shorter, wider apple trees that yield more fruit and make it easier to engineer a robot that can identify and pick apples from their branches. Couple that with broader avenues between the rows of apple trees, and you have an environment that is ripe for automation.[10]

So while agriculture was once an arena in which human dominance was clearly expressed, it is now a testament to the growing power of the machine and the slow and steady march toward human obsolescence.

Human Obsolescence in Manufacturing

Since I started with the agricultural revolution, the next logical step is the Industrial Revolution. From about 1750 onward, our predominantly agricultural economies have been gradually displaced by predominately industrial ones. Era-defining technological developments in the processing and capturing of energy from fossil fuels led to dramatic increases in industrial output and productivity. Starting in the United Kingdom and spreading across the rest of the Western world, masses of workers migrated from the countryside to the city.[11] This led to significant social and political upheaval, particularly with the emergence of the middle class and their bourgeois values and sensibilities.[12]

The story of the Industrial Revolution was initially a story of human ingenuity and dominance. A handful of key technological innovations, such as the steam engine and the mechanical loom, yielded enormous gains in economic output. They also necessitated a significant redeployment of human labor. But unlike the agricultural revolution, the Industrial Revolution has always been premised on human obsolescence. It brought with it the first major wave of automating technologies. Skilled human labor was replaced by the relentless, and sometimes brutal, efficiency of the machine.[13]

Since then, the automation of manufacturing has been normalized and extended. The assembly line of a modern factory is the paradigm of automation. It is deeply etched into the cultural imagination as such. In some ways this is unfortunate because, as we are about to see, it is only the most visceral and obvious manifestation of automation. The industrial robots that assemble our cars and computers are impressive technological artifacts, to be sure, but they are bulky and conspicuous. There are far more pervasive and "hidden" automating technologies that are pushing back the border of human relevance.

The long, melancholy withdrawing roar of humanity can be heard throughout the modern economy.

Human Obsolescence in Finance

One place where the roar is loudest is the realm of finance. The financial system plays an important role in the efficient allocation of capital throughout the economy. Our cartoon image of the financial sector is one in which humans play a central role. The boisterous and noisy floor of the stock exchange, where densely packed traders bark "buy" and "sell" orders at each other all day long, is often at the top of people's minds when they are asked to describe the business of finance. The news media continues to promote this image by broadcasting interviews with key financial sector players from the floor of the leading stock exchanges. Furthermore, we often now lament the way in which the financial sector sucks up human labor. We complain that we are losing our "best and brightest"—where "best and brightest" means something like "Ivy League–trained mathematicians and Oxbridge–educated physicists"—to the trading houses of Wall Street and the City of London.

But this paints a misleading picture. The financial world is undoubtedly a world of outsized egos but it is not some black hole that is gradually enveloping human labor. The business of finance is the business of machines. The once-bustling floors of the stock exchanges are largely empty, little more than soundstages for the news networks.[14] The real work is conducted electronically, through underground cables and computer terminals, facilitated by hordes of trading algorithms and AI decision-support tools. These systems analyze data and execute trades. Humans continue to oversee the process, making decisions based on the data fed to them by the machines, but increasingly they don't do all that much. Although it is difficult to estimate precisely, the general consensus is that at least 50 percent of trades on US equity (namely, stock) markets are conducted by trading bots or algorithms.[15] And that figure doesn't take into account the use of AI to assist human traders in the processing and analysis of data, nor the rampant use of automation throughout the banking sector.

There are good reasons to think that the march of financial automation has only just begun. The reality is that finance, and particularly financial trading, is an area of economic activity in which automation is not just possible but essential. The markets are the natural habitats of the machine. They are electronically mediated. They are highly liquid and dynamic: there is lots of activity taking place over short timescales. The core business model of finance requires traders to spot arbitrage opportunities (price differentials between functionally equivalent assets on different markets) before their competitors do. The arbitrage opportunities can be precisely defined in mathematical and formal terms—the native language of the machine—and it can be difficult for humans to spot and calculate them in real time. They need machine assistance. As Wellman and Rajan point out, "Markets generate huge volumes of data at high velocity, which require algorithms to digest and assess. The dynamism of markets means that timely response to information is critical, providing a strong incentive to take slow humans out of the decision loop."[16]

This is creating problems. Inaptly designed automated systems can act in unpredictable and unexpected ways. And the sheer speed at which they operate can lead to sudden drops in market prices (so-called flash crashes).[17] For the time being, our "best and brightest" can work on refining these systems and ironing out their kinks. But there is every reason to expect that their role will be an increasingly diminishing one: the machines are likely to get better at spotting, executing, and possibly even creating arbitrage opportunities than their human creators could ever hope to be.

Human Obsolescence in the Professions

Knowledge has always been a valued resource. Most societies enable suitably qualified individuals to earn a premium price for dispensing their specialized knowledge to those in need. These are the so-called "professionals," with doctors and lawyers ranking among the most common and widely known. Doctors and lawyers are perennial players in the human drama, present, in some form or other, since the dawn of civilization. The practical details of their training has changed, and the specific constituents of their expert knowledge has altered, but their basic methods of service delivery have remained remarkably consistent. Doctors and lawyers meet with clients / patients, assess their cases, and, using their expert knowledge, come up with solutions to their problems. This basic business model has flourished for centuries and enabled doctors and lawyers to become highly respected, and highly rewarded, members of society. But for how much longer?

Consider the future of doctors. The job of the medical professional can be divided into three components: (i) diagnosis; (ii) treatment, and (iii) care. Medical professionals have long embraced the use of technology to assist in the performance of these tasks. For much of the history of this embrace, the belief has been that technology complements and enhances professional performance. More recently, the tide has begun to shift: the fallibility of humans, their lack of precision, their susceptibility to error and tendency toward overconfidence, makes them an obvious source of risk in the provision of medical care. Machines are now being designed, built, and implemented to replace, not simply complement, their human coworkers.

The automation of diagnosis is perhaps the best example.[18] Pioneers in the field of machine learning, such as Geoff Hinton, think the future for diagnosticians is bleak. He says it is "completely obvious" that artificially intelligent machines will replace diagnostic specialists such as radiologists within the next decade, and likens their position to that of Wile E. Coyote in the *Road Runner* cartoons: they have run off the cliff of human obsolescence but just have not looked down yet.[19] The founder of Google X, Sebastian Thrun, agrees, but provides a vision of the diagnostic future that is at once more optimistic and more dystopian. As Siddartha Mukherjee describes it, in an excellent *New Yorker* article on the use of AI in medicine, Thrun wants to create a future "medical panoptican" where we are constantly under the diagnostic scrutiny of machine-learning algorithms that can detect cancers faster, earlier, and more accurately than humans could ever hope:

> Our cell phones would analyze shifting speech patterns to diagnose Alzheimer's. A steering wheel would pick up incipient Parkinson's through small hesitations and tremors. A bathtub would perform sequential scans as you bathe, via harmless ultrasound or magnetic resonance, to determine whether there's a new mass in an ovary that requires investigation. Big Data would watch, record, and evaluate you: we would shuttle from the grasp of one algorithm to the next.[20]

There is little room for human diagnosticians in this picture. Nor is there likely to be more in other areas of medical practice either. Evidence-based medicine demands that doctors keep up-to-date with the latest research and best practices when it comes to both diagnosis and treatment. But humans cannot possibly do this. According to one calculation, a new medical paper is published, on average, every forty-one seconds. If only 2 percent of those studies were relevant to the average medical practitioner, they would have to read for twenty-one hours every day just to keep up.[21] Similarly, surgeons have long practiced their craft through the medium of robotic hands, often sitting at impressive-looking control panels while their robotic brethren tend to the patient on the table. But soon there may be no need for the control panels. Recent trials have suggested that robot surgeons can plan and perform some surgical tasks better than humans.[22] It is early days still, but we may not have long to go before human surgeons are reduced to merely supervisory roles.

The provision of the *care* element of healthcare is slightly different. Care has often struck people as something that might (and probably should) remain resistant to automation.[23] The idyllic notion is that care is a *relationship:* an interpersonal connection between a vulnerable, dependent patient and their understanding, sympathetic carer. To perform the task effectively, the carer must have some inner life: the capacity to feel and emote. Surely machines could never do that? I have my doubts,[24] but even if we would prefer it if humans performed care-related functions, we have to accept that care is also something that is increasingly subject to automation. Our world is ageing. Our growing elderly populations need to be cared for, and there are proportionately fewer young people around to shoulder the care burden. Significant resources are being invested in the design of carebots that can step in to carry this burden. Carebots are already commonplace in Japan, with some people saying that they prefer carebots to human carers, and they are being trialed across Europe, particularly for patients with dementia and early onset Alzheimer's.[25]

In short, the future of the medical profession is not one in which humans seem likely to play a major part.

What about the legal profession? The picture there is much the same. In many countries, legal professionals form tightly knit guilds, constantly resisting reform and innovation. They remain wedded to archaic work practices, dress codes, and dining rituals.[26] If you ever wander around Chancery Lane and Fleet Street in London—the traditional home to the barristerial branch of the legal profession—you would feel like you have stepped back in time. This is not just because of the architecture. The impeccably attired, occasionally bewigged lawyers also seem like they have been frozen in time in the heart of London since the seventeenth century.

This facade of antiquity masks an interior of considerable innovation and automation. Away from the Tudor facades and colonnades of Chancery Lane, the commercial law firms of London (and New York, Paris, Tokyo, and beyond) are eagerly experimenting with technological substitutes for human labor. This is happening at a remarkable pace. Much legal work involves the preparation and filing of routine documents such as boilerplate contracts, divorce proceedings, property conveyancing, personal injuries claims, court summonses, and so on. Automated document assembly systems have been developed that can generate these documents with ease.[27] Various companies specialize in providing these documents directly to the consumer, via online platforms, thereby cutting out the need to rely on a professional consultation with a lawyer. Related to this, the process of document review, long the bane of a young lawyer's life due to its mind-numbing tediousness, is being routinely automated at many firms, with companies like Deloitte offering it as a key service to their clients.

And there is more. In early 2017, a number of news outlets got quite excited about the arrival of Ross, billed as the world's first robot / AI lawyer, and being trialed by a number of leading law firms.[28] Ross, which is premised in part on IBM's Watson technology, can understand natural language, perform legal research, and assist a human lawyer in preparing materials for their clients. There are also other services, like Lex Machina, that can perform legal research and advise on case strategy, offering predictions of likely success.[29] These are just the tip of the iceberg. Big data–based modelling and AI are now being used throughout the legal system to predict, advise, and, in some cases, enforce the law.

The reality is, just as with medicine, law is a profession that is ripe for automation. More laws and regulations are being produced every year—more than any human lawyer can possibly keep up with. I can testify to this personally. I teach law to college students and am married to a professional lawyer. The increased levels of anxiety and panic associated with keeping on top of everything and making sure that you haven't overlooked some crucial new regulation or judgment that would benefit your client are palpable. Machines can manage this world far better than humans ever could.

Human Obsolescence in the Service Sector

Finance and the professions, of course, represent an elite of human workers. If their jobs are deskilled and automated, there may be little to lament. What about everyone else? Where do they find work? The answer seems to be: in the wider services sector. The obsolescence of humans in manufacturing and agriculture in Western economies has gone hand-in-hand with the rise of the services sector.[30] The term "services sector" is somewhat loosely defined, but covers skilled, dexterous physical work, such as hairdressing and food preparation, as well as emotionally intelligent affective labor, such as customer support and client relationship management. Some people think that this sector is among the greatest hopes for humanity because dexterous physical work and emotional affective labor have been historically hard to automate.[31]

But the services sector is also losing the battle. We witness this every day. Most of us will have had the experience of using self-service checkouts in supermarkets, dutifully scanning and packing the items by ourselves, and paying for them by cash, card, or phone. The use of self-service kiosks of this kind is now widespread and represents a curious mix of worker displacement and customer exploitation. The genius of the self-service kiosk is that it reduces the need for human workers (one or two workers can now supervise dozens of kiosks) and forces the customer to perform some of the labor traditionally performed by paid employees. The total automation of retail is not far away. The internet has already significantly disrupted the retail sector and automated the matching and fulfilling of customer orders. One of the pioneers in internet retail, Amazon, has created a physical grocery store that uses computer vision and sensors to track the items taken by customers from the shelves and charge them directly via an app as they leave the store. It looks like humans will prowl the stores of the future like ghosts under the watchful eye of the machine.[32]

And this is just one example of automation in the services sector. The automation of customer support services has been a long-standing source of frustration. Who has not been forced to navigate through a tedious menu of preprogrammed options just to find the answer to a simple request? But the frustration may not last long. Advances in the natural language-processing power of AI is set to revolutionize the automation of customer services, particularly with the use of chatbots to handle customer queries. In early 2018, Google wowed audiences when it demoed its AI Assistant software's ability to replicate the natural human voice when making phone calls.[33] The replication was so good that the human callers at the other end of the line seemed to have been unaware that they were dealing with a machine. According to a report published by Oracle in 2017, 78 percent of surveyed companies are already using or planning to use AI in the provision of customer services by the year 2020.[34]

The world of dexterous physical labor also looks set for considerable technological displacement. Food preparation and service had been tagged as a major growth sector for employment by the US Bureau of Labor Statistics in 2013, but there have been impressive developments in the world of robotic food preparation in the intervening years.[35] Momentum Robotics, a San Francisco–based start-up, specializes in the development of fast food–preparing robots, including a robot hamburger-chef that can churn out 400 hamburgers an hour.[36] And many bars and fast-food retail outlets are now either partially automating their services or investing in automation. And why wouldn't they? As Alex Vardakostas, founder of the automated burger restaurant Creator, observes, a robotic chef can make a perfect gourmet burger using premium ingredients for the price of a Big Mac.[37] Human workers just add cost to the bottom line.

Again, these examples just scratch the surface of the "automation wave" that is hitting the services sector.[38] The biggest wave of all is about to crash down on delivery services due to the emergence of self-driving cars, robotic ships, and delivery drones. This could displace millions of jobs in the United States alone.[39]

Human Obsolescence in Government

The picture painted thus far might seem pretty bleak. The rise of the robots is pushing humans out of the traditional sources of economic employment. But to say that we are being pushed out of the traditional sources of economic employment is not to say that we are being rendered completely obsolete. Historical consciousness is important. We must not forget that there has always been a leisured class—a set of people loosed from the necessity of labor, free to engage in "higher" pursuits. One of those higher pursuits has, classically, been seen as managing the business of government. As André Gorz notes, "in all pre-modern societies, those who performed [labor] were considered inferior. They belonged to the realm of Nature, not the human realm. They were slaves to necessity and therefore incapable of the high-mindedness and disinterestedness which would have rendered them capable of taking charge of the city state."[40]

Perhaps the retreat from the economic world of work can allow us to re-visit the premodern ideal of democratic governance, only now in a more perfect form? Instead of there being a privileged leisure class and a laboring underclass, perhaps we can all be members of the leisure class, capable of the high-mindedness and disinterestedness that is needed for the business of governance?

There is little prospect of this. The business of governance is radically different now from what it was when Socrates roamed through the agora corrupting the youth of Athens. The reason for this has to do with the evolution of social organization in both business and government. With the rise of industrialism came the rise of scientific management.[41] Managers of manufacturing plants came to view the production process itself as a machine, not just as something that involved the use of machines. The human workers were simply parts of that machine. Careful study of the organization and distribution of the machine parts could enable a more efficient production process. Much the same view has taken hold in the world of government. Sociologists since the time of Max Weber have noted the ways in which the legal-bureaucratic organization of a state is subject to the same modernizing trends as the design of industrial factories.[42] The tasks of governance are subdivided, and roles are specialized so that the business of governance can be performed as efficiently as possible. This depends on the collection and analysis of data about the society and citizens to whom the system applies, and from the dawn of the computer age attempts have been made to automate some or all of that process. Key figures in the cybernetics movement, for example, advocated the use of computerized systems of data collection, processing, and decision-making in social governance.[43] With the emergence of mass surveillance, big data, and predictive analytics, the dream of those early cyberneticists is now becoming a reality, with many processes of governance being automated or rendered susceptible to automation.[44]

One of the most striking manifestations of this comes from the world of automated law enforcement. In an effort to cut costs, and increase efficiency, many police forces are experimenting with predictive policing technologies. These technologies use data-mining algorithms to process data inputted by individual police officers about crime rates and arrest rates in different locations.[45] They then produce "heat maps" for the officers that tell them where crimes are most likely to occur, so that they can intelligently distribute scarce policing resources. This changes the nature of policing. Police officers become less reliant on judgment and intuition; they become more reliant on advice handed down to them by machines. Even more striking is the total automation of certain law enforcement activities.[46] Speed camera systems are the most obvious example of this. Speed cameras can be placed in fixed locations to record speeding data, along with license and registration details. This information can then be fed to a central processor that issues automatic speeding tickets or penalty points for your driving license. Such systems are in use in a number of countries around the world. In a similar vein, some states in the United States have experimented with the use of facial recognition algorithms in an effort to catch people using fake identities.[47] The algorithms automatically search through databases of driver license photographs, flagging any faces that look suspiciously similar, and automatically revoking the licenses of the flagged parties. This all takes place without direct human supervision or control.

Much of this automation of law enforcement is hidden from view. We have some awareness of the surveillance cameras and IT systems that make it all possible, but we often do not "see" them at work. This makes the trend toward automation in governance less salient than it might otherwise be. But it will be difficult to ignore the reality much longer. Knightscope in California has created physical robot security guards that can patrol parking lots and shopping centers.[48] The gulf state of Dubai has installed robot police officers at tourist attractions and rolled out a fleet of robotic police cars with facial recognition technology and companion drones to patrol its streets.[49] If other countries and jurisdictions follow suit, the reality of automated law enforcement may become much more tangible in the not too distant future.

You may argue that this example misses the point. Sure, we are gradually automating the provision of government services and the implementation of laws, but that's just the messy day-to-day business of government. It is not the high-minded job of making policies and settling societal values. This is the job of governance that was beloved by the leisured class of Ancient Greek males, and it is the job that may still be open to us in an era of rampant automation.

The precise role of humanity in the future of government is a topic that deserves more scrutiny.[50] The important point to make here is that although humans may continue to have input into the system of governance, we have to consider how significant that input will be. Remember that we have created governmental infrastructures that rely on the surveillance, collection, and processing of data about the citizens to whom it applies. This infrastructure has evolved and hardened over time, becoming a highly complex, not always efficiently organized, machinery of state. It makes the automation of governance not only possible but, in many instances, essential. The business of government is now too large and too complex for any individual human to truly understand. Government has to rely on machine assistance to process data and, increasingly, recommend policy and decisions.

Therefore, although we may well continue to have human legislators and human politicians—no one is envisaging a robot president or king just yet—their role in the business of government will be much diminished. They will simply supervise the machinery of state—machinery that will be made up of fewer and fewer human parts.

Human Obsolescence in Science

Although the term "Homo sapiens" translates roughly as "wise man," we are a remarkably ignorant species, evolved to make sense of the world of middle-sized objects, moving at moderate speeds, in three dimensions.[51] One of the main fruits of the modern scientific revolution, commencing around the year 1500, is the discovery of just how ignorant we are.[52] This scientific revolution has gone hand-in-hand with many of the economic and technological reforms mentioned above, and has consequently often been the catalyst of automation and human obsolescence. Nevertheless, the craft of the scientist, discovering important truths about the world and advancing the course of human knowledge, has been viewed as a more noble, humane art. It is the pursuit of knowledge for knowledge's sake, one of the highest expressions of human nature.

What's also remarkable about the history of the scientific craft is how many of its finest practitioners have come from, or been patronized by, the leisured classes. Charles Darwin, for example, was the son of a wealthy doctor and landowner, and was able to pursue his scientific inquiries in relative peace and tranquility because he was freed from the necessity of earning an income. Furthermore, Darwin was not an isolated example—many of the leading scientific lights of the time were, in effect, gentlemen of leisure, seeking knowledge without the need to worry about the economic necessities of life.[53] One could argue that this has continued to be true to the present day, since many of the leading research scientists work in universities which are, to some extent, quarantined from the economic realities of life (although this argument holds less water than it once did, as university life has become riddled with performance reviews, metrics, and targets in order to discipline the once-pampered residents of the ivory towers).

This is not the place for a lengthy diatribe about the management culture in the modern university. The important point here is that the pursuit of knowledge for knowledge's sake—if we are to take the example of history seriously—looks like something that can be pursued by a leisured class. So, once again, maybe there is no cause for concern when the wave of automation comes crashing down upon us? Maybe humans will be rendered obsolete in the world of work but will remain free to pursue scientific (and other scholarly) inquiry, much like the gentlemanly geologists of Darwin's era?

Alas, history is but a poor guide to the future of scientific inquiry. Just as the business of government (and medicine, law, and finance) has become too complex and interdependent to be conducted without machine assistance, so too has the business of science. The low-hanging fruits of scientific inquiry have all been plucked. Science is now a big data enterprise. We have entered the era of big science, where large international teams use algorithms to sort through mountains of data and computer programs to test and develop hypotheses. For now, the machines remain tools, handmaidens to their human commanders, but this is beginning to change. Two examples illustrate the shift that is underway.

The first is the emergence of automated theorem proving in the world of mathematics.[54] The prospect of this was implicit in the work of Gottlob Frege, Bertrand Russell, and Alfred North Whitehead in the late 1800s and early 1900s. They worked hard to axiomatize and formalize mathematics, laying much of the groundwork for modern computer science. The actual use of computer programs to prove mathematical theorems first made headlines in the 1970s when Kenneth Appel and Wolfgang Haken used a computer program to help them prove the four-color theorem (roughly: why do you only need four colors to color in a political map of the world?).[55] Since then, as mathematical proofs have grown in complexity, mathematicians have increasingly come to rely on computer programs to check the validity of their proofs. This has turned out to be a major boon to researchers, enabling them to prove conjectures that have remained resistant to proof for centuries.[56] While many mathematicians are skeptical of the prospect, some, such as Cambridge University's Timothy Gowers, are pushing ahead with the design of robotic mathematicians that will be able to generate and test their own mathematical conjectures.[57]

In doing so, Gowers and his colleagues can draw inspiration from a second example: the automation of biomedical research. Designing and testing drug treatments and understanding the mechanics of biomedical disease is, like all other areas of science, an increasingly complicated business. In addition to using algorithms to assist in the testing and interpretation of data, researchers have begun to create robotic scientists that are capable of generating and testing their own hypotheses. ADAM, a robot designed by researchers at Aberystwyth University in Wales, was announced as the first robot to independently discover scientific information in 2009.[58] ADAM was fed all the current scientific information about baker's yeast and used this to generate and test twenty hypotheses about its genome. It successfully identified the genes that code for certain enzymes that are crucial to the growth of baker's yeast. Since then, the same team of researchers have created another robot, EVE, which has been put to work on malaria research. It has discovered a chemical (known as TNP-470) that effectively targets an enzyme that is key to the growth of one of the parasites that causes malaria.[59]

These are still early days. The robotic scientists we have in place right now are yet to have the dramatic effects on science that they have had on agriculture and manufacturing, but the proof of concept is there. Given the historical trends, it seems like it is only a matter of time before the human scientist is rendered obsolete.

The Road Ahead

I could go on. This brief tour of the past, present, and future of human obsolescence has not even touched on the ways in which machines are helping us to solve the moral problems associated with the distribution of scarce resources, surpassing our recreational abilities at games like chess and Go, creating art, poetry, and music, and managing our interpersonal relationships.

Despite its omissions, the brief tour should impress upon the reader one critical point: everywhere you look, humanity is in retreat. The reason for this is straightforward: technology is advancing and the world is becoming more complex. These two trends go hand-in-hand, a mutually reinforcing cycle. This brings us great rewards. We are healthier, live longer, and are more productive than ever before. Nevertheless, while our societies advance, we ourselves remain relatively static, still trapped in the biological form bequeathed to us by evolution long before the agricultural revolution even began. Our achievements have been great. We have built this technologically advanced and socially complex reality. But those achievements have made it more likely that it will be machines, not humans, that manage our future. We are not built for that task.

To be clear, this litany of examples should not be mistaken for an argument. It would be all too easy to interpret this opening chapter as claiming that because humans are being replaced in various domains it follows that their obsolescence is imminent. But there are some problems with this. The most obvious is that the conclusion does not follow from the premise: just because humans are being rendered obsolete in certain domains does not necessarily imply that humans are being rendered obsolete across the board. Furthermore, this book is not in the prediction game. The intention is not to claim that some future is inevitable or unavoidable. Human agency can make some difference to how the future unfolds. The point is to think carefully about how we use that agency to craft a future worth wanting. To this end, more robust arguments in favor of the possibility and desirability of obsolescence will be presented in Part 1 of this book, when we look in more detail at the automation of work and life.

So if the purpose of this chapter has not been to make a logically watertight case for the imminence of obsolescence, what has it been? The answer: encouraging readers to undertake a perspectival shift. We live our lives in such narrow, specialized niches. We work on specialized tasks and interact with an infinitesimal fraction of our fellow human beings, and so we get a limited sense of what really is happening out there. From our specialized niches, the obsolescence of humanity may seem fanciful and far-fetched. By providing detailed examples of the trend toward obsolescence, I hope to have shocked you out of any complacency in this regard. The reality is that automation is proceeding apace on all fronts. It is happening in areas that many of us don't fully appreciate or understand, often behind closed doors, sometimes hidden in plain sight. When you finally see the scale and scope of automation, you cannot avoid the questions that motivate this book: What are we going to do as we continue to obsolesce? How will we flourish and thrive? By defending the four propositions outlined earlier in this chapter, I hope to provide some answers.

PART ONE

Automation

Proposition 1: The automation of work is both possible and desirable: work is bad for most people, most of the time, in ways that they don't always appreciate. We should do what we can to hasten the obsolescence of humans in the arena of work.

Proposition 2: The automation of life more generally (outside of work) is a less positive thing: there are important threats to human well-being, meaning, and flourishing that are posed by the use of automating technologies in everyday life. We need to carefully manage our relationship with technology to limit those threats.

CHAPTER 2

The Case for Technological Unemployment

WE SPEND MOST OF OUR LIVES DOING IT, preparing for it, talking about it, investing in it, studying for it, and complaining about it. In this chapter, I want to argue that it is possible, with the help of automating technologies, to eliminate it from our lives. I'm talking, of course, about work. Whether it is, in turn, desirable to eliminate work from our lives is a separate question, one we will consider in the next chapter. Combined, this chapter and the next will defend the first of the four propositions outlined in the introductory chapter.

In saying that it is possible to eliminate work from our lives, this chapter contributes to the "technological unemployment" debate. This is the debate about the plausibility and feasibility of widescale, technologically induced unemployment—a debate that has generated quite of lot of heat in recent years. A number of books, reports, and articles have been published examining the possibility of technological unemployment.[1] Some of these publications argue that technological unemployment is worth taking seriously; some are more skeptical. My goal in what follows is to offer a succinct, novel, and compelling argument for thinking that widescale technological unemployment is possible, even if it is not inevitable. This argument will clearly outline the logic of the case in favor of technological unemployment and will engage with the most up-to-date evidence and criticisms thereof. Even those who are familiar with the ins and outs of the technological unemployment debate should derive some value from this presentation of the argument. Nevertheless, readers who are already firmly convinced of the possibility of technological unemployment may find this novel presentation unnecessary. To those readers, I recommend skipping ahead to the diagram at the end of this chapter, which summarizes the case for technological unemployment, and proceeding to Chapter 3.

Can "Work" Really Be Eliminated?

Still here? Good. To make the case for technological unemployment, I first need to consider the nature of work itself. When I say that work can be eliminated through automation, what exactly do I mean? This is a surprisingly difficult question to answer. Any suggested definition of "work" is subject to death by a thousand objections and qualifications; and any failure to define work renders the argument for technological unemployment hostage to fortune. I know this all too well. I have been writing and speaking on the topic of work and automation for several years. Whenever I make a claim such as "work is going to be automated" or "we must prepare for a postwork society," I am quickly greeted by irate objectors who insist that work is a fundamental part of the human condition, that humans have always worked, and that we will always work, no matter how sophisticated or intelligent machines may become. In many instances I agree with these objectors, but that's because we are using the term "work" in different senses. So I have learned my lesson. It is essential to define your terms.

But in defining terms I face a dilemma. The easiest thing to do would be to use a *stipulative definition* of "work." In other words, to simply ignore everything that has been written or said about the topic of work and declare, for the purposes of this discussion but no further, that whenever I refer to "work" I am referring to a phenomenon with properties X, Y, and Z, where properties X, Y, and Z are ones that I deem important. If I follow this approach, I risk making an argument that no one really cares about. Furthermore, the word "work" is largely irrelevant to what I am doing. I may as well use the word "snuffgoogle" and proceed from there. The alternative approach is to use a definition that tracks *ordinary language usage.* Such a definition would not ignore everything that has been said and written on the topic of work. On the contrary, it would pay very close attention to it and try to set out a definition that best captured the sum total of what has been said and written. The problem with this approach is that you run into the difficulties I noted above: people use the word "work" in different, sometimes contradictory senses.

A few examples help to illustrate the problem. Bertrand Russell once said that "work is of two kinds: first, altering the position of matter at or near the earth's surface relatively to other such matter; second, telling other people to do so. The first kind is unpleasant and ill paid; the second is pleasant and highly paid."[2] As I have argued before, this is a strange definition, though it carries all the hallmarks of Russell's sardonic wit.[3] The first part adopts a broad, scientifically inspired, definition of work; the second part adopts a narrow, managerial, or consultancy-oriented definition of work. Both forms of work are then characterized in value-laden ways, with the first being viewed as unpleasant and menial and the second as parasitic and unfairly rewarded. No doubt Russell's definition captures something of the truth. But it is also deeply misleading. The first part covers pretty much all physical activity, including what we would usually call "recreation" or "play," which is not always unpleasant, and the second part is unfair to the reality of many managerial jobs.

Consider another example, this time from Peter Fleming's wonderfully pessimistic diatribe *The Mythology of Work.* The definition here is implicit rather than explicit. Fleming does not claim to be defining work, but he implicitly identifies some of what he takes to be its necessary and sufficient conditions:

> Once upon a time, in some faraway corner of that universe which is dispersed into countless solar systems, there was a planet upon which clever animals invented "work." Slowly, work lost its association with survival and self-preservation and became a painful and meaningless ritual acted out for its own sake. Taking on a hue of endlessness and inescapability, the curious invention consumed almost every part of the clever beast's lives.[4]

There is a lot of interesting stuff going on this passage. First, Fleming suggests, contrary to Russell, that work is not some basic property of the physical world (not something that takes place simply whenever matter is moved against the force of gravity); rather, it is an "invention" or, to use the philosophical term, a "social construction." He does, however, suggest that there are two types of work: work carried out solely for self-preservation and survival, and work carried out as part of a meaningless ritual. Again, I think Fleming is on to something here. I think work, as currently understood in society, is in large part a social construction, and I also think it has lost any deep connection to survival and self-preservation (although there is some connection, since we need an income to survive and work is a way of securing it). This is a theme that is taken to its logical extreme by David Graeber in his book *Bullshit Jobs*.[5] That said, I think there are also several problems with Fleming's implied definition of work. For one thing, if there is a type of work that is carried out for the purposes of survival, it is probably not best characterized as a meaningless ritual or social construction: it is essential to life. And even if we limit ourselves to the second kind of work, there is the problem that it is being defined in a wholly negative way, as a soul-destroying ritual of capitalism. Although I am, ultimately, sympathetic to this view, I do not think that it should be built into the definition of work.

I think we should strive for a definition of work that is not *over-inclusive*—does not include every physical or cognitive activity that we perform, and not *value-laden*—does not presuppose the undesirability of work. I suggest that we can avoid the sin of over-inclusivity by focusing on work in the "economic sense."[6] This is work that is done for the purposes of achieving some kind of economic reward, usually monetary or, if not monetary, easily convertible into monetary terms (so-called benefits in kind). Furthermore, I suggest that we can avoid the sin of value-ladenness by simply avoiding any presumption that work in this economic sense is necessarily evil or degrading. We may reach that conclusion eventually, through reasoned argumentation, but not through definitional fiat. Consequently, my own preferred definition of work is this:[7]

> Work: Any activity (physical, cognitive, emotional etc.) performed in exchange for an economic reward, or in the ultimate hope of receiving an economic reward.

I add the clause "in the hope of receiving" an economic reward in order to include within the remit of the definition things like entrepreneurial activities or unpaid internships that may not be immediately rewarded but are not done purely as exercises of good will or charity. I argue that the focus on work in the economic sense covers most of what people care about when they talk about work, and most of what we care about when it comes to understanding debates about the automation of work. Under this definition work is not so much an activity or set of activities, but rather a condition under which certain activities are performed. This means that what counts as work is somewhat open-ended: anything could, in principle, count as work if performed under the right conditions. Nevertheless, I freely admit that the definition does, at the present moment, exclude some activities that people often like to include within the remit of "work." For example, difficult hobbies and artistic activities not pursued for economic reward, as well as most domestic work (cleaning, cooking, childcare)—at least when performed by spouses and partners without hope or expectation of economic reward—are excluded from the definition. This is controversial since some people argue that the economic value of the latter type of labor is underappreciated. I agree with this, but its exclusion from the definition seems appropriate since the argument in this chapter (and the next) is concerned with the current status quo with respect to economically rewarded work, and not with any historical or future ideal. This is, incidentally, why the definition would also exclude things like subsistence farming or slavery from its remit. These activities would often be described as work, but would not be economically rewarded, at least not in the sense described in this chapter.

The bottom line then is that when I argue that work can and should be automated, what I mean is that *work in the economic sense* can and should be automated.[8] I do not mean that all forms of activity, be they pleasant or unpleasant, can and should be automated. Indeed, this distinction becomes critical in later chapters when I highlight and accept some of the problems with automation. It is absolutely crucial that you keep this definition and distinction in mind as you proceed. In most instances, I will simply refer to "work" in what follows. However, since my preferred definition of work is so bound up with the concept of an economic reward, I may occasionally refer to it as "paid work" or "economic work." I mean the same thing by all these terms.

The Argument for Technological Unemployment

Now that we have a clearer sense of what work is, we can make the case that the automation of work is possible. But let's be clear about the limitations of the argument from the outset. No one who argues for the possibility of technological unemployment thinks that technology is going to eliminate all forms of work. Even if we create perfect, human-equivalent androids—machines that can do everything we can do, only better, faster, and without getting tired—it is still likely that at least some humans will be gainfully employed. Instead, what proponents of technological unemployment argue is that technology will make a significant number of human workers unemployed in the near future, to such an extent that these workers will be unable to find alternative forms of work. To put it another way, what proponents of technological unemployment claim is that there will be significantly fewer workers in the future. What is meant by "significantly fewer" is open to some debate. A future in which only 10–15 percent of the population is working would certainly count; a future in which 30–40 percent are working would probably also count. This would represent a sizeable reduction from the current labor-force participation rate of approximately 60–70 percent in most developed countries. In Marxist terms, this would mean that the *surplus population* (that is, the number of people who are no longer needed for capitalistic production) is going to see a large increase as a result of technological displacement.

What argument can be made for this thesis? In a simplified, logical form, the argument is this:

(1) If technology can and will replace more and more forms of human work, and if there will be fewer and fewer alternative forms of work to which humans can migrate, then there will be technological unemployment.

(2) Technology can and will replace more and more forms of human work, and will do so in a way that results in fewer and fewer alternative forms of work to which humans can migrate.

(3) Therefore, there will be technological unemployment.

This argument is taken, with some minor modifications, from an article I previously wrote.[9] As I mentioned in that article, the first premise of this argument should be relatively uncontroversial. It is effectively a truism. The real heart of the argument is the second premise. This is the one that is likely to garner most opposition, and we will spend the majority of this chapter assessing its merits.

The initial case in its favor can be set out straightforwardly enough. It is obviously true that technology has, in the past, replaced human workers. I tried to give a full and vivid illustration of this in the first chapter. The examples discussed clearly highlight the *displacement potential* of technology. The initial case in favor of premise (2) is that current developments in the world of AI and robotics have even greater displacement potential than past technological innovations. This will result in the widescale replacement of human workers.

Chapter 1 offered only a qualitative survey of the displacement potential of modern technology. That qualitative survey may suffice for some people, but others will like some quantitative estimates of the displacement potential of AI and robotics. Fortunately, there is no shortage of such estimates. Several reports and surveys have been published over the past few years that point to significant displacement potential. The most widely cited is the report (and later article) from Osborne and Frey, which claims that 47 percent of all occupations in the United States are capable of being "computerised" in the next ten–twenty years.[10] Similar reports include (a) the McKinsey Global Institute report suggesting that 49 percent of the tasks workers currently perform have the potential to be automated through adopting current available technologies;[11] (b) the PriceWaterhouseCooper report arguing that 110 million jobs around the world are at risk of automation in the next twenty years;[12] and (c) the Institute for Public Policy Research report, which claims that one in three jobs in the UK are at risk of technological displacement.[13]

These reports would seem to bolster the case for premise (2), but we should be careful in how we interpret them. The headline figures from these studies are often cited but rarely scrutinized. Critics have argued that the figures are alarmist and based on faulty logic.[14] How exactly did the researchers arrive at them? What do they really mean? We need to dig into the details of the reports in order to answer those questions. I will do this by considering two of them in some detail: the Frey and Osborne report and the McKinsey report.

The Frey and Osborne report is, to borrow a legal term, the *locus classicus* in this field. Its headline figure—that 47 percent of all occupations in the United States are susceptible to automation—is dramatic and easy to understand. Add to this the fact that it was published by a pair of academics from a prestigious university (Oxford) and you have the perfect fodder for newspaper headline writers. But to derive this figure, Frey and Osborne adopted an abstruse methodology that provides some grounds for skepticism.

It worked like this. Frey and Osborne started by reviewing the history of automation and the current developments in AI and robotics. The history clearly highlighted to them the displacement potential of technology, and the current developments clearly suggested that machines will be capable of performing more routine workplace tasks, as well as some non-routine tasks, in the near future. Nevertheless, reviewing the current developments also revealed to them that humans would retain dominance over machines in certain forms of *perception and manipulation, creative intelligence,* and *social intelligence* for the foreseeable future. Building upon these assumptions, they then tried to create a formal estimate for the number of jobs that are likely to be automated (to be precise, they said "computerised") in the next two decades. They did this by consulting the O*NET database of US occupations. This is a database maintained by the US Department of Labor that identifies all the occupations performed by workers in the United States and gives a detailed description of the tasks performed within those occupations. This is an important database because any particular job—for example, a lawyer—is going to be made up of many different tasks—like document review and analysis, legal research, persuasion, schmoozing with clients and so on. Some of these tasks may be readily susceptible to automation, others may not. This means that if you are interested in the susceptibility of an occupation to automation it is often a mistake to focus on a high-level description of the job and better to focus on the tasks that make up the job. Frey and Osborne were cognizant of this and used the O*NET database, along with the Bureau of Labor Statistics information on employment in the United States, to correlate task lists with 702 different occupations performed by workers in the United States.

With this dataset in place, they developed some estimates for the susceptibility of these occupations to automation. They did this through a combination of subjective and objective methods. First, they organized a workshop at Oxford and, along with a group of machine-learning researchers, they "subjectively hand-labelled" seventy occupations, assigning them a score of 1 (if they thought the occupation was automatable) or 0 (if they though it was not).[15] Second, they used what they described as a more "objective" method that correlated the O*NET database's description of occupations and tasks with the three tasks that they think are currently most difficult to automate (namely, tasks involving perception and manipulation, creative intelligence, and social intelligence). They identified nine different "variables" (general descriptions of skills required for occupations) in the O*NET database that corresponded with the three types of task that are currently difficult to automate. This then allowed them to develop an algorithm that probabilistically classified the occupations based on their automation potential.

Using these two methods, they were able to divide the set of occupations up into those that were at high risk of automation (probability assessed at being greater than 0.7), medium risk (probability between 0.3 and 0.7), and low risk (probability less than 0.3). They focused solely on the list of occupations in the O*NET database as of 2010, and did not make any predictions regarding potential future occupations that could come onstream as a result of technologically induced change. This is what led them to the estimate that 47 percent of US occupations are at a high risk of automation in the next two decades.

That's the Frey and Osborne study. What about the McKinsey one? They followed a very similar approach, except that instead of focusing on occupations, they focused only on tasks, arguing that this is the correct level at which to assess automation potential.[16] They also used the O*NET database and US Bureau of Labor Statistics information to get detailed descriptions of the tasks performed by different workers. Doing so, they identified over 2,000 different work activities performed across more than 800 different occupations. They broke these activities down into eighteen performance capabilities, divided into five groups (sensory perception, cognition, natural language processing, social and emotional capacity, and physical capacity). They then estimated the level of performance for each capability required for each of the relevant tasks using *human-likeness* as the standard. This gave them a four-part classification, dividing tasks up into those that (a) did not require human-level ability; (b) required below-median level human ability; (c) required median-level human ability; and (d) required high-level human ability. They used the same classification system for assessing the performance capabilities of existing technologies. This enabled them to come up with an estimate for the likelihood of the relevant tasks being performed entirely by machines in the short- to medium-term future.

Following this method, they estimated that some tasks—for example, predictable physical activities in a predictable environment, data collection, and data processing—were highly susceptible to automation, whereas other tasks—for example, managing others, applying expertise, and unpredictable physical activities—were less susceptible to automation. By combining this assessment with an estimate as to how much time is spent in the relevant tasks across the 800 different occupations, they were able to come up with an overall assessment of the automation potential of different occupations. They repeated this methodology for forty-five other economies. They concluded that less than 5 percent of current occupations are fully automatable, but that 60 percent of occupations have at least 30 percent of activities that are automatable. Furthermore, they estimated that 49 percent of the activities that people are paid to do in the global economy could be automated by adapting currently available technologies, and the activities that fall within the "most susceptible" bracket make up 51 percent of total employment in the United States as of 2017.[17]

I have described both of these studies in considerable detail to make an important point. If you just focus on the headline figures from both reports, you might go away with the impression that the case for technological unemployment is pretty strong: just under half of all the work currently done in the world is capable of being automated in the very near future. This provides support for at least the first part of the claim made in premise (2) of the argument for technological unemployment—the claim that technology is replacing more and more forms of human work. But once you burrow into the details, you realize that things are a little more nuanced and less clear-cut. The estimates are not based on alchemy or soothsaying, but they are hardly on the level of astronomy or even weather forecasting. They depend on a lot of assumptions and subjective assessments: what is currently possible with technology, or is likely to be possible in the near future; what capacities are relevant to different tasks, and so on. Furthermore, neither study purports to address the impact of automation on future forms of work. They both focus on the automation potential of current tasks and occupations, not future ones. This is significant because it means that these studies do not address what is perhaps the major objection to the case for technological unemployment. This objection is so important that it is worth addressing it in some detail.

The Luddite Fallacy and the Complementarity Effect

The major objection to the case for technological unemployment is that it commits the "Luddite fallacy."[18] That is to say, it makes the assumption that the kinds of work we do—the tasks that are economically rewarded—are fixed in nature. If that were true, it would mean that there is only a certain number of work tasks out there, and once machines become good enough to replace humans at each of them, there will be nothing left for humans to do. The problem with this assumption, according to critics, is that it is false. There isn't a fixed amount of work out there to be done (a fixed "lump of labor"). Economies are subject to innovation and dynamic change. New jobs come onstream in line with new technologies.[19] If we take a static snapshot of the economy as it stands today, which is what the Frey and Osborne and McKinsey studies do, it may indeed be correct to say that most human workers are likely to be replaced by machines, but we cannot think about it in these static terms.

There are a few different ways to support this critique. The first, and most obvious, is to point to history. There is a reason why this is called the Luddite fallacy. The Luddites—the groups of disgruntled and displaced workers who smashed machinery in British factories in the early 1800s—were afraid of technological unemployment but—so the argument goes—they were wrong to be afraid. Employment has not vanished in the intervening 200 years. In fact, there are more people working today than ever before. They are just doing different things. This seems to be the lesson of history: human wants and needs know no obvious limit: as technology changes the material conditions of our existence, so too does it change the landscape of labor. Jobs that were unheard of 100 years ago—like computer programmer or social media adviser—become both possible and economically desirable. The critic argues that we can and should expect this historical trend to continue.[20]

There are also theoretical arguments in support of the critique. Two of the most important stem from (i) the productivity effect and (ii) the complementarity effect.[21] The effects are closely related. They both point to the same job-creating potential embedded within automating technology. The idea is this: if machines replace human workers, it will be because they perform work-related tasks in a manner that is better and / or faster and / or cheaper than human workers. This should lead to a net productivity gain, that is, more being done for less. This should have several knock-on consequences. It should reduce the costs of certain outputs on the market, which means there is more money to hire workers in other areas. Those other areas could include new industries or forms of work made possible by the technology (for example, programmer or designer of the machine) and, crucially, forms of work that are complemented by the technology and in which humans have a comparative advantage relative to machines.[22]

David Autor is one of the most forceful proponents of this critique.[23] He argues that those enamored with the idea of technological unemployment focus too much on the *substitution effect* of technology and not enough on the *complementarity effect.* Like Frey and Osborne and the authors of the McKinsey report, he emphasizes the fact that jobs are not typically made up of a single task. They are, rather, agglomerations of many tasks. Each of these tasks constitutes an input to the job as a whole. These inputs are usually complements to one another: the better you are at one of the them, the better you can become at others. This means that improving competency across the full range of job-related tasks can have a synergistic effect. The aggregate benefits, in terms of productivity or profitability, are then what count for most, not the individual tasks themselves.

To give this more flesh, consider once more the job of the lawyer. He or she must have a good working knowledge of the law, must be able to use legal research databases, must be able to craft legal arguments, meet with and advise clients, and socialize with them if needs be, negotiate settlements with other lawyers, manage their time effectively, and so on. Each of these tasks constitutes an input that contributes to their overall economic value. They

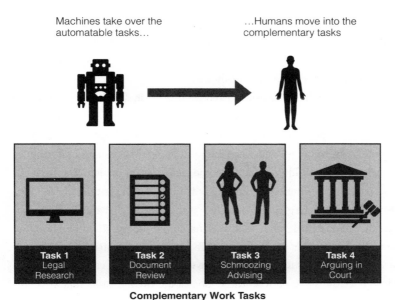

Machines take over the automatable tasks…

…Humans move into the complementary tasks

Task 1	Task 2	Task 3	Task 4
Legal Research	Document Review	Schmoozing Advising	Arguing in Court

Complementary Work Tasks

Figure 2.1 The Complementarity Effect

all complement each other: the better the lawyer is at legal research, the better the arguments they craft, and the better the advice they can provide (and so on). Now, many times these inputs are subject to specialization and differentiation within a given law firm: one lawyer will focus on schmoozing, another on negotiation, another on research and case strategy. This specialization can be a positive sum game (as Adam Smith famously pointed out): the law firm's productivity can greatly increase with the specialization. This is because it is the sum of the parts, not the individual parts, that matters.

This is important when it comes to understanding the impact of technology on labor. Experience to date suggests that when machines replace human workers they tend to replace them at specific tasks, not the full range of tasks that are relevant to the specific occupation or workplace. But since the economic value of any particular work process tends to be produced by a set of complementary input tasks, and not just a single specialized task, it does not follow that this will lead to less employment for human beings.

Humans can be redeployed to the complementary tasks, often benefitting from the efficiency gains associated with machine substitution. Indeed, lower costs and increased output in one specialized domain can increase labor output in other complementary domains.

Autor's analysis has been supported by others, including by a report on the future of jobs commissioned by the World Economic Forum. In contradistinction to the reports from Frey and Osborne and McKinsey, this report argues that, far from being a net displacer of jobs, advances in AI and robotics could help to create additional jobs. To be clear, the report is not entirely inconsistent with the other reports discussed above. It accepts that technology's share of job tasks in the global economy is going to increase from 29 percent to 42 percent between 2018 and 2022, and that in the process 75 million jobs are going to be displaced (nothing to be sniffed at). But, consistent with Autor, it argues that the very same technologies have the potential to create 133 million new jobs over the same period. These jobs would involve tasks that are complementary to the abilities of the machines. The challenge—and it is a big one—would be in retraining or reskilling workers to fulfill those roles.[24]

Four Reasons to Reject the Critique

This is, hopefully, a charitable reconstruction of the critic's view. The question is whether it has any bite. In general, I think we should be cautious about any argument that claims to know exactly what the future of work will be. This includes my argument for technological unemployment. The future is uncertain because it is subject to many difficult-to-quantify feedback loops and effects. One of the strengths of the critique is to highlight how a naive case for technological unemployment ignores these effects. Nevertheless, even if we acknowledge this uncertainty, I think there are four good reasons to think that the future of work tells against the critic's view.

To appreciate these four reasons, we need to consider the abstract structure of the critic's argument. They are arguing that technology will have a net positive (or at least neutral) feedback effect on work: it may replace humans in some work-related tasks in the short term, and thereby destroy some jobs, but it will create other opportunities in complementary tasks. They draw support for this view from historical evidence and theoretical models. To undermine their argument one simply needs to argue that there is either some flaw in these models, at least when applied to advances in robotics and AI, or some reason to think that the historical examples are not analogous to our current predicament.

The first reason to think this might be true comes from initial empirical work on the job-displacing effects of robots on the workforce. This evidence is preliminary, and I don't rest too much weight on it here, but it is nevertheless suggestive. It comes from a paper by Darren Acemoglu and Pascual Restrepo, economists at MIT and Boston University, respectively.[25] In this paper, they try to measure, empirically, the net effect of robots on the labor market. Do they displace more jobs than they create? They answered this question by studying the impact of robotization on the labor market in certain commuting zones in the United States from 1990 to 2007. They picked the commuting zones with the most exposure to robotization for this purpose, and observed that this exposure was weakly correlated with other job-displacing effects (such as offshoring). This enabled a reasonably pure estimate of the net impact of robotization on the workforce in those areas.

Their findings were significant. They estimated that the introduction of one robot worker into a given commuting zone displaced, on net, 6.2 workers in that commuting zone.[26] They were, however, careful in reading too much into this. They realized that somebody enamored with the productivity or complementarity effects of robotics could come back at this point and say, "Yes, there may be a net reduction in employment *within a particular commuting zone,* but that doesn't mean that there will be net reduction in the economy as a whole. Other commuting zones or other regions could benefit from the automation and see net increases in employment." So they looked into this possibility as well. They modeled a number of different scenarios and found that, in the aggregate, one robot would be likely to replace 5.6 workers and decrease the average wage by about 0.5 percent, across the US economy as a whole, not just within the relevant commuter zone. Nevertheless, they found that there was a range of possible outcomes and that the displacing effect could be as low as one robot replacing three workers, with a decrease of 0.25 percent in the average wage.[27]

These findings were significant for a number of reasons. First, they actually tried to empirically assess the feedback effect of robotization on employment and, in the process, found that the assumptions underlying the Luddite fallacy critique were incorrect (at least in this instance). Second, although the period of time covered by the study saw a fourfold increase in the total number of robots in the US workplace, it was still a period of time in which the overall level of robotization was relatively low: about 1 robot per 1,000 US workers.[28] Given advances in the physical and cognitive capacities of robots in the past few years, we can expect to see this figure increase more dramatically in the future. This suggests that, going forward, the displacing effect is likely to be even greater. Third, Acemoglu and Restrepo's study showed that although workers performing routine jobs in manufacturing industries were affected the worst by robotization, no class of worker saw a net gain from robotization. This is significant because it goes against one of the arguments made by Autor and others, which is that highly skilled workers with college educations are likely to gain from increased automation. Finally, the study is significant in that its authors, in their more theoretical work, are quite sympathetic to the claim that the complementarity effect should help to protect human employment.[29]

So much for the empirical findings. Another reason to doubt the Luddite fallacy is the problem of *accelerating change* and the impact it has on workers' abilities to migrate into machine-complementary work tasks. It has been widely documented that certain types of technology are subject to exponential improvements. This is particularly true in the world of information technology, where we see exponential improvements across a range of performance metrics for computer chips and processors. Futurists like Ray Kurzweil make much of these trends, as do proponents of the technological unemployment thesis like McAfee and Brynjolfsson.[30] The reason they do so is because we often underestimate the speed at which technology improves, and thereby underestimate the possibility of replacing humans in certain tasks. McAfee and Brynjolfsson point out that as recently as 2004, technological prognosticators were arguing that self-driving cars were several decades away from becoming reality, and yet here we are, a little over a decade later, with hundreds and millions of miles driven by such cars. The job-displacing potential of this development alone is breathtaking. Some 3.5 million adult Americans are directly employed in trucking, with millions more employed in subsidiary industries (like roadside motels, gas stations, and diners).[31] Many (though probably not all) of them could see their liveli-hoods evaporate in the next decade.

Accelerating change is important when it comes to understanding the case for technological unemployment because it creates a positive feedback loop between technology and the displacement of employment.[32] Remember, the critic is not claiming that machines do not replace human workers—the Luddites were not wrong: their jobs were replaced by machines—they are simply claiming that machines will complement other human skills and create other opportunities. This implies that in order to maintain their em-ployability, humans will need to retrain or upskill themselves. That is all well and good if humans are faster at retraining and upskilling than machines are at improving and developing new capacities. The problem is that this is un-likely to remain true in a world of accelerating technological change. This is compounded by the fact that retraining and upskilling large groups of humans is not a cost-free exercise. It requires significant resources and insti-tutional backing. This can be difficult in a world of political and institutional inertia.

The problem of accelerating change may be particularly challenging for younger generations. As Pol and Reveley argue, robot-induced unemploy-ment could mean that younger generations get trapped in a "cycle of immis-eration."[33] Young people are often sold college educations on the basis that it will help them find better jobs. There is reasonable empirical support for this, with evidence suggesting those with a college education earn consid-erably more over the course of their lifetimes than those without, though there is also debate about the cause of this effect.[34] This has led to a notice-able increase in the percentage of young people attending university around the world. This could be viewed in a positive light as it will enable them to develop the high-level skills they need to remain relevant in a world of in-creased automation. But there is a catch. Attending university is not cheap. Even if the tuition fees are low or free (or their payment is delayed through some conditional loan agreement), there is still considerable expense asso-ciated with accommodation, food, textbooks, and so on. Many students are required to work part-time jobs to get by. The problem is that the kinds of jobs they often work in—customer services, food service, and other forms

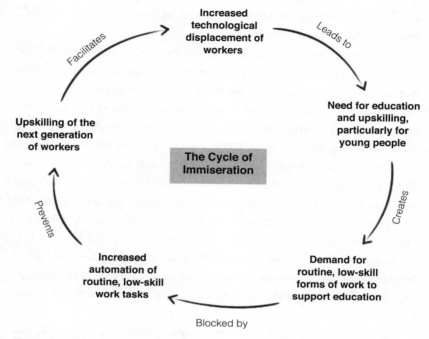

Figure 2.2 The Cycle of Immiseration

of low-skilled labor—are now becoming increasingly susceptible to automation. This creates a potential cycle of immiseration: machines increasingly substitute for young, unskilled labor, which limits the ability of young people to invest in their own skill acquisition (education) and physical capital (housing, etc.). This means they face a double disadvantage: increased susceptibility to automation and decreased capacity to upskill. The ability of the human population as a whole to renew itself in the face of technologically induced displacement is, consequently, limited.

This point about accelerating technological change and institutional / human inertia needs to be finessed. Accelerating change is not an immutable law of nature. Rapid innovation and technological disruption themselves require considerable institutional and societal support. When new discoveries are made and new technologies invented, there is often a flood of improvements and advances early on—as the low-hanging fruit of innovation are plucked—then it gets more difficult. More time, money, and effort have to be invested to secure the same, or reduced, returns.[35] There is some sign of a recent slowdown in Moore's Law (the most famous example of accelerating technological improvement in the ICT industry), and recent research by Nicholas Bloom and his colleagues at Stanford University and MIT—reported in their paper "Are Ideas Getting Harder to Find?"—suggests that we are only maintaining current rates of innovation through increased spending.[36] It's possible that we will stop doing this and thus the disruptive impact of technology on work will be halted. But let's be clear that we don't currently know when that will be. There are still plenty of applications of existing automating technologies that have yet to be tried and refined, and these applications are likely to have a significant impact on employment opportunities, based on what we currently know (again, the nascent impact of automated transport should be borne in mind). And recall that it is relative rates of change that matter: even if the rate of technological innovation eventually slows down, to make a difference it will have to slow down to below the rate at which humans can improve or enhance themselves. Since it is currently taking twenty to thirty years to train humans into increasingly precarious jobs, that does not appear to be a likely prospect. Furthermore, even if we do have to invest more to maintain accelerating change, and even if that ultimately comes at the expense of human workers, we may wish to make that tradeoff if doing so unlocks the potential of a post-work world. The desirability of workplace automation is a crucial factor in how we think about the merits of any investment strategy. The desirability of such automation will be the focus of future chapters.

A third reason to doubt the critic's argument stems from the nature of automating technology itself. The current furor over technological unemployment is caused by advances in AI and robotics. These technologies have certain properties that make their employment-displacing effects larger than might be appreciated. As Brynjolfsson, Rock, and Syverson point out, AI (and by extension robotics) is a "general purpose technology" (GPT), that is, something that changes how work gets done in general, and not just in specific industries.[37] Historical GPTs would include electronics, steam power, and information technology. These technologies took a while to get fully embedded in society, but once they did, they radically changed how commerce worked. This was because developments in the GPTs tended to *complement* one another. Consider the example of the steam engine:

> The steam engine not only helped pump water from coal mines, its most important initial application, but also spurred the invention of more effective factory machinery and new forms of transportation like steamships and railroads. In turn, these co-inventions helped to give rise to innovations in supply chains and mass marketing, to new organizations with hundreds and thousands of employees, and even to seemingly unrelated innovations like standard time, which was needed to manage railroad schedules.[38]

The rebuttal to the critic's argument is that developments in AI and robotics could have similar complementarity effects: improvements in one aspect of AI—for example, natural language processing—could complement improvements in other aspects of AI—for example, data mining and predictive analytics. What's more, these improvements could be integrated on top of existing technological infrastructures, such as those provided by information communications technologies, to create an economic environment in which human workers become ever less relevant. Indeed, we already see this happening. Take the world of finance and trading. As noted in Chapter 1, trading algorithms are now responsible for more than half of all trades executed on securities markets. Why is this? Because the trading environment is one that rewards an ability to respond quickly to changes in information, to spot patterns, and to make predictions. These are capacities at which machines excel and humans do not. The trading ecosystem is, consequently, one in which machines complement one another. You can imagine this complementarity extending even further when these high-speed trading algorithms are combined with developments in natural language processing and speech recognition, to create a world in which investors not only have all their investing done by machines, but are also informed and reassured by tireless teams of robo-advisers.

The complementarity of machines to one another undermines the argument made by David Autor concerning the complementary of humans and machines. Autor's complementarity effect is too narrow. It focuses on how the advent of machines that are good at one particular work task can prompt human workers to move into complementary work tasks. This ignores the fact that developments in technology do not proceed along a single track. There are multiple complementary technological developments occurring at any one time. We ignore this at our peril. When combined, multiple complementary technological developments can create a work environment that is not fit for humans and where humans have no complementary tasks to which they can migrate.

Autor himself might like to resist this argument by claiming that there are certain things that humans will always do better than machines, and hence there will always be complementary tasks to which they can migrate. But how confident can we be of this? Autor uses the work of Michael Polanyi to argue in favor of enduring human complementarity.[39] Polanyi was famous for writing about the "tacit dimension" of human knowledge. He argued that, to a large extent, human know-how depended on skills and rulesets that are often beneath our conscious awareness—ones that are transmitted to us via culture, tradition, evolution, and so on. These forms of knowledge are not easily describable or formalizable. It has long been known by computer scientists and roboticists that this tacit dimension to human knowledge is the hardest to automate. Hans Moravec observed back in the 1980s that it was relatively easy to automate highly abstract cognitive abilities, such as the ability to play chess, because those abilities were easily translatable into computer code. It was much more difficult to automate low-level sensorimotor skills, such as the ability to catch a ball, because these skills were tacit.[40] This subsequently became known as Moravec's Paradox. For some odd reason, Autor decides to rename this Polanyi's Paradox and argues that it provides a significant bulwark for humanity in the face of machine domination. It means that tacit human know-how will be a continuing source of human-to-machine complementarity.

But this is not really that reassuring. For one thing, as Autor himself acknowledges, the dexterous sensorimotor skills that are most difficult for machines are not particularly well-rewarded in the labor market. Indeed, they are often the most precarious and poorly paid (more on this in Chapter 3). For another thing, Autor's argument fails to fully appreciate the robotics and AI revolution that has taken place over the last thirty years. This revolution is enabling machines to develop the tacit know-how—natural language processing, image recognition, speech recognition, and even driving—that was once the exclusive domain of humans. If the revolution continues, there is every reason to doubt whether even these poorly paid forms of work will remain viable for humans.

Autor claims to be unimpressed by these developments. He thinks that technologists really only have two techniques for creating machines that can overcome Moravec's / Polanyi's Paradox. They are (a) *environmental control*—control, manipulate, and simplify the task environment in such a way that it is easier for machines to perform the task; and (b) *machine learning*—get the machine to mimic tacit human judgment by using bottom-up machine-learning techniques that train computer programs on large datasets rather than top-down programming. Autor thinks that both techniques are limited. Simplifying the task environment is only appropriate in some cases, and also means that machines are unable to adapt to sudden changes in the task environment. Human dexterity is still essential. Autor pours similar cold water on the machine-learning revolution, though his argument here is more opinion driven, claiming that he is unimpressed and underwhelmed by machine-learning systems like recommendation algorithms and IBM's Watson. Autor accepts that we are still in the early days of this technology but he thinks there may still be fundamental problems with the systems being developed, particularly when it comes to creating machines that can reason about purpose and intention. He concludes that there will continue to be a range of skilled jobs that require human flexibility and adaptability and that they will continue to complement the rise of the machines, and that the real problem is not so much the continuing relevance of humans but the fact that our educational systems (and here he is speaking of the United States) are not well set up to provide the training that future workers require (not an insignificant hurdle).[41]

But Autor's argument is unconvincing. Predictions about future technologies should definitely be grounded in empirical realities about current technologies, but there is always a risk of narrow-mindedness when it comes to drawing inferences from those realities to the likely future of work. Autor's critique is narrow-minded in that it fails to consider the impact of accelerating, broadly distributed, technological change on the labor market. Autor is unimpressed by what he sees, but what he sees is a static and faulty picture of how machines are likely to replace human workers. Autor assumes that if machines are not as flexible and adaptable as we are, they won't fully replace us. But this ignores the critical point that advances in robotics and AI can complement one another (namely, that there is a *machine complementarity effect*), and in doing can unlock advantages to non-human-likeness in the design of work environments and the performance of work-related tasks.[42]

This is something that Jerry Kaplan illustrates quite nicely in his book *Humans Need Not Apply.*[43] Kaplan makes the point that you need four things to accomplish any task, be it work related or not: (i) sensory data; (ii) energy; (iii) reasoning ability; and (iv) actuating power. In human beings, all four of these things have been integrated into one biological unit (the brain-body complex). In robots, these things can be distributed across large environments in unusual ways: teams of smart devices can provide the sensory data; reasoning can be centralized in server farms or in the "cloud"; and signals can be sent out to teams of actuating devices. Kaplan gives the example of a robot painter. You could imagine a robot painter as a single humanoid object, climbing ladders and applying paint with a brush; or, more likely, you could imagine it as a swarm of drones, applying paint through a spray-on nozzle, controlled by some centralized or distributed AI program. The entire distributed system may look nothing like a human worker; but it still replaces what the human used to do. This replacement is what matters, not the surface appearance. When Autor looks at warehouse-stacking robots or self-driving cars, he may be unimpressed because they don't look or act like human workers, but he overlooks how they may be merely one component in a larger integrated robotic system that has the net effect of replacing human workers. In other words, he draws a faulty inference about technological limitations by assuming that technology must be humanlike. This criticism is reinforced by the fact that, in his discussion, Autor appears to treat environmental control and machine learning as independent solutions to Moravec's/Polanyi's Paradox. But they are not: they are complementary solutions. Technologists work on simplifying work environments and improving machine-learning problem solving. The combination of both has much greater displacing potential than either in isolation.

This brings me to the fourth and final reason to doubt the critic of technological unemployment: the growth of "superstar" or "winner-takes-all" markets. Remember, a key assumption of the critic's position is that technology will create new employment opportunities: jobs that don't exist yet will become both possible and economically feasible in the wake of technological progress. There is no reason to doubt that this will happen to at least some extent. But there is reason to doubt that it will result in many new jobs. That reason has to do with the growth of superstar markets. The idea of a superstar market was first formalized by the economist Sherwin Rosen in the early 1980s. He defined a superstar market as being one "wherein relatively small numbers of people [the 'superstars'] earn enormous sums of money and dominate the activities in which they engage."[44] Famous examples of such markets include markets for musicians, sports stars, and artists. Rosen suggested that the phenomenon was becoming more pronounced in the 1980s. Since then it has blossomed even further.[45] This is due, in large part, to information technology and globalization. These twin phenomena have created global markets for producing and distributing physical and digital goods and services. Within such global markets, it is possible for a few superstar companies to dominate their respective markets (think Amazon, Alibaba, Google, Facebook, and Apple) and to do so without employing that many people, certainly not as many as the large commercial enterprises of the past. Add to this the fact that many of the technological developments that make such markets possible—increased internet penetration; the digitization of goods and services; the rise of wearable / portable computing and 3D printing—also enable people to produce goods and services at near-zero marginal cost and you have a recipe for fewer jobs and less profit.[46] The net effect for consumers may be terrific; for workers, much less so.

In sum, these four reasons—*initial evidence on the equilibrium effects of robotization, accelerating technological change, the general purpose nature of AI and machine complementarity,* and *the growth of superstar markets*— call into question the critic's view. At the very least, they make the elimination of most forms of work through automation a real possibility.

Two Further Doubts about Technological Unemployment

There are two additional concerns about the case for technological unemployment that are worth addressing before moving on.

The first is that the case described so far overlooks the social and regulatory impediments to workplace automation. The story of William Lee is often trotted out to make this point.[47] Lee was an English clergyman who lived in the second half of the sixteenth century. He invented the world's first knitting machine, a device that partly automated the task of knitting garments, and which is still in use, in slightly modified form, to this day. Lee was famously refused a patent for his machine by Queen Elizabeth I on the grounds that its widespread use would threaten the livelihoods of knitters.[48] This is supposedly a classic example of how legal and regulatory authority can be used to slow down the technological displacement of human workers. Recently, some authors have argued that similar impediments could help slow down the next wave of automation. Upchurch and Moore, for instance, argue that the much-touted revolution in self-driving cars is going to be scuppered by both social unease and legal resistance (liability issues, lack of insurance, etc.) to their widespread deployment.[49]

But this is a weak objection. Legal and regulatory impediments to automation are usually only temporary in nature, and typically fail if the technology has some genuine economic advantages over human workers. William Lee's knitting machine is, in fact, an illustration of this. Once rejected by Queen Elizabeth I, Lee went to France and found that the king of France (the Huguenot Henry IV) was willing to grant him a patent. In the long run, his device became commonplace, and the knitters that so concerned Elizabeth I were replaced. Something similar is likely to happen with the self-driving car and other innovations in automation. Some countries or jurisdictions may be resistant, but others will be more willing to experiment (if only to signal a willingness to do business with powerful tech companies), and in the long run no legal barrier is likely to remain if self-driving cars are, as the manufacturers claim, safer and more reliable than human-driven vehicles. Furthermore, legal and regulatory impediments to automation are, strictly speaking, optional. If, as I will argue in the next chapter, the automation of work is often desirable, they are an option we should be reluctant to exercise.

The second concern about technological unemployment is that it is unsustainable. A capitalist consumerist economy, it is argued, cannot function if a significant percentage of the adult population is unemployed. This concern is often illustrated by the story of Henry Ford Jr and Walter Reuther. Reuther was the head of a trade union representing automobile workers. He was given a tour of one of Ford's new factories. The factory was replete with new machinery, all capable of automating the tasks of assembly line workers. As Reuther was contemplating this brave new world, Ford asked, with some glee, how Reuther was going to get these machines to pay union dues. Reuther, quick off the mark, responded by asking Ford how he was going to get them to pay for his new cars. This story is probably apocryphal, but too good not to tell. It perfectly illustrates the *unsustainability concern:* capitalist economies depend on consumers, and consumers depend on wages; if automation eliminates workers, it also eliminates consumers. The system can absorb some of this loss—perhaps by wealthier individuals taking on more consumption—but there are limits. If the consumer base is too depleted, the whole system will unravel: capitalists will stop making money and so will not be able to afford any more investment in automation.

This concern sounds plausible in broad outline—there must be some upper limit to the amount of automation the capitalist system can sustain without precipitating a major crisis—but there are three problems with it. First, it's not clear when the crisis point will be reached. As many a world-weary Marxist will tell you, capitalism has weathered past crises surprisingly well. How many unemployed people does it take for it to become truly unsustainable? Nowadays, the labor participation rate hovers around 60–70 percent in most developed countries. Could it drop as low as 30 percent or 15 percent and still remain viable? There is no way of knowing for sure right now. Second, the unsustainability argument overlooks ways in which the system could adapt in order to sustain a larger population of unemployed people. Increased tax and transfer, and the possibility of a guaranteed minimum income, are just some of the options that have been touted in recent years as a response to the problem of unsustainability.[50] Third, the argument doesn't address the issue of desirability. If automation results in masses of unemployed, surplus populations living in destitution, that would undoubtedly be a terrible thing. But if the state of unemployment could be better than that of working—if we have good reason to desire the automation of work—then unsustainability may not be an issue after all.

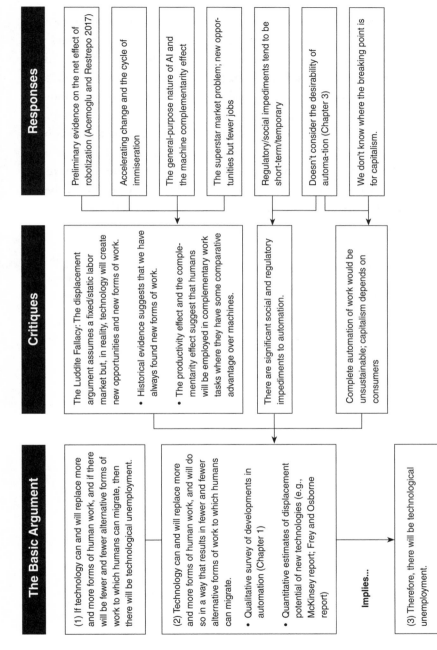

The Basic Argument

(1) If technology can and will replace more and more forms of human work, and if there will be fewer and fewer alternative forms of work to which humans can migrate, then there will be technological unemployment.

(2) Technology can and will replace more and more forms of human work, and will do so in a way that results in fewer and fewer alternative forms of work to which humans can migrate.

• Qualitative survey of developments in automation (Chapter 1)

• Quantitative estimates of displacement potential of new technologies (e.g., McKinsey report; Frey and Osborne report)

Implies...

(3) Therefore, there will be technological unemployment.

Critiques

The Luddite Fallacy: The displacement argument assumes a fixed/static labor market but, in reality, technology will create new opportunities and new forms of work.

• Historical evidence suggests that we have always found new forms of work.

• The productivity effect and the complementarity effect suggest that humans will be employed in complementary work tasks where they have some comparative advantage over machines.

There are significant social and regulatory impediments to automation.

Complete automation of work would be unsustainable; capitalism depends on consumers

Responses

Preliminary evidence on the net effect of robotization (Acemoglu and Restrepo 2017)

Accelerating change and the cycle of immiseration

The general-purpose nature of AI and the machine complementarity effect

The superstar market problem; new opportunities but fewer jobs

Regulatory/social impediments tend to be short-term/temporary

Doesn't consider the desirability of automa-tion (Chapter 3)

We don't know where the breaking point is for capitalism.

Figure 2.3 The Case for Technological Unemployment (Summarized)

Conclusion

Let's get our bearings before moving on. The purpose of this chapter was to defend the claim that the automation of work is possible. To that end, I offered a definition of work as the performance of skills or activities for economic reward ("paid work" or "work in the economic sense"). I then set out the basic argument for technological unemployment—namely, the wide-scale automation of work in the economic sense. I identified the leading objection to it—the Luddite Fallacy—and offered four responses to this objection. I also noted some additional concerns—social / regulatory impediment and unsustainability—but suggested that they did not undermine the basic case for technological unemployment and left unresolved the further question of the desirability of workplace automation. It is to the desirability question that we turn in the next chapter.

CHAPTER 3

Why You Should Hate Your Job

YOU PROBABLY HAVE A JOB. You may like that job, possibly even love it. It may be the essence of who you are: the thing that gets you out of bed in the morning and gives you a sense of purpose in life. My goal in this chapter is to convince you that you are wrong to feel this way. Even if your job seems good to you right now, you should resent living in a world that requires you to work for a living. To put it bluntly: I will be arguing that work is bad and getting worse, and we should welcome its technological elimination. This is the desirability claim that forms the second half of the first proposition introduced in Chapter 1.

Let me start, however, with a confession: I'm one of those people who loves their job. It is the core of who I am. So in arguing that work is bad, I'm arguing against my own day-to-day experience of work. This makes the argument I'm defending a tough sell, even to myself. It is, consequently, important to clarify the structure and scope of the argument.

There are a few different ways to defend the view that work is bad. One way would be to point to specific forms of work and argue that they are bad in one or more senses (for example, bad for your health, poorly paid, physically and mentally abusive, and so on). I call this the "contingency" strategy because its persuasiveness depends on the contingent features of specific forms of work. It's obviously not a very robust way of defending the badness of work since it may be possible to reform or eliminate these contingent features or to simply find another form of work. It also would not be consistent with the definition and understanding of work that was outlined in Chapter 2, wherein work was not defined as a specific activity or set of activities, but rather a condition under which activities are performed. An alternative strategy would be to argue that all forms of work are, necessarily and inherently, bad (for example, because working for economic reward is inherently unjust or freedom undermining). I call this the "necessity" strategy because it claims that the badness of work is not dependent on contingent features of particular jobs, but rather is inherent to all jobs. This would be consistent with the previous definition of work, and in an earlier article I endorsed this line of argument since it is obviously the strongest way in which to defend the badness thesis.[1] But I now think that the necessity strategy goes too far, partly because it contradicts many people's day-to-day experience of work, and partly because some of the features to which it points (injustice and unfreedom) are present in the absence of work, as I shall be keen to point out in later chapters.

Consequently, I now favor an alternative strategy for defending the badness of work. This strategy hovers between the two extremes of contingency and necessity. It argues that work is structurally bad.[2] This means that its badness is not wholly contingent on the form of work nor intrinsic to all forms of work, but is the result of the social or institutional structure within which it takes place. To state the idea more clearly:

> *Structural Badness of Work:* The labor market in most developed countries has settled into an equilibrium pattern that makes work very bad for many people, that is getting worse as a result of technical and institutional changes, and that is very difficult to reform or improve in such a way as to remove its bad-making properties.

Another way of putting it—which will be described in more detail later—is that the badness of work is the result of a *collective action problem,* whereby the individually rational behavior of workers and employers is resulting in a social arrangement that is bad (and getting worse) for most workers.

If this claim seems *prima facie* absurd to you, it will be useful to remember from Chapter 2 that I am not claiming that all forms of physical or mental activity are bad—that would obviously be absurd. Some people have very broad definitions of work and they sometimes think that this is what I am trying to argue. I am not. I am only arguing that the performance of physical and mental tasks in return for economic reward, given the structural and institutional features of our modern economy, is bad. Furthermore, because my claim is about the structure of work in modern society, I am perfectly willing to accept that particular forms of work could be very good for some people (myself included). There may be pockets of joy within the structure of suffering.

In what follows, I will defend the structural badness of work by describing five specific features of work in the modern world that make it structurally bad. I will respond to the major criticisms of this negative view of work as I go along.

Five Reasons to Hate Your Job

The structural badness argument has two parts to it. The first part consists in identifying the features of work in the modern world that make it bad for most workers; the second part consists in arguing that these features are difficult to reform or change. I'll start by focusing on five features of work in the modern world that make it bad for most workers. In brief outline, they are:

> *The Problem of Dominating Influence:* Employment contracts, and, more generally, the state of being employed, typically give employers an unjust dominating power over the lives of workers. This significantly undermines the freedom of workers.
>
> *The Problem of Fissuring and Precarity:* The working environment is becoming increasingly *fissured,* and working conditions are becoming increasingly *precarious* for many workers. This makes working life more unpleasant and stressful.
>
> *The Problem of Distributive Injustice:* Work is distributively unjust. Technology is resulting in an increasingly *polarized* workforce in

which a small number of highly paid individuals reap most of the economic rewards, and these rewards are not, in any obvious way, proportional to effort or merit.

The Problem of Temporal Colonization: Work colonizes our lives. Most of our mental and physical effort is taken up with preparing for, performing, or recovering from work. What's more, this colonization is getting worse as a result of technology.

The Problem of Unhappiness and Dissatisfaction: Most people are dissatisfied with their work and think they could do better, and this makes it difficult to justify the other bad-making features of work.

I will present each of these five problems as distinct antiwork arguments. As will become clear, they reinforce and complement one another.

The Problem of Dominating Influence

The first argument claims that work is a significant source of freedom-undermining domination in our lives. We will build up to this argument gradually by considering a general question: What system of governance is the most antithetical to individual liberty? The communist dictatorships of the twentieth century must be up there. Consider Elizabeth Anderson's description of what it would be like to live under such a system:

> Imagine a government that assigns almost everyone a superior whom they must obey. Although superiors give most inferiors a routine to follow, there is no rule of law. Orders may be arbitrary and can change at any time, without prior notice or opportunity to appeal. Superiors are unaccountable to those they order around. They are neither elected nor removable by their inferiors. Inferiors have no right to complain about how they are being treated, except in a few narrowly defined cases. They also have no right to be consulted about the orders they are given. There are multiple ranks in the society ruled by this government. The content of the orders people receive varies, depending on their rank. Higher-ranked individuals may be granted considerable

freedom in deciding how to carry out their orders, and may issue some orders to inferiors. The most highly ranked individual takes no order but issues many. The lowest-ranked may have their bodily movements and speech minutely regulated for most of the day.[3]

Would you like to live under such a system of government? Surely not. It has all the hallmarks of injustice and tyranny. Unless you were lucky enough to be the highest-ranked individual, you would live your life at the arbitrary mercy of others, always trying to ensure their good graces and avoid their wrath. The psychological turmoil and constriction would be immense.

There is a philosophical term for this kind of injustice: it's called *domination*. It is the antithesis of freedom. Freedom is usually thought to be a good thing. Contemporary liberal democratic societies place great emphasis on freedom. Their legal and political apparatuses are usually conditioned upon respect for and protection of individual liberty.[4] But what exactly does freedom require? This is something that has been widely contested since the birth of liberalism.[5] Generally speaking, there are two main schools of thought:[6] (i) freedom requires non-interference; and (ii) freedom requires non-domination.

The former is probably the most popular, having been shaped by some of the leading philosophers of liberalism, including Thomas Hobbes and John Locke.[7] It states that you are free just so long as you are able to act without being interfered with by another person. Interference can take many forms, from direct physical manipulation of your body to coercive threats and psychological manipulation. The key feature of freedom as non-interference is that as long as other people leave you alone, you are deemed to be free.

The other school of thought—the non-domination school—sees things rather differently. It argues that it is possible for someone to live their entire life without any active interference by another person and yet remain in a condition that no one would describe as being free. Phillip Pettit, who is probably the leading contemporary defender of the non-domination ideal, uses Henrik Ibsen's play *A Doll's House* to illustrate the problem. The play's main characters are Torvald and his wife, Nora. Torvald is a young successful banker. By law, he has considerable power over his wife. He could, if he so desired, prevent her from doing many things. But he doesn't exert those powers. He is happy for Nora to do whatever she desires, within certain limits. As Pettit describes it, "Torvald has enormous power over how his wife can act, but he dotes on her and denies her nothing—nothing, at least, within the accepted parameters of life as a banker's wife . . . She has all the latitude that a woman in late nineteenth-century Europe could have wished for."[8] But is she free? Pettit says she is not. The problem is that Nora lives under the *domination* of Torvald. If she wants to do anything outside the accepted parameters of activity for a banker's wife, she will have to seek his permission. He may not interfere with her actions on a daily basis, but he stands poised to do so if she ever gets out of line. She consequently has to ingratiate herself to him, and match her preferences to his, if she is to live a trouble-free life. Her growing awareness of her dominated state is one of the major themes of the play. Pettit argues that this is contrary to true freedom: "To be a free person you must have the capacity to make certain central choices . . . without having to seek the permission of another."[9] In other words, freedom requires not just the absence of interference but the absence of domination. Only when domination is removed are we truly free.

It should be obvious that Nora's situation is very similar to that of the person living under Anderson's hypothetical communist dictatorship. Both are subject to the arbitrary whim of a master or *dominus;* both live at the mercy of this master. It is also very similar—and here's the argument—to the predicament of many employees in the modern economy. In any small-to-large corporate enterprise, employees work within a hierarchical structure that makes them answerable to, and dependent on, a superior. They must ingratiate themselves to these superiors and act within the parameters determined by those superiors. In other words, they live in a state of freedom-undermining domination. Indeed, I must now reveal that the description of the "communist dictatorship" that I took from Anderson was not, in fact, intended to be a description of what life would be like under such a regime; it was, rather, Anderson's description of life as an employee in a modern corporation. Anderson merely compared it to a communist dictatorship in order to support her view that employment is an unjust, freedom-undermining system of *private government.*

If Anderson's description of what life is like as an employee is reasonably accurate, it gives us good reason to object to the system of work. It means that work is a significant source of unfreedom in human life. But, of course, many people will object to Anderson's description of what life is like as an employee. Surely things aren't so bad, they will say. Surely there are mitigating factors that mean work is not the terrible source of domination that she claims it to be? Let's consider four objections to her line of thinking.

First, let's consider Tyler Cowen's claim that it is really only a small subset of workers who are subject to the kind of extreme dominating influence that concerns Anderson.[10] Most of us are not so bad off. Perhaps, but the plight of those who do suffer from extreme domination should not be ignored and should be taken seriously. As Anderson herself points out, many low-paid workers in retail and manufacturing are subject to routine body searches and random drug testing, as well as various forms of harassment by managers and customers.[11] Employers also exert considerable control over the work schedules of these workers, subjecting them to draining split shifts and changes in shift work patterns.[12] This is a particularly debilitating form of domination because it has knock-on effects on how the workers are allowed to spend their time outside of work (more on this below).

On top of this, it may not just be a small subset of workers who are subject to these extreme forms of domination. More totalizing forms of surveillance and monitoring are now being encouraged even among higher-paid workers. This surveillance and monitoring enables domination. Consider the various corporate wellness programs that are now in place in companies around the world. These programs are often instituted first among high-paid, creative workforces.[13] One example is the sleep-monitoring program that was introduced by the US insurance company Aetna. Realizing that getting a good night's sleep was essential to physical and mental well-being, and realizing that a healthy worker was a productive worker, Aetna decided to offer its employees bonus payments of $25 for every twenty days that they slept for at least eight hours.[14] Other companies encourage surveillance and monitoring of both work-related activities and recreational health and fitness activities in an effort to boost productivity.[15] Submitting to programs of this sort requires workers to record and share information about activities that are ordinarily free from the surveilling gaze of employers. At the outset, programs of this sort tend to be voluntary, but as I will argue below, they often end up becoming effectively compulsory. Workers don't like to mark themselves out as being different from their peers, particularly when the difference has a potentially negative connotation. Consequently, people become obliged to submit to the increased domination of the employer. Furthermore, and this is critical, it does not matter whether employers use the information they are recording to make their workers' lives more unpleasant. This is the critical insight of the "freedom as non-domination" ideal. As Pettit points out, Nora's life under the dominion of her husband Torvald is often quite pleasant, as long as she is willing to play his game; it is the mere fact that he could exercise his dominating power at any time that makes her unfree. When she makes this realization in the play, she sees how limited her life has been. The same is true for employees that are subject to extensive forms of corporate monitoring and surveillance. It all seems fine, until they step out of line.

A second objection to Anderson's argument is that the existence of legal protections for employees moderates the dominating power of employers. What an employee is legally obliged to do on behalf of an employer is determined by the contract of employment they agreed to at the commencement of the employment (as modified by subsequent negotiations). This contract will have certain terms and conditions implied into it (if they have not been explicitly provided for), on foot of employee rights legislation that protects the employee from the worst excrescences of arbitrary power (for example, rights to breaks, holidays, sick pay, and protection against discrimination and unfair dismissal). When you add this to the potential for collective bargaining through the activities of trade unions, you seem to end up with a far less oppressive picture of what life is like under the dominion of an employer.

But there are several factors that count against this rosier picture. For starters, legal protections for employees vary greatly. European countries (largely through the efforts of the EU) have reasonably robust protections for employees (particularly against discrimination and unfair dismissal), but other countries do not. Anderson notes that the United States, through its acceptance of at-will employment, has a much less protective regime that subjects its workers to much greater potential for arbitrary dominion.[16] Furthermore, even in countries with seemingly robust protections for employees it is important to distinguish between the de jure and de facto protections (that is, between what it says in the legislation and what actually happens on the ground). Employers increasingly use novel or temporary forms of contracts to avoid employee protection legislation—witness, for example, the normalization of short-term and even zero-hour contracts in recent years. And many employees (and employers!) are simply unaware of what their legal rights are, or are too afraid to assert them because they are desperate for employment. Unions might be able to assist in this regard, but unions are in decline around the world. The net result is that the law often does little to protect against the dominating influence of employers.

A third objection to Anderson's argument is that employment is a voluntary arrangement. No one is forced to accept the dominating influence of their employers. They can leave their employment at any time. If they do accept the dominating influence of their employers, it must be because they see it as a good deal for them (for example, because the financial reward compensates them for any loss of freedom). Where's the harm in that?

But this is not a persuasive objection. Employment is not a voluntary arrangement for the vast majority of people: it is a necessity. People need an income to survive and they have to work in order to earn that income. Welfare payments are an alternative source of income, but they are typically conditional upon either (a) showing that you are actively seeking work or (b) showing that you are unfit for work (due to physical or mental disability). Reforms to welfare could change this—the much-discussed universal basic income guarantee would remove the conditionality of welfare—but until this happens it is simply not true to say that employment is voluntary. Even those who manage to game the welfare system for a while often face enormous anxiety and social pressure to work, as David Frayne evidences in his ethnography of modern-day work avoiders, *The Refusal of Work*.[17] Furthermore, it is not true to say that people have lots of choice over who their employers are, and can easily exit jobs with unpleasant working conditions. This may be true for some highly skilled workers, and in some job markets, but the increasing "labor glut" that is arising as a result of automation and globalization means that employers have most of the power of selection, and the alternatives available to most workers are unlikely to be better than what they currently have (see the discussion of fissuring and precarity, below, for further illustrations of this).

A final, and related, objection to Anderson's argument is that maybe there is a way to avoid the dominating influence of employers by either (a) clambering your way to the top of the corporate ladder or (b) becoming self-employed. But the sad reality is that neither is likely to eliminate dominating influence from your life. Corporate CEOs and entrepreneurs are often subject to another, often more pernicious, type of dominating influence, namely: the dominating influence of their investors. And self-employed individuals are subject to the dominating influence of the market of potential contractual partners. They have to constantly prove their employability / desirability to this market, often by subjecting themselves to more pervasive forms of surveillance and monitoring. I will discuss this in more detail when talking about the temporal colonization problem, below.

There is, however, an objection to this response from within the theoretical literature on freedom as non-domination. Pettit, for example, has argued that we should not stretch the concept of freedom as non-domination too far, suggesting that it would be unhelpful to say that people live under the dominion of natural forces like the weather. Only persons, natural or corporate, should be seen as masters for the purposes of freedom as non-domination. This would seem to rule out something abstract like the market as a source of domination.

In the interests of conceptual purity, we could accept this view and simply argue that being subject to the whims of the market is a distinctive problem, but I think there is some reason to push back against the restriction. The market is not like the weather: it is a social institution, something produced through the aggregated behavior of many human individuals. There may be no single agent guiding or directing the market, but if we ignore the dominating influence of such "functionally agentless" social institutions over our lives we would end up ignoring many of the most significant sources of freedom-undermining domination.[18] After all, in the case of Nora and Torvald it wasn't just Torvald who exercised the dominating influence: it was Torvald plus the social institution of marriage (how it was viewed and understood by society at large) that did this. It's the same for the worker, CEO, or self-employed person. They are subject to many masters, each of whose power and influence is reinforced by an institutional framework that constrains their options.

The Fissuring and Precarity Problem

The second argument for the structural badness of work focuses on the phenomena of *fissuring* and *precarity*.[19] "Fissuring" happens when activities that were once performed under the umbrella of a single corporate enterprise are spread across several fissured organizations. To give an example, suppose you had a large corporation whose primary business activity was to manufacture cars. In the mid-twentieth century, we might expect that company to house all of the activities that were essential to that primary activity under the same corporate umbrella.[20] This could include things like designing the cars, maintaining factory machinery, maintaining company IT systems, payroll and accounting, catering and gardening, transportation, and so on. In the early twenty-first century we can expect to see a more fissured corporate design. The car manufacturing company is likely to outsource many of the peripheral support activities to companies that specialize in those activities. Its IT workers are likely to be contracted / seconded from firms that specialize in IT; its payroll and accounting services are likely to be outsourced to firms that specialize in providing those services; its gardeners are likely to be private contractors; and so on. "Precarity" refers to the predicament of many workers in the modern economy. The idea of a permanent job for life is at an end, and the situation of workers has become increasingly precarious. Many workers now find themselves on temporary, short-term contracts and classify themselves as self-employed workers, operating as part of the growing gig economy.

Fissuring and precarity are related. The former tends to precipitate the latter. They are also well documented. Weil provides detailed case studies of how fissuring has affected the American labor market in his book *The Fissured Workplace*, focusing in particular on the rise of subcontracting, franchising, and changes in how corporate supply chains are managed. In terms of the latter, one of the more striking examples he gives concerns the way in which a technology giant like Apple manages its supply chain. As of 2014, approximately 63,000 workers were directly employed by Apple, but over

750,000 were employed worldwide in its supply chain.[21] This is made possible through fissuring. Surveys of employers suggest that subcontracting and outsourcing are on the rise, and surveys of workers, both in the United States and across the Organization for Economic Cooperation and Development (OECD), suggest that there has been an increase in the number of contingently employed workers since the mid-1990s.[22]

One of the most noticeable manifestations of fissuring and precarity is the rise of so-called platform work.[23] Technology companies like Taskrabbit, Uber, AirBnB, Etsy, and Deliveroo all now specialize in providing digital platforms for linking buyers and sellers of human labor. They are, to use Guy Standing's term, digital "labor brokers."[24] And these companies are just the most well-known: there are similar platforms available for graphic designers, home cleaners, computer programmers, legal service providers, tradespeople, and more. Platform workers are essentially self-employed gig workers. Their platform providers take a cut from every transaction, and they often have to work according to the platform providers' algorithmically mediated terms and conditions.[25] Although this sometimes results in platform providers exercising a lot of control over workers, the platform providers themselves are keen to deny that they have any direct employment relationship with those workers, often classifying them as independent contractors. Platform workers are pushing back against this classification, and there has been an upsurge in unionization and litigation among such workers. I'll discuss this development in more detail below. Despite this emerging resistance, it seems fair to say that platform work is a growing phenomenon. Although precise predictions about the future are always worth treating with skepticism (as mentioned in Chapter 2), the McKinsey Global Institute claims that up to 200 million workers worldwide will be working via these platforms by 2025.[26]

The argument here is that the rise of fissuring and precarity is another manifestation of the structural badness of work. To support this claim we need to consider *why* this trend has arisen, and *what* its consequences are.

The "why" question is easy to answer: it's due to a combination of economic logic, regulatory facilitation, and technological innovation. As Weil argues, you can divide the history of the modern corporation into two distinct phases. The early-to-mid twentieth century (roughly from 1920 to 1970) was the era of *centralization.* Corporate enterprises grew larger by organizing and managing their essential and peripheral support services in-house. Doing so had economic advantages. Ronald Coase developed the leading theory as to why in his famous article "The Nature of the Firm."[27] Pre-Coase economists were puzzled by the existence of large corporations. They wondered why one couldn't organize all corporate activity through a network of private contracts. Coase answered that it all had to do with transaction costs: it would be very costly to bring all the necessary individuals together to negotiate those contracts, and it would be very costly to monitor and enforce those contracts once they came into existence. It was easier to internalize the network of contracts inside the corporation, where you could keep a closer eye (and hand) on what was going on.

The second era began in the 1970s. This was the era of *fissuring.* Many corporations from the earlier era grew too large. Consultants and business gurus urged corporations to start focusing on their core competencies instead of peripheral or tangential services. The idea was that if you are really a technology design company (like, say, Apple), you should focus on the design; if you are really a clothing brand (like, say, Nike), you should focus on the brand. Let some other company specialize in manufacture, transportation, payroll, and accounting. There was an obvious economic logic to this: those peripheral support services were cost centers within large corporations, not profit centers. If you could outsource them, and pay less as a result, fissuring would be an economic no-brainer. But to truly benefit from fissuring, certain other innovations were needed. After all, the coordination problems identified by Coase were not illusory. Companies needed some "glue" to enable coordination across a set of fissured workplaces.[28] This glue came in the shape of new legal agreements that facilitated fissuring (for example, franchising agreements), and also new surveillance and monitoring technologies that ensured that subcontractors or outsourcers were complying with the standards required by their contractual partners. Onboard computing in trucking is the perfect example of this.[29]

According to Weil, we are still living through the era of fissuring. More of the "technological glue" needed to facilitate coordination becomes available each year. Indeed, platform work could be viewed as the latest and most extreme variant on the fissured workplace: the algorithmically mediated platform providing the perfect glue for one host company to coordinate (and extract rent from) vast networks of private contracts. The consequences for workers are grim. Three in particular are worth noting. First, workers are pushed into less secure forms of work, with fewer non-pay benefits and employment protections. This is either because they are classed as independent contractors and hence responsible for their own insurance, health care, equipment, and related costs; or because if they work for a subcontracting firm (or franchisee), those firms offer fewer benefits than larger companies used to offer, or simply do not comply with legal regulations requiring payments and protections.[30] Second, and in addition to this, the workers have to subject themselves to more monitoring and surveillance in order to enable the fissuring. This compounds the dominating influence problem discussed earlier. Finally, fissuring and precarity result in much less pay for workers. There is a simple economic logic to this too. Fissuring changes how the benefits of corporate activity are shared among the key stakeholders in any corporate enterprise: consumers, investors, and workers. Fissuring typically results in a better deal for investors and consumers: costs are reduced and profits go up. But this comes at the expense of the workers, who are pushed out and contracted in at reduced rates.[31]

You could object to this and argue that fissuring and precarity aren't all bad because they provide workers with greater autonomy and flexibility. This is the defense usually offered by platform providers like Uber and Deliveroo. They claim that people love working for them because they can determine their own work schedules and be their own bosses. Furthermore, they claim that people use these platforms to supplement other employment-related activities (like other part-time work or education). There may be some truth to this—although we should be skeptical about the claim that platforms provide workers with greater autonomy for reasons I'll discuss below—but the mere fact that this type of work has advantages for certain types of workers does not mean that we should judge it better, all things considered. Platform work is merely one manifestation of the larger trend toward fissuring and precarity, and that larger trend is worse for workers in two distinct ways. First, it is worse for workers relative to *what used to be the norm*, namely, secure, well-paid work with a greater number of benefits. And second, it is worse for workers relative to *the non-work possibilities*, namely, how they could be spending their time if they did not have to work. The first point is obvious from the historical record; the second point is what I will be arguing in subsequent chapters of this book. A precarious, fissured workplace may be better than nothing, and individual workers may be thankful for having some way to make a living if the alternative is no income at all, but we shouldn't be comparing it to nothing.

Another potential objection to the argument is that it undercuts the case for technological unemployment that I presented in Chapter 2. Remember, the key contention there was that technology is (and could be) reducing the total number of employment opportunities in the economy. And yet, here we seem to have an example of technology doing the opposite: creating more employment opportunities through the advent of new digital platforms. This is not necessarily the case. For one thing, the new employment opportunities created by digital platforms may result in a significant amount of underemployment—more part-time work and unpaid work.[32] For another, the opportunities may be fleeting. The kinds of services people provide via digital platforms are subject to the same forces of automation as other types of work. Uber is famously bullish about the prospects of self-driving cars and wishes to replace its fleet of drivers with such vehicles in the future. Services like home cleaning, food delivery, basic legal advice, and so on are also being actively automated, decimating the platform workers who currently provide them.

A final objection to the argument is that regulatory reform could stop fissuring and precarity from being so bad. Legal systems are often slow to adapt to technological change, but once they catch up they can introduce reforms that provide protections for workers who have been disadvantaged. As mentioned above, the attempt to classify platform workers as independent contractors, and thereby avoid duties under employment protection law, has started to meet with some resistance. In November 2017, Uber lost an Employment Appeals Tribunal case in the UK.[33] They were trying to argue that their drivers should not be classed as employees and hence should not be entitled to protections under the Employment Rights Act of 1996, Working Time Regulations of 1998, and the National Minimum Wage Act of 1998. The judge held that the amount of control Uber exercised over those drivers was inconsistent with this claim. This verdict was upheld by the Court of Appeal for England and Wales in December 2018.[34] Furthermore, in July 2017, the British government released the *Taylor Review*, which argued for legal reform to provide greater protection for workers in the gig economy.[35] These are certainly welcome developments but their capacity to redress the structural badness of fissured work can be doubted. At roughly the same time that Uber lost its case, Deliveroo won a case against forty-five workers, entitling the company to continue classifying them as independent workers and to avoid any duty to pay them a minimum wage or holiday pay.[36] Furthermore, it is well to remember that legal rulings and regulatory reforms can create perverse incentives. We can expect any attempts to increase protections for gig workers to (i) incentivize companies to further adjust their relationships with workers to avoid regulatory burdens (for example, Uber could start looking to Deliveroo as a model and adjust its agreements with workers to avoid legally mandated duties); and (ii) incentivize investment in automation to displace the increasingly costly workers. We should definitely be rethinking how we share the benefits of technologically facilitated productivity, and legal and regulatory reform to working conditions will be essential to that task, but it is not clear that the best solution to the problem is to retain our commitment to work if its consequences are unpleasant for workers. Abandoning our commitment to work may be our best hope.

The Distributive Injustice Problem

The third argument for the structural badness of work is that work is "distributively unjust." By this, I mean that the rewards of work (particularly income)[37] are not shared in a fair or proportionate manner: a small group of individuals take most of the income, to the detriment of the majority. This claim needs to be interpreted properly. I would neither expect nor desire a world of perfect pay equity. Some differences in pay are justifiable due to differences in skill and effort, and some differentiation might be desirable in order to spur innovation.[38] My claim is that the kinds of differentiation we currently witness are not justifiable in these terms, and are being exacerbated by technological change.

To support this claim we first need to establish that there is significant inequity in the distribution of income. An easy way to do this would be to cite some of the headline-grabbing figures that have been produced in recent years. For example, it was estimated in 2017 that the eight wealthiest individuals in the world owned more than the bottom 50 percent combined.[39] Figures like this certainly drive home the reality of inequality, but they ignore some of the complexity in income distribution that is important for the present argument. The empirical databases constructed by Piketty and Atkinson are more helpful.[40] As Piketty points out, there are two main sources of income: labor and capital.[41] Total income inequality is determined by the aggregation of both. According to the figures produced by Piketty and his colleagues, ours is a world of increasingly stratified income inequality: the top 10 percent get a disproportionate share of total income; the top 1 percent receive a disproportionate share of this; and the top 0.1 percent receive an even more disproportionate share.[42]

To give some numbers: in most European countries (c. 2010) the top 10 percent of the income distribution received approximately 35 percent of total income, with the top 1 percent receiving 10 percent. In the United States (c. 2010) the top 10 percent received 50 percent of the total, with the top 1 percent receiving 20 percent. These aggregate figures mask deeper inequities in the ownership of capital. When you break out capital income from labor income, you find that in Europe (c. 2010) 60 percent of capital was owned by the top 10 percent, with 25 percent of that being owned by the top 1 percent; and in the United States (c. 2010) 70 percent of capital was owned by the top 10 percent, with 35 percent of that being owned by the top 1 percent.[43] This is significant when it comes to assessing the likely impact of technology on income distribution. Technology after all is a kind of capital. When you automate a worker's tasks, you effectively replace that worker with machine capital. Consequently, we can expect the gains of automation to flow primarily to the owners of capital. Which means we can expect automation to result in greater income inequality.

But does this mean that the system is distributively *unjust?* One reason for thinking that it does comes from David Autor's work on the *polarization* of the job market.[44] Despite his skepticism about the long-term prospects for technological unemployment (discussed in Chapter 2), Autor does think that technology is having a significant effect on the distribution of jobs and income. He argues that the labor market can be divided into three main types of work: (i) *manual work,* which consists of dexterous physical tasks in unpredictable environments; (ii) *routine work,* which consists of repetitive, routine cognitive or physical tasks; and (iii) *abstract work,* which consists of creative problem-solving tasks that often require intuition and persuasion. As noted in Chapter 2, it is unlikely that a single job consists of only one type of work / task, but it's still likely that jobs cluster around similar sets of tasks. Broadly speaking, these three forms of work correspond to different income brackets: manual work is generally classed as low-skilled work and is relatively poorly remunerated and often quite precarious; routine work is generally classed as middle-skilled work and sits in the middle of the (labor) income distribution; abstract work is classed as high-skilled and is often well rewarded. Autor argues that between 1980 and 2015, technology had a dramatic effect on routine work. Robots and computers were really good at performing routine cognitive and physical tasks and consequently displaced workers in the middle income bracket. This is borne out by data from the US labor market, which shows zero or negative growth in routine work from 1979 to 2012, coupled with increases in manual and abstract work.[45] However, those increases are not equally shared. Abstract work, which usually requires high levels of education and has high barriers to entry, is concentrated among relatively few actual workers. Furthermore, these abstract workers are the ones who are best positioned to increase their overall productivity as a result of the automation of routine work. They can earn premium income rates due to their relative scarcity and this boost in productivity. Manual workers have neither of these advantages. They are oversupplied and unable to boost productivity through machine assistance. The majority of workers displaced since 1980 have been pushed into manual work, with its lower incomes and more precarious working conditions, which has had obvious repercussions for wage inequality.[46]

I would argue that this polarization effect is a clear manifestation of the distributive injustice of work as it is currently structured. Routine workers have not been displaced because of a lack of skill and effort, nor because of any personal moral or cognitive failing, but because their jobs happened to be relatively easy to automate. They were the low-hanging fruit: the first to be cut down by the machines. Furthermore, they were not displaced into better opportunities and better working conditions. On the contrary, they have been left in a worse predicament than before. It is hard to see how this outcome could be justified by any of the leading theories of distributive justice.

The case for distributive injustice is particularly strong when we focus on the polarization at the top end of the labor income distribution. As Piketty notes, in certain countries increasing disparities between the top 10 percent and the bottom 90 percent, as well increasing disparities within the top 10 percent, are responsible for most of the increase in inequality that has been observed since the 1980s.[47] This is particularly true in Anglo-Saxon countries (the United States, the UK, Canada, Australia), but also true, to a lesser extent, in continental Europe and Japan.[48] In the United States and the UK the top 0.1 percent have seen their incomes increase from 20 times the average wage in 1980 to 50–100 times the average wage in 2010; in countries like France and Japan, they have seen their incomes go from 15 times the average wage to 25 times the average wage.[49] These changes are even more significant when you consider that over that period most people have seen their purchasing power stagnate.[50] This means that the increase in economic power for the top end of the income distribution is even greater than the headline figures suggest.

There is, however, a standard economic explanation for this inequality—one that, while it does not justify the inequity, may partially excuse it and provide a solution. The standard explanation is that the inequality is due to a "race" between technology and education.[51] The idea is that workers are paid according to their marginal productivity (how much they add to the output of a firm), and their productivity depends on their skill. If their skills are in high demand and short supply, they can expect to see their wages go up. The problem is that technology changes the kinds of skills that are in demand: a capacity for routine, cognitive work (like bookkeeping) might have been in high demand in the 1960s or 1970s, but due to advances in IT and automation it no longer is. The supply of skills is determined by the educational system. If people lack access to education, or if the educational system does not train them in relevant high-demand skills, it will result in fewer people with high demand skills. This will have an impact on wage inequality. Highly educated people with skills that complement the current technological infrastructure will see their wages go up disproportionately while others will see their wages go down. The claim is that many people are now losing the race between technology and education, and this explains the current distribution of income.

As I said, this is hardly a moral justification for what we see: if labor inequality is due to a mismatch between education and technology, then the people who suffer as a result of that mismatch are hardly to blame for their predicament. That said, the race argument may provide some hope for redressing the imbalance. We just need to improve the access to, and relevance of, the educational system.

There are, however, problems with the race argument. For starters, the assumptions underlying it—that the educational system trains people in work-relevant skills and that the marginal productivity of an individual worker can be easily determined—are doubtful.[52] Likewise, the notion that we could easily restructure the educational system in order to train people in skills that complement our current technological infrastructure is fanciful. It is very difficult to predict what skills will be in high demand in twenty years' time, and if the arguments in Chapter 2 about accelerating change and machine complementarity are correct, there may not even be that many technology-complementary skills in high demand in the years to come. Furthermore, as Piketty argues, it's pretty clear that the race argument cannot explain the current patterns we see in income distribution. In particular, it cannot explain the differences in the fates of the top 10 percent, 1 percent, and 0.1 percent that we see across different countries. The United States and France have been subject to the same technological forces, but senior managers in the United States earn significantly more than senior managers in France. It also cannot explain the differences in income within the top 10 percent. These workers have usually attended the same elite universities and received similar educations, and yet there are remarkable discontinuities between the incomes earned by the top 1 percent and the other 9 percent.[53]

So what does account for the current patterns? Piketty argues that "institutional factors" must be playing a significant role, namely, the current set of business norms, legal and regulatory rules, and political influence over how wages are set. It's clear from historical experience that legal and political interference can have an impact on remuneration. For example, wages were deliberately (and by agreement) suppressed in many countries during WWI and WWII.[54] For better or worse, most countries now favor institutional systems in which senior managers and company shareholders have significant autonomy in how wages are set. For obvious, and self-interested, reasons they tend to set wages in a way that means they benefit most. This means they underpay workers for their contribution to firm productivity, and / or invest more in labor-replacing technologies, and / or encourage fissuring and precarity (as we saw in the previous section). This is sometimes moderated by the impact of minimum wage laws and collective bargaining agreements. In the United States the inequality is worse because of the relatively low federal minimum wage and the stark decline in unionization. It is better in France, which has a higher minimum wage and stronger culture of unionization.[55] But this provides little solace: the general trend is toward declining unionization, greater labor market flexibility over wage setting, and increasing income inequality.[56] In other words, the institutional structure that is currently in place is one that compounds and reinforces the distributive injustice of work. This is yet more evidence for the structural badness of work.

The Temporal and Mental Colonization Problem

The fourth argument for the structural badness of work focuses on the way in which work colonizes our lives, in particular on the ways in which it occupies our time and our mental space. The concern here is twofold: (i) that we spend more time working than is ideal, and (ii) that even when we are not working, work is the lens through which all other activities are interpreted and valued. While (i) is certainly a problem, (ii) is the more serious concern since it contributes to the totalizing and dominating power of work. It means that our free time is not really free time at all. It is time that we spend recovering from and preparing for work. As David Frayne puts it in his book *The Refusal of Work*, "true leisure . . . [is] that sweet 'oasis of unmediated life' in which people detach from economic demands and become genuinely free for the world and its culture."[57] The modern institutional structure of work does not allow for such true leisure.[58]

There are three ways in which to make the case for the colonizing power of work. The first is to use a combination of intuition and common experience; the second is to focus on evidence suggesting that people have "lost time" to work in the past half century; and the third is to use a game theoretical model that explains why people increasingly allow work to colonize their lives. I'll use all three tactics to make the case.

I start with intuition and common experience. At first glance there is some reason to doubt the claim that work now colonizes our lives. After all, statistics on the average number of working hours suggests that people are officially working fewer hours nowadays than at certain times in the past.[59] The picture, however, varies depending on which historical era you pick as your comparator. In a famous essay entitled "The Original Affluent Society," the American anthropologist Marshall Sahlins argued that the shift from hunter-gatherer lifestyles to agricultural lifestyles was to blame for our loss of time to work.[60] Based on anthropological evidence from modern-day tribes, Sahlins argued that the hunter-gatherer lifestyle was awash with genuine leisure time: people had to "work" very few hours every day in order to secure their basic needs. It was when we became settled and yoked to the land that we found our days filled with backbreaking labor. Sahlins's view of the hunter-gatherer lifestyle may be somewhat idyllic, and there is no direct analogue to "work" (as I understand that term) in such societies to make the comparison a fruitful one; nevertheless, if you fast-forward to the early and darkest days of the Industrial Revolution—when work in the economic sense undoubtedly existed—you do get evidence to suggest that people worked more than they do today. There were no official legal limits on the number of hours people could be asked / forced to work by their employers: twelve–fourteen-hour days of physically exhausting labor were not uncommon. Nowadays there are, in many developed countries, some legally mandated limits on the number of hours you can be asked to work. The limits vary but typically lie in the range of thirty-five–fifty hours per week.

But these official limits are meaningless in the lives of many workers. They may have made sense in early to mid-twentieth century, when the concept of "industrial time" was prominent: people clocked in and clocked out, and their economic productivity could be easily measured in units of time. Today, particularly for knowledge workers, this idea is antiquated. There are no obvious links between time and productivity. There is always the sense that you could be doing more and that you have the technological infrastructure to make this relatively easy: you don't need to be physically located in your office or workplace to write that report you have been putting off for the last week, or answer more emails, or engage in more online promotion of your personal brand. Furthermore, in several sectors of the economy—for example, technology, finance, consultancy, law—the dominant work culture is one in which you must be seen to be "putting in the hours," otherwise you are assumed to be slacking and are at risk of being fired.

The boundaries between the working day and the rest of one's life have consequently blurred beyond all recognition. The classic slogan of the labor movement—"eight hours for work. eight hours for sleep, and eight hours for what we will"—is quaint and naive. Jonathan Crary makes the point in stark and pessimistic terms in his book *24/7: Late Capitalism and the End of Sleep.*[61] He argues that we have created a digitally mediated, globalized workplace. It is open 24 hours a day, 7 days a week, 365 days a year. It is always there, always demanding more from us. Crary argues that its ultimate purpose is to bring an end to sleep (and he discusses several scientific research programs that have aimed at reducing sleep time to illustrate the point). That's probably extreme, but the point is well taken. It is clear that when you have a job you are encouraged to get the most out of it, and when you do not have a job you are encouraged to use your time to prepare for work by building your CV and making yourself employable.[62] University students often interpret their activities in terms of employability and resist anything that does not seem to contribute to this end. This is something that many universities actively encourage, getting their graduates to catalogue their extracurricular activities into employability portfolios that they can hawk to potential employers. And the employability agenda has filtered into the minds of younger children too. Frayne describes one encounter he had with a twelve-year-old boy who had participated in a research program at his local school. When asked why he enjoyed the program, the boy said that it was because "it will look good on my CV."[63]

Beyond intuition and common sense, is there any evidence to suggest that we are in fact losing time to work? There is. Heather Boushey's study of work-life conflicts in American families is particularly illuminating in this regard because it focuses on what is happening to families as opposed to individuals.[64] Most people live most of their lives in family units of some sort, whether they be single-parent, dual-parent, or otherwise. Within those family units there is a constant struggle to maintain some semblance of work-life balance, particularly when it comes to juggling care commitments (to children or elderly family members) with career commitments. Boushey looks at how American families have managed these conflicts since the late 1970s. She does so by considering families across three major income brackets: middle, low, and professional. She argues that the common experience of all three is that "they have lost time," but the reasons for this vary across the different income brackets.

For middle-class families there are two main reasons for the loss of time: (i) the increased number of hours that women work outside the home and (ii) the stagnation (and sometimes decline) in wages for men. The increased number of hours worked by women is partly caused by (positive) changes in legal and cultural values, but also partly necessitated by the stagnation of male wages and the increasing costs of child care, education, healthcare, and housing.[65] In order to keep up with these rising costs, middle-class families have to give up more time to work, which means they have less time and energy for their care commitments. This results in increased feelings of stress and work-life conflict.[66] This is compounded by the fact that the expectations around parenting and other care commitments have increased, with both women and men reporting an increased amount of time spent performing these activities each week.[67]

For low income families, the causes are different. They experience greater levels of family breakdown, with approximately 50 percent of families in this income bracket being classed as single-parent (the vast majority of whom are female).[68] They are typically under-educated and hence shut out from higher-income jobs, and they experience higher levels of poverty and financial desperation. As a result, they are often forced to take the precarious and poorly paid jobs that I described in previous sections. These jobs can come with unpredictable and non–family-friendly schedules (for example, just-in-time scheduling or split shifts), and a lack of job security and non-income benefits.[69] This puts increased time pressures on this group when it comes to balancing the need for an income with care commitments. There is an interesting feedback cycle between the struggles of this group and the rise of the 24/7 economy. On the one hand, the rise of the 24/7 economy is the cause of their problems: it is what leads to more unpredictable, less family-friendly work schedules. On the other hand, it is the solution to them, since they need to be able to do their shopping and access services outside of the ordinary working day.[70] This leads to a self-perpetuating squeeze on time.

For professional families, things are different again. They are well educated and well paid (in Boushey's study they average approximately $200,000 per year). Our hearts do not bleed for them. But they are feeling the time pinch too. Their jobs are often the ones that demand the longest working hours—for professional men, the average number of hours worked per year (as of 2012) was 2,186; for professional women it was 1,708—and they often take their work home with them and are on call outside of the ordinary work day. Speaking from my own knowledge and experience of professional law, I see this reality first hand. The majority of my friends and colleagues work twelve hours per day, and expect to work several weekends every month. When important deadlines loom, working until after midnight is not uncommon. The obvious advantage that they have over the others is that they have more money to pay for necessary services. But this is itself a manifestation of the colonizing powers of work. They have to live what Arlie Hochschild calls the "outsourced life": they are cash rich, but time poor and hence pay others to organize their non-work lives (childcare, elder care, party planning, dating services, etc.).[71]

The final way to defend the colonizing powers of work is the game theoretical one. This focuses in particular on the "employability agenda" and how it encourages us to constantly perform and present our activities in terms of their contribution to our employability. As already argued, work is increasingly precarious, and more people are being shifted into the gig economy. This means that more people have to be constantly on the lookout for employment opportunities. They have to signal their availability and willingness to work, and they have to do so in such a way that marks them out from the crowd. How can they do this? The answer: by disclosing information about themselves. This can obviously include information about job-relevant skills, but it can also include information about peripheral or tangential matters. For example, sharing information about all the volunteering work that you do, or the marathons that you have run, signals to potential employers that you are dedicated and public spirited. Both are qualities that employers look for. Sharing information about positive customer ratings, or newspaper reviews, signals to people that you offer a good-quality service. These kinds of information disclosure make sense from the individual perspective.

The problem is that there is a dangerous strategic logic to such disclosures. As soon as one person starts making them, everyone has to do the same in order to avoid others making unwarranted assumptions about them. The legal theorist Scott Peppet calls this the "unravelling problem."[72] He explains it with a very simple example. Imagine you have a group of people selling crates of oranges on the export market. The crates carry a maximum of 100 oranges, but they are carefully sealed before sale so that a purchaser cannot see how many oranges are inside. What's more, the purchaser doesn't want to open the box prior to transport because doing so would cause the oranges to go bad. But the purchaser can, of course, easily verify the total number of oranges in the box after transport by simply opening it and counting them. Now suppose you are one of the people selling the crates of oranges. Will you disclose to the purchaser the total number of oranges in the crate? You might think that you shouldn't because, if you are selling less than the others, that would put you at a disadvantage on the market. But a little bit of game theory tells us that we should expect the sellers to disclose the number of oranges in the crates. Why so? Well, if you had 100 oranges in your crate, you would be incentivized to disclose this to any potential purchaser. Doing so makes you an attractive seller. Correspondingly, if you had 99 oranges in your crate, and all the sellers with 100 oranges had disclosed the number of oranges in their crates to the purchasers, you should disclose the number of oranges in your crate. If you don't, there is a danger that a potential purchaser will lump you in with anyone selling 0–98 oranges. In other words, because those with the maximum number of oranges in their crates are sharing this information, purchasers will tend to assume the worst about anyone not sharing the number of oranges in their crate. But once you have disclosed the fact that you have 99 oranges in your crate, the same logic will apply to the person with 98 oranges, and so on, all the way down to the seller with 1 orange in their crate.

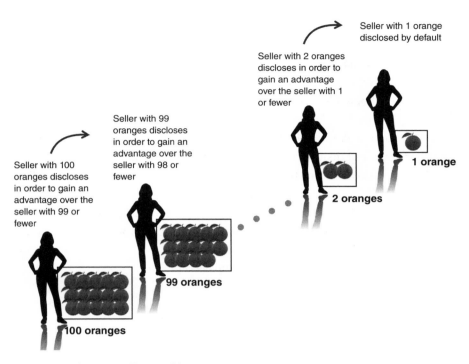

Seller with 1 orange disclosed by default

Seller with 2 oranges discloses in order to gain an advantage over the seller with 1 or fewer

1 orange

Seller with 99 oranges discloses in order to gain an advantage over the seller with 98 or fewer

2 oranges

Seller with 100 oranges discloses in order to gain an advantage over the seller with 99 or fewer

99 oranges

100 oranges

Figure 3.1 The Unravelling Problem

This is unravelling in practice. The seller with only one orange in their crate would much rather not disclose this fact to the purchasers, but they are ultimately compelled to do so by the incentives in operation on the market. Unravelling of this sort is already happening on the employment market (just ask any Uber driver forced to share their customer ratings or any academic who has to share information about their student ratings), and is likely to increase in the future as the competition for work becomes more intense. The more valuable information we have about ourselves, the more we are incentivized to disclose this to potential employers in order to maintain our employability. Those with the best information will do so voluntarily and willingly, but ultimately everybody will have to do so in an effort to differentiate themselves from other, potentially inferior, workers. What's more, digital surveillance technology makes it easier for people to participate in this unravelling. By providing people with data directly uploaded from smart devices, you provide people with what they *perceive* to be a high-quality, easily verifiable source of information about you. Peppet argues that the apotheosis of this trend is the "full disclosure" future—a future in which we share absolutely everything about ourselves in a personal digital dossier.

Let's hope this is some way off. For now, all I would say is that unravelling is a perfect illustration of both the colonizing power of work and its structural badness. For not only will it mean that people share more information about themselves, it also means they will be incentivized to *generate* more positive information about themselves, that is, to always be building their employability credentials. This has nothing to do with malevolent bosses or evil corporate overlords. It's the incentive structure of the market that does all the damage. Soon there will be no escape from the grasp of work, and we will all rationally want it to be that way. This is the collective action problem at the heart of the modern malaise of work.

The Unhappiness and Dissatisfaction Problem

The final argument for the structural badness of work is that the vast majority of people are not happy doing it. This argument is distinct from the preceding ones. To this point, I have been lodging philosophical / ethical objections to work. These objections focus on negative structural properties of the work, not on what workers themselves think about their work. Indeed, if you recall, I started this chapter by suggesting that even if you love your job, you are wrong to feel that way about work in general. I am well aware that the structural properties of work that make the present system so bad are not always in the mental spotlight of most workers. My goal to this point has been to raise their consciousnesses in order to see the problem. It would, however, be patronizing and paternalistic if I completely ignored how people actually felt about their work. These feelings have to be part of the overall assessment of the badness of work. Fortunately, the evidence we have on these feelings supports the general contention that work is structurally bad.

The polling company Gallup has been conducting "State of the Global Workplace" surveys for several years. These surveys are large, typically involving over 200,000 respondents from over 150 countries, and they assess a number of work-related issues. Their 2013 report grabbed headlines around the world when it reported that only 13 percent of workers, globally, are "engaged" by their work, and over 24 percent are "actively disengaged."[73] Gallup measures engagement by testing people's responses to twelve statements. These statements cover the worker's sense of motivation, inclusion, and purpose at work. It is a plausible way in which to assess work-related satisfaction and happiness. We might expect the engagement figures to improve in line with the fate of the economy, but this does not appear to be the case. In the 2017 iteration of their survey, Gallup reported that 15 percent of workers globally were engaged at work, a very slight uptick from 2013.[74] The figures vary from country-to-country and company-to-company. Gallup proudly boast, for example, that 70% of workers in their 'top performing' companies are engaged.[75] Nevertheless, the overall trend is negative. In no country does the engagement figure exceed 40 percent, and it is shockingly low in some regions: only 6 percent of workers in Asia and 10 percent of workers in Western Europe are engaged at work. This compares with just over 30 percent in the United States, which is ranked as one of most highly engaged workforces.[76]

These figures help to underscore a point that has been implicit in the discussion up to now. The modern system of work is one that encourages a great deal of competitiveness and anxiety: good jobs are difficult to come by, you have to work exceptionally hard to make yourself employable, and once you do, you end up locked in a system that doesn't necessarily provide you with fair remuneration for the work you are doing. What is all this anxiety and competitiveness for? Not much, seems to be the answer. The Gallup surveys suggest that the majority of people who find work don't enjoy it or think they could do better. And other studies (based on similar datasets) support this view. For example, climbing the corporate ladder and earning more money does not seem to improve emotional, day-to-day experiences of well-being. There is, rather, a threshold of income where this reaches its peak, estimated to be approximately $75,000 in the United States in 2010, but varying (of course) depending on the cost of living. It seems that you need to make enough to meet basic needs and wants, but earning more than that is self-defeating.[77]

This is not to say that all the work that gets done in the economy contributes nothing. Increases in national income and productivity do correlate with increases in self-reported levels of happiness and life satisfaction, and innovation and productivity obviously help in the distribution of important goods and services (like food and healthcare).[78] But the critical question is whether humans should be the ones doing all the work to increase productivity. My answer is that we shouldn't, not if it doesn't make us happy and not if the system has the other four properties discussed in the preceding sections.

Does Any of This Make Work Structurally Bad?

Hopefully, I have said enough now to convince you that the system of work is bad. The next question is whether it is "structurally" bad. Recall how I earlier defined this concept. I said that the system of work would count as structurally bad if it had "settled into an equilibrium pattern" that made it bad for many people, and would be "very difficult to reform or improve in such a way as to remove its bad-making properties." I also said that structural badness could be seen to be the result of a *collective action problem* around work and its pursuit.

I think it is reasonably obvious that the five features of work outlined above satisfy these conditions of structural badness. They are each the product of forces that are larger than any one individual or group of individuals and would be very difficult for such individuals to reform. For instance, the problems of fissuring and colonization are attributable to basic economic forces (the need for profit and employability) and technological change that makes it possible to respond to those forces in a particular way (more surveillance and control). They are the product of choices made by individual employers and employees that are perfectly rational from their perspective but that, when multiplied across an entire industry or society, result in a system that is worse for all workers. This is a classic collective action problem. Similarly, the problems of domination and distributive injustice are the result of long-standing legal and social norms, combined with technological innovation and economic forces. Consequently, addressing these problems would require reform of the basic rules of capitalism, some suppression or ban of widely used technologies, as well as reform of the legal and social norms that apply to work. It's not something that employees and employers can easily rectify by themselves.

But let me be absolutely clear before moving on. I am not claiming that these structural features of work are completely beyond repair. Someone could accept everything that I have said so far and nevertheless come back and say, "why don't we just reform the features that make it bad?" All I would say to such a person is that it is important to appreciate the enormity of that task. It would require significant changes across several dimensions of our current social system, and those changes would in turn require significant cooperation and coordination. I would liken the challenge to that of addressing climate change: even if everyone agreed on the problem and on the solution, it would be exceptionally difficult to get them to comply with the solution if there were some short-term gain to be derived from perpetuating the current system (as there clearly is for some workers and employers). Because of this, I argue that it is worth considering the more radical alternative—that of abolishing the system of work—and accepting the automation of most economically productive labor. There are three reasons for this: not working would be better, all things considered, for human flourishing; that radical alternative is, to some extent, implicit in the current trajectory of technological change; and, to the extent that it would require significant social cooperation and coordination to achieve, it would seem to be no greater a challenge than trying to reform the current system.

Three General Objections to the Structural Badness Thesis

I want to close out this chapter by considering three general objections to the argument I have made.

The first of those is something I will call the "structural goodness" argument. It is the antithesis of the view I have presented so far. I have been harping on the structural properties of work that make it bad; but surely there are structural properties that make it good? Anca Gheaus and Lisa Herzog have defended something like this view in a paper entitled "The Goods of Work (Other Than Money)."[79] They start from the obvious point that work is a source of income and this is good because it allows people to pay for essential goods and services. But they then accept that this "good-making" property of work could be redressed by reforming the welfare system to give people income in other ways. So they move on to consider good-making properties of work that are not income-related. They identify four such properties:

Mastery: Work is a privileged forum in which to master certain skills, and this is a process and state of being that people find very rewarding.

Contribution: Work is the main way in which people make a positive contribution to the societies in which they live.

Community: Work provides people with communities with whom they can interact and collaborate.

Status: Work is the main way in which people attain social status and esteem. This gives people a greater sense of self-worth.

Gheaus and Herzog's argument is that these good-making properties need to be taken seriously in any debate about the justice (or injustice) of a particular system of work and non-work. If some people are no longer employed, we must ask: Are they being adequately compensated for the loss of the non-income-related goods of work?

I am perfectly willing to accept that the four properties identified above are structural goods of work (though I have some qualms about social status, depending on how it is interpreted) and that they should be factored into any assessment of the badness of work.[80] The question that concerns me is whether the goods identified are so intimately connected with work that if we eliminated it we would no longer be able to attain them. The answer, I believe, is a firm "no." Gheaus and Herzog implicitly acknowledge this when they point out that work is currently a "privileged" forum for the realization of these goods. This is undoubtedly true, but this is largely because of the colonizing power of work. It is because we spend (and have to spend) so much of our time performing, planning for, and worrying about work that we rely on it for mastery, contribution, community, and status. It is not as if those goods are impossible to obtain outside the confines of the workplace. People can and do achieve mastery over their hobbies and pastimes; people can and do contribute to their societies through volunteering and charity; and people can and do collaborate with others and build a sense of community in the process. These other forums are less accessible to us at the moment because of the overwhelming importance of work in our lives. If work lost its privileged status, they would open up once more.

In short, although there are undoubtedly structural goods associated with work as it is currently constituted, they are not so firmly embedded in the system as the structural bads: there are other viable pathways to those goods that could become more widely available if we encouraged more widescale automation of work. Furthermore, it should be remembered that there is considerable injustice in how these four non-income-related goods are distributed within the current system of work. Some jobs provide far more opportunities for mastery, contribution, community, and social status than others.[81] Thus, the four goods become a double-edged sword: the unfair distribution of them within the current system, just like the unfair distribution of income, may actually contribute to its structural badness.

The second general objection to the structural badness thesis is something I shall call the "why should I care?" objection. Remember, a key feature of the structural badness thesis is that it is the entire system of work that is the problem, not specific jobs. Some people work in jobs that are, from their perspective, very good indeed. As noted, I count myself as one of them. I am fortunate to have a job that pays reasonably well and gives me a lot of freedom to pursue my own interests. Why would someone in my predicament want things to change?

There are two responses. One is to appeal to our common sense of moral and social justice. Taking an impartial "view from nowhere" is often thought to be an essential ingredient in being a moral person.[82] The moral person should care about the well-being of everyone in their communities and societies (and possibly in the entire world). They should not be content with a system of work that just happens to reward them at the expense of others. But not everyone wants to be a moral person, so the second response is to appeal to enlightened self-interest. One's contentment within the current system of work is a fragile thing. The jobs that get easily displaced by technology are not necessarily the ones that pay the worst and have the worst conditions. To repeat the point made earlier, the middle-income, middle-skill jobs that have been devastated by information technology were solid, dependable, and life-sustaining for those who worked within them. Everything was going fine for these people until it wasn't. Automation is now creeping into the higher end of the pay and conditions spectrum, with complex cognitive tasks like financial analysis, trading, scientific experimentation, legal research, and medical diagnosis all being gradually automated, and subject to the forces of fissuring, precarity, and colonization that beset other jobs. Anyone who is well rewarded within the current system should be adopting a "there but for the grace of God go I" mentality. They should not become complacent. They should be willing to entertain the notion that their lives could be better outside the system.

The third general objection to the structural badness thesis is the "opportunity cost" objection. To this point, I have said a lot about what makes work bad, but I haven't said much about the alternatives. Why assume that they will be any better? Work might be pretty awful as it currently stands, but a world without work might be much worse. It might be a world of deprivation, listlessness, social conflict, lack of purpose, and so on. This is a common dystopian belief. You cannot build an argument for the desirability of the automation of work while ignoring its consequences for other aspects of our lives. The naive, anti-work view simply assumes that the post-work world will be better for all. But that's not something that can be taken for granted in a world in which people derive a sense of social purpose and meaning from work. It is something that needs to be carefully evaluated and defended.

I agree. That's why the remainder of this book will be dedicated to evaluating and defending different versions of the post-work world. Suffice to say, I think some of those versions have great potential, and others are less appealing. Creating the right kind of post-work future will be key to making good on the claim defended thus far in the book, namely, that the automation of work is both possible and desirable.

CHAPTER 4

Giving Techno-Pessimism Its Due

ONE OF MY FAVORITE FILMS IS *WALL:E*. It is an animated movie about a love-sick robot living on a future Earth. In this future, the environment on Earth has been completely despoiled. Wall:E spends his days sorting through mountains of trash and industrial detritus. Things have gotten so bad that all the humans have fled. They now live onboard gigantic interstellar cruise ships, looking for a new home. Their lives onboard these ships are pure, technologically mediated luxury. They no longer have to lift a finger. Hordes of robots control and maintain the ship, catering to their every need. They float around on motorized armchairs. They have become grossly obese. They are fed a constant stream of junk food and light entertainment. They are satiated, stupefied, and compliant.

Although undoubtedly satirical in nature, *Wall:E* provides us with one vision of a fully automated, post-work future. But the *Wall:E* vision of the future is hardly anyone's idea of a utopia. In fact, it seems downright dystopian: it shows how a fully automated future could bring out the worst in us, not the best. It seems like we are going to need to avoid this if we are to truly reap the benefits of escaping from the world of work.

The purpose of this chapter is to develop a field guide to the threats that need to be avoided if we are to secure a desirable post-work future. In the course of developing this field guide, I will defend the second of the four major propositions that were set out in chapter 1:

> **Proposition 2:** The automation of life more generally (outside of work) is less desirable than the automation of work: there are important threats to human well-being, meaning, and flourishing that are posed by the use of automating technologies in everyday life. We need to carefully manage our relationship with technology to limit those threats.

I will do this in three steps. First, I will explain what it is that humans need in order to flourish and what will need to be preserved (and enhanced) in order to sustain our flourishing in the post-work future. Second, I will present a theoretical framework for thinking about the threats that automating technologies may pose to our flourishing. Third, I will argue for the existence of five such threats. This will set the stage for the second half of the book wherein we consider two major strategies for avoiding these threats.

The Good Life

What is the good life? This is a perennial question among philosophers. Many ancient schools of philosophy (Stoicism, Epicureanism, Cynicism, etc.) were dedicated to answering it, and many words have been written in the intervening millennia defending different answers to it. I cannot do justice to all those different positions here, nor can I make an original contribution to the vast philosophical literature on the topic. My aims are more modest. I want to take advantage of the best work that has been done to date on the question of what makes for a good life and use this to figure out whether automating technologies could help or hinder our capacity to live a good life.

I will do this by isolating some generic and widely accepted conditions for a flourishing and meaningful existence. When combined with the framework set out in the next chapter, this will allow me to sketch an abstract landscape of possibility for a "good" (or utopian) post-work future. I will then use this landscape to evaluate and compare different visions of the post-work future. This should enable me to avoid a common pitfall in the writings of techno-utopians and optimists: a singular failure to say anything concrete or meaningful about what the ideal future should look like.[1]

To start, I need to clarify some of the terminology I will be using in this chapter and in the remainder of the book. From here on out, I will frequently talk about the need for a flourishing and meaningful existence. I use both terms to refer to different aspects of what a good life is. I use "flourishing" to refer to how well someone's life is going *for them*, that is, to their well-being. I use "meaningful" to refer to some additional component of the good life that is not always reducible to well-being, that is, the overarching significance or worthwhileness of an individual's life. There is some overlap between the two concepts, as we shall see in a moment, but there are also some relevant distinctions. I believe that both properties come in degrees. An individual's life can be more or less flourishing and more or less meaningful. I also think we can measure these properties over different timescales. We can judge that someone's life is flourishing / meaningful over a short timeframe (an hour, a day, a week) or over a longer timeframe (years, decades, entire lifespans). What interests most philosophers are the longer timeframes, particularly the "whole life" assessment, since it is possible for an individual's fortunes to wax and wane over the course of their lives. What we usually want to know is how good their lives are "on net" or "in the aggregate" not at some particular moment.[2]

To understand what it means to live a flourishing life, we must become familiar with the philosophical debate about the nature of human well-being.[3] There are two main schools of thought in this debate. There is the *subjectivist* school, which sees well-being as something that arises from subjectively determined states of being, such as pleasure or preference satisfaction.[4] And there is the *objectivist* school, which sees well-being as something that arises from the satisfaction of objectively determined states of being.[5] Theories within this school are sometimes referred to as "objective list theories" because they commonly list the conditions that they think need to be satisfied in order to ensure well-being. These can include things like education, knowledge, friendship, sense of community, physical and mental health, income, and so on.[6] The most well-known and influential objective list theory is probably the "capabilities theory" of Martha Nussbaum and

Amartya Sen, which sees developing basic human capabilities as the key to flourishing.[7]

To understand what it means to live a meaningful life, we must familiarize ourselves with the philosophical debate about meaning.[8] The positions within this debate are a little more complex, but we can simplify by saying that there are three main schools of thought.[9] Once again, there is the *subjectivist* school, which sees meaning as something that arises from the satisfaction of subjectively determined states of being, usually desire fulfillment or attaining a sense of achievement.[10] There is also the *objectivist* school, which sees meaning as something that arises from the satisfaction of objectively determined states of being. The big difference between this and the objectivist perspective of well-being has to do with the objective conditions that are deemed important. In the meaning debate, it is generally agreed that an individual's life needs to *add value* to the world in order to count as objectively meaningful. In other words, the individual must address themselves to solving or ameliorating some moral problems, adding to the sum total of human knowledge, or creating works of artistic significance. So, for example, we say that Martin Luther King Jr. lived a meaningful life because he advanced the cause of civil rights in America; that Albert Einstein lived a meaningful life because he developed the theories of relativity; and that Mozart lived a meaningful life because he composed wonderful operas. These three pathways to an objectively meaningful life are sometimes referred to as the Good, the True, and the Beautiful and have played a prominent role in the history of human thought.[11] In addition to the subjectivist and objectivist schools of thought, there is a third, which we can call the *hybridist* school. According to this, a combination of subjective and objective states of being need to be satisfied in order for someone to live a meaningful life. What this usually boils down to is the need for some relevant connection between the individual's mind and the objective value that they add to the world. For example, Susan Wolf argues that a meaningful life is one of *fitting fulfillment*.[12] It is a life in which an individual is subjectively fulfilled by pursuing and contributing to projects of objective value. In this respect, Wolf's hybridist theory corrects for an obvious flaw in purely subjectivist theories: that one could be subjectively fulfilled by doing many trivial things.

Imagine someone who really loves polishing their glasses and spends as much time as possible doing so. They might be subjectively fulfilled but they are hardly living a meaningful life.

That's the main lay of the land when it comes to understanding what it takes to live a meaningful life. There are, however, some other conditions of meaning that are discussed in the philosophical literature and that may be relevant to understanding the good life in a post-work world. There is, for example, a long-standing tradition of thought that links the existence of God to meaning in life.[13] Religious theories of this sort can be categorized as a type of objectivist theory because they effectively argue that an individual must contribute something of value to the world in order for their life to count as meaningful. It is just that the "something of value" in their case is something like "contributing to God's plan for salvation" or "worshiping God." There is also a long-standing tradition of thought that argues that death or the eventual heat-death of the universe pose problems for meaning because they wipes out any valuable contributions one might make during one's lifetime.[14] This leads some to suggest that immortality and eternal existence are necessary for meaning.[15] A less extreme version of this concern arises when people worry about the fragility of value in life, namely, the fact that one's fortunes are so easily reversed by things like war, natural disasters, ill health, and so on.[16] In previous writings, I have argued that we might want to add an "existential robustness" condition to our theory of meaning in order to address this concern about fragility.[17] In other words, in order to live a meaningful life we might need some assurance that our lives / projects will not be so easily disrupted.

Table 4.1 summarizes the constituent elements of the good life, as identified in the preceding discussion.

As mentioned at the outset, I am not going to stake out an original position on what makes for the good life. I am going to be guided by the best of what has been thought to date. Consequently, I am going to take an ecumenical approach to the different theories that have just been outlined. I will assume that in order to live a flourishing and meaningful life you need to satisfy some combination of subjective and objective conditions; and I will assume that these conditions include, in the case of flourishing, things like

Table 4.1   Conditions of Meaning and Flourishing

Flourishing	Meaningfulness
What makes an individual's life go well for them, i.e., what contributes to their well-being.	What makes an individual's life meaningful, i.e., what makes it significant or worthwhile.
Subjectivist Theories	*Subjectivist Theories*
You need to satisfy subjective states of being in order to flourish • Hedonism (pleasure) • Preference satisfaction	You need to satisfy certain subjective states of being to have meaning • Desire fulfillment • Sense of achievement
Objective List Theories	*Objectivist Theories*
You need to satisfy objective states of being and develop certain capabilities in order to flourish • Education • Health • Family • Friendship • Community • Knowledge • Practical reason • Cognitive ability	You need to contribute something of value to the world in order to have meaning • Make some contribution to the Good, the True and the Beautiful • Participate in God's plan
	Hybridist Theories
	You need to contribute something of value *and* be subjectively oriented to it in the right way • Fitting fulfillment theory • Fitting achievement theory
	Additional Conditions on Meaning • Immortality? • Eternity? • Existential robustness?

pleasure, education, health, friendship, developed cognitive ability, and in the case of meaning, things like fulfillment, achievement, and contributions to the Good, the True and the Beautiful. The more of these conditions that can be satisfied, the better, on average, the life.[18] In later chapters, I will explore in more detail the extent to which a life can flourish and have meaning if only subjective or objective conditions are satisfied, and I will also address the precise nature of the objective conditions that are appealed to in the different theories, but for now I will assume that both are necessary. On top of this, I will assume that some *connection* between the objective and subjective is required, particularly if you are to live a meaningful life.

The only conditions that I will decisively reject at this point are the religious / supernatural ones. I do so for three reasons: (i) I am not personally religious and so do not find these relevant or persuasive; (ii) there is too much disagreement about the specific content of particular religious worldviews for this to provide guidance, particularly when it comes to our relationship with automating technologies; and (iii) most of the secular conditions to which I appeal are also ones that feature in some of the world's leading religious traditions and so should appeal to members of those traditions.[19] Finally, I should add that I will assume that the arguments made in the preceding chapters also say something important about the conditions for a good life. For example, I assume that individual freedom (and the absence of domination) is important, as is some degree of distributive / social justice. These could be understood as part of the objective list needed for well-being.

In sum, when assessing whether an automated post-work future is one in which humans can flourish, it is important to consider the extent to which that future enables us to satisfy the subjective and objective conditions of flourishing and meaning, as well as the extent to which it facilitates a relevant connection between the two. To do this effectively it is essential that we have a good mental model for understanding our relationship to automating technologies.

How to Think about Our Relationship to Automating Technologies

In early 1991, the French media theorist and philosopher Jean Baudrillard wrote three provocative essays arguing that the "Gulf War did not take place."[20] At the time, the First Gulf War was actually taking place. An international coalition, led by the United States, was busy repelling the Iraqi invasion of Kuwait, through a combination of aerial and naval bombardment, and an eventual land invasion. Consequently, Baudrillard's thesis seemed a little odd.

There have been many interpretations of exactly what he meant over the years, but the most straightforward, and the one I favor, is that he was not denying the actual occurrence of the war but rather making a point about how the war was presented to the West through the media. The First Gulf

War was notable for the fact that it was one of the first times that journalists were embedded with troops during a conflict and were presenting live broadcasts from the battle lines. Baudrillard was arguing that these media representations of the war distorted and misrepresented the true reality. What we experienced in the West was a simulacrum of the war, not the actual war.

I mention this because it illustrates an important, and obvious, point about the effect of technology on our relationship to the world. Technology *mediates* our relationship to the world around us by creating new *affordances* in our environments.[21] When our distant ancestors created the Acheulean hand ax (some one million years ago), they created new possibilities for action and interaction with the world around them. With the ax, they could hunt and butcher animals in ways that their ancestors never could. Since then, humans have created a plethora of new technologies, each of which changes our relationship to the world around us. One only has to wander down a busy high street to see the evidence of this. It is a highly constructed environment. People drive cars, ride bikes, and gaze intently into the screens of their smartphones. No one interacts with the environment in a pure, unmediated form. They live and breathe in a technological ecology.

The mediating effects of technology have an important impact on our capacity to live a flourishing and meaningful life. By changing our relation to the external world, and by affording us new possibilities for action, technology changes our capacity to satisfy the subjective and objective conditions of flourishing and meaning. It also alters the relationship between the subjective and objective. In many instances, the effects of technology are a net positive. Technology often removes impediments to goal fulfillment: if you want to travel from your house to the city center, it's much easier to do so by bike or public transport than by foot; if you want to talk to your brother in Australia, it's much easier to do so via Skype than via letter or even traditional telephone line. By removing impediments to action, technology often helps us to satisfy the objective and subjective conditions of the good life.

But sometimes this can go too far. The example I used to open this chapter—of future humans in the movie *Wall:E*—provides a striking illustration of this. In the world of *Wall:E*, technology seems to be too good at removing impediments to action: it makes it too easy for humans to satisfy pleasurable and immediate desires (for food and entertainment), to the detriment of others. The lives of these humans might be very subjectively satisfying, but they would score low on any objective assessment of well-being and meaning. Technology has made them lazy and stupid.

This has been a long-standing concern. One of the founding texts of Western philosophy is Plato's dialogue *The Phaedrus*. In it, Socrates laments the invention of writing, arguing that if people spend too much time committing their thoughts to paper (or papyrus), they will lose the capacity for memory, and their minds will wither and atrophy: "their trust in writing, produced by external characters which are no part of themselves, will discourage the use of their own memory within them . . . they will read many things without instruction and will therefore seem to know many things, when they are for the most part ignorant and hard to get along with, since they are not wise, but only appear wise."[22]

To a modern audience, Socrates's lament seems overwrought. Have we really lost that much through the invention of writing? Have we not, in fact, gained by it? Writing has enabled new forms of cultural transmission and learning, new forms of institutional governance (through written law and written constitution), and more complex thinking. Socrates overlooked—or perhaps could not see—these advantages. In retrospect it looks like he was being short-sighted. If we are to avoid making his mistake again, we need to think carefully and rigorously about the consequences of automating technologies for our relationship to the world.

Is there any way to do this? I believe there is. I believe that the theory of situated / distributed cognition gives us a framework for thinking systematically and rigorously about this relationship between humans and technology. The essence of this theory is that human cognition (and anything humans do that is linked to cognition, including problem solving and goal achievement) is not just a brain-based phenomenon. It is, rather, a distributed and situated phenomenon. It arises from interactions between humans and the environment in which they operate, where that "environment" includes any technological artifacts that might have been created to assist in cognitive processing.[23]

Take a simple everyday example: solving a mathematical puzzle with the help of pen and paper. In this example, the solving of the puzzle is not something that takes place solely in the human mind. It is, rather, something that takes place as the result of a dynamic, interdependent relationship between the mind, the pen, and the paper. The essential insight of distributed cognition theory is that these kinds of interactions are pervasive, not just exceptional. This basic insight has been honed into a complex theoretical framework over the years, several aspects of which are useful for the present inquiry.

One aspect that is particularly useful in the present context is that it encourages us to think about the importance of so-called cognitive artifacts in the pursuit of the good life. Cognitive artifacts can be defined as any tools, objects or processes that assist in the performance of a cognitive task.[24] Artifacts of this sort are abundant and integral to human life. As the philosopher Richard Heersmink notes, "we use maps to navigate, notebooks to remember, rulers to measure, calculators to calculate, sketchpads to design, agendas to plan, textbooks to learn, and so on. Without such artifacts we would not be the same cognitive agents, as they allow us to perform cognitive tasks we would otherwise not be able to perform."[25]

Cognitive artifacts are important for a number of reasons. Cognitive artifacts help to reduce the cost of thinking (that is, make it less mentally intensive and time-consuming), and enable and facilitate new forms of cognition. They do this by creating external platforms for representing, organizing and combining information in novel and distinctive ways.[26] However, not all cognitive artifacts are equal in this respect. Some provide assistance by genuinely enhancing human abilities, others do so by distorting or undermine human abilities. Again, distributed cognition theory gives us the tools for understanding why this happens. There are two features of the theory that are important in this respect. First, the theory allows us to identify different categories or types of cognitive artifacts and see how these different categories might support or undermine our capacity to live flourishing and meaningful lives. Second, it allows us to think about the different ways in which those artifacts alter the cognitive tasks that humans perform, for better or for worse. Let's consider both of these features in more detail.

In terms of the different categories of cognitive artifacts, the complexity theorist David Krakauer has proposed a taxonomy that is specifically designed to help us to understand the role that advances in AI and automation might play in human cognition.[27] I offer a refined version of his tax-onomy here. This taxonomy distinguishes between three main categories of cognitive artifact:

> *Enhancing Artifacts:* These are cognitive artifacts that enhance innate, brain-based cognitive abilities. Krakauer's go-to example is the abacus. The abacus creates an external platform for representing and performing mathematical operations. People who are trained with abaci are often exceptionally fast and proficient mathematical problem solvers. What's more, although the abacus itself is invaluable during the learning phase, it is possible for it to be removed and for the trained individual to perform the operations just as well without the artifact. The reason for this is that the individual can recreate the artifact in virtual form inside their minds and solve mathematical problems with the virtual artifact. In this way, the artifact functions like a pair of training wheels that can be taken away once proficiency is attained.

> *Complementary Artifacts:* These are artifacts that enhance innate, brain-based cognitive abilities, but in a way that requires an ongoing reciprocal causal interaction between the human and the artifact. An example would be solving a mathematical puzzle with a pen and paper. This allows the human to create an external representation of the algorithm needed to solve the mathematical puzzle, but the external representation is always needed in order to be able to perform the operation. There is, consequently, genuine complemen-tary interdependency between the human and the artifact. It is not simply like a pair of training wheels that can be taken away.

> *Competitive Artifacts:* These are artifacts that assist in the perfor-mance of cognitive tasks, but not necessarily in a way that enhances or complements human cognitive ability, because they largely replace / outsource cognition. The classic example would be a digital calculator. This allows people to solve mathematical puzzles more quickly and accurately than they could hope to do by themselves, but the artifact does all the hard work. Humans input some basic

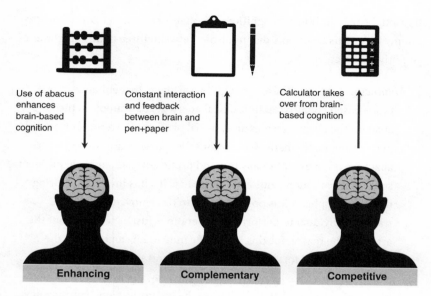

Figure 4.1 Three Kinds of Cognitive Artifact

commands and the artifact does the rest. This often has the exact opposite effect of an enhancing artifact because it makes people less good at performing mathematical operations by themselves and more dependent on the artifact.

The argument that I make here, and that Krakauer makes in his work, is that advances in AI and robotics tend toward the competitive end of this spectrum. They assist humans in the performance of cognitive tasks, and sometimes do so in complementary or enhancing ways, but often tend towards replacing or outsourcing human cognition. Krakauer thinks this is bad because it breeds technological dependency, which could have a knock-on effect on our autonomy and resiliency. I will consider this in more detail below. For now, I would just caution against any general denouncement of automating artifacts on the grounds of technological dependency. We need to be on guard, once more, against the danger of lapsing into the Phaedrus fallacy in being too narrow-minded in how we think about the effect of automating technologies on our pursuit of the good life.

This is where the second element of distributed cognition theory can help. As Donald Norman pointed out in a seminal 1991 article on cognitive artifacts, we need to think about our interactions with cognitive artifacts at two different levels: the *system level* (our brains / bodies plus the artifact) and *the personal level* (how we interact with the artifact).[28] At the system level, cognitive performance is often enhanced by the presence of an artifact: me-plus-pen-and-paper is better at math than me-without-pen-and-paper; me-plus-smartphone is better at remembering people's phone numbers than me-without-smartphone. But this system-level enhancement is usually achieved by *changing the cognitive task* performed at the personal level: instead of imagining numbers in my head and adding and subtracting them using some mentally represented algorithm, I visually represent the numbers on a page, in a format that facilitates the easy application of an algorithm; instead of mentally encoding and recalling phone numbers, I input search terms on the screen of my smartphone. The artifact thus changes one cognitive task into another (series) of cognitive tasks.

It is important to think about the changes rendered by automating cognitive artifacts at both levels. If we focus on the system level, we might think the net effect of automating technologies is overwhelmingly positive: they enable us to do more and get more of what we want, with less effort. Indeed, this net positive effect was what motivated many of the arguments that I made in Chapters 2 and 3. But if we focus on the personal level, things become less clearly positive. At the personal level, the effect can be both positive and negative: the artifacts can change the tasks that we have to perform in a way that either (a) opens us up to new and better experiences / interactions, tests our abilities to their limits, and facilitates our flourishing and meaning or (b) requires little effort and input, and thus breeds complacency and dependency. We need to be sensitive to both possibilities when we think about whether or not automating technologies enable us to live the good life.

Five Arguments for Techno-Pessimism

That's enough scene setting. I now turn to the main purpose of this chapter. As mentioned at the outset, I want to present five arguments for being pessimistic about the impact of automation on human flourishing and meaning. These arguments are intended to cast serious doubt on our ability to live a good life in a fully automated, post-work world. Each of the arguments focuses on a different way in which the widespread availability of automating technologies mediates and thereby changes our relationship with the world around us, in particular by changing how we relate to the subjective and objective conditions of meaning and flourishing. The arguments should be interpreted in conjunction with the case against work that was defended in the previous chapter. In other words, everything I say here presumes that work is, indeed, bad and getting worse. But before we run off into the post-work world, we need to pause to consider what kind of world we are escaping into. This is my attempt to paint a bleak picture of that world. It is only by fully acknowledging this potential bleakness that we can embrace the more optimistic views defended in later chapters.

Before I get into the five arguments, I need to say a word or two about the problem of deprivation in a post-work world. Obviously, any world in which the need for paid work has been eliminated would be a world in which a large percentage of the population would risk losing their ability to pay for the basic goods and services they need to survive. After all, a consistent income is *currently* essential for these things. Without it, we would perish. This is what I call the "deprivation problem." Any world in which mass deprivation is a reality, automated or otherwise, could not be conducive to human flourishing and meaning. People need a basic platform of health and well-being before they can truly flourish and pursue projects of great meaning. Consequently, any post-work world worth its salt will need to solve the deprivation problem.

But I am not going to solve or propose a resolution to the deprivation problem in this book. It is not my goal: I want to consider what happens even if we do manage to solve that problem. I do because it strikes me as being the more interesting inquiry. It forces us to confront fundamental questions about what it means to be human in an automated future. But to confront those questions in a substantive way, I have to bracket issues associated with the deprivation of basic goods and services, and I accept that these are big issues to set to the side. I feel confident in doing so, however, because I think the deprivation problem is solvable. There are two reasons for my optimism. First, the technologies we use to replace human labor should help to create a world of *abundance,* that is, a world of extremely cheap goods and services. Just imagine a world in which the world's best AI doctor, lawyer, architect (etc.) is readily accessible on your smartphone, and in which you can "print" any physical object you desire at the press of a button. That is the kind of world we are building with automating technologies. It may take us some time to fully realize and distribute its potential, but such technologically fa-cilitated abundance is feasible. Second, any residual problems associated with the lack of an income could be resolved through *redistributive* changes to the welfare system. The most obvious and widely discussed of which would be the introduction of a basic income guarantee. There are many books that already do a better and more comprehensive job of making the case for both the likelihood of abundance and the viability of a basic income than I ever could. I direct the interested reader to them.[29]

With that important caveat out of the way, let's consider the five argu-ments for thinking that we should be pessimistic even if we do solve the de-privation problem. In presenting these arguments, I will resort to the philo-sophical practice of presenting arguments as a series of numbered premises and conclusions. I do this both for ease of analysis and to help the reader clearly identify the strengths and weaknesses of the arguments being pre-sented. This is part of my effort to not simply defend a set of conclusions, but to demonstrate how to think about those conclusions. To do that, I try to be honest and upfront about the hurdles that my optimistic vision of the future must clear.

The Severance Problem

The first argument for pessimism is the most general. It claims that the widespread availability of automating technologies is a problem because it threatens to *sever the link* between humans and the objective world. This is bad because some link between humans and the objective world is integral to flourishing and meaning. For example, I cannot make meaningful contri-butions to scientific knowledge if I am not actually investigating, interpreting, and responding to the world around me; I cannot address the moral prob-lems of the world if I am not acting in it. One of the obvious features of automating technologies is how they tend to obviate the need for human action. They allow us to achieve outcomes without doing anything particularly strenuous. Indeed, this is a presumption underlying all the arguments for the automation of work outlined in Chapter 2: that machines can produce economic goods and services with minimal human assistance.

In more formal terms, the argument works like this:

(1) If humans are to live lives of flourishing and meaning, there must be some significant connection between what they do and what happens to them and the world around them.

(2) The widespread availability of automating technologies severs the significant connection between what humans do and what happens to them and the world around them.

(3) Therefore, the widespread availability of automating technologies undermines the capacity of humans to live lives of flourishing and meaning.

Let's consider each premise in more detail. I have alluded to the "significant connection" idea several times already in this chapter, but it's worth being more precise. What makes for a significant connection between what someone does and what happens to them? There are several different accounts of this in the philosophical literature. We can start by considering the "fitting fulfillment" connection discussed in the work of Susan Wolf. This account focuses on the subjective enjoyment of things that are objectively good. On the face of it, this does not seem to require much effort or strenuous activity on the part of the person being fulfilled. I could sit back and enjoy all the objectively wonderful things that machines produce in the world—new scientific discoveries, new cures for disease, new reductions in suffering—and still live a life of fitting fulfillment. All that matters is that I *respond* to changes in the objective world in the right way. This would seem possible no matter what the advances in automating technologies might be.[30] This reveals an interesting truth, which is that theories of flourishing and meaning that are primarily subjective in nature (even if the subjective has to respond to the objective) can embrace a fully automated future more easily than primarily objective theories. They do so by denying or attenuating the need for human activity in the pursuit of flourishing and meaning. This is the antithesis of the significant connection appealed to in premise (1).

I will have more to say about primarily subjectivist theories later in this book. For now, I would just argue that the idea that one could simply sit back and enjoy the ride is anathema to the most intuitive conception of the good life. We need something more than mere responsiveness to the objective world to live a good life. We need to actually bring about the changes in the objective world that lead to our fitting fulfillment. We need to be able to say that we have made the world a better place. In short, we need to be able to say that we *achieved* the things in the objective world that provide us with fitting fulfillment. According to Gwen Bradford, we only have a right to say that when three conditions are satisfied: (i) we have followed some *process that produces* the outcome in which we are interested; (ii) that process is *sufficiently difficult*; and (iii) that process is *non-lucky* (meaning, it requires some skill or competence on our part).[31] Suppose I just completed a marathon and I feel good about it. That's a legitimate achievement because it satisfies the three conditions: I followed a process (training/running) that produced that outcome; the process was difficult (many months of arduous physical activity and a final race); and it was non-lucky (I couldn't just fluke my way through the twenty-six-mile run). Contrast that with winning the lottery by buying a ticket. That's not an achievement because the process that produced the outcome wasn't particularly difficult (buying a ticket is easy), and the outcome produced was purely a matter of luck (my numbers just happened to come up).

Achievement is the significant connection we need to satisfy premise (1). It is also the connection that is most threatened by advances in automating technologies. Why so? Because automating technologies undermine two of the three conditions needed for achievement: (i) they replace human processes with machine ones; and (ii) they make it much easier to produce relevant outcomes (the flick of a switch or a voice command is enough). They do not make outcomes a pure matter of luck, but they ensure that human competence and skill is less needed and more attenuated. This isn't to say that achievement is completely undermined. The producers and designers of the machines may have some rightful claim to the achievements of machines, but their claim will be minimal if the machine learns and develops on its own (just as parents have less claim to the achievements of their children over time) and they will be relatively few in number compared to the large masses of people whose achievements are displaced by automating technologies.[32] This in turn provides support for premise (2): as automating technologies develop in scope and power, there is reason to think that human achievement will be undermined, which results in the severing of the connection we need to live lives of flourishing and meaning.

You may have noticed that the severance argument is quite similar to the general argument for technological unemployment outlined in Chapter 2. Both make grand claims about the power of automating technologies to displace human activity, and both are consequently susceptible to same kind of objection. Where proponents of the technological unemployment argument had to deal with the Luddite fallacy, proponents of the severance argument have to deal with a very similar alleged fallacy. The alleged fallacy is this: the argument just outlined may succeed in showing that human achievement will be undermined in certain domains of activity—to pick a random example: in medical diagnostics and drug discovery (both of which contribute to the objective good)—but surely there are many other domains of activity in which humans can flourish and seek meaning? What's more, mightn't some of these domains of activity be complemented by the availability of automating technologies? For example, I might be a much better and more creative scientist if automating technologies can do some of the experimental drudge work on my behalf.

As you might imagine, some of the responses to the Luddite fallacy argument also apply here, particularly since we currently rely on the labor market to provide access to the kinds of activities we need for flourishing and meaning. That said, if automating technologies reduce the need for work, we would then be free to choose other (non-economically rewarded) domains of activity that are conducive to flourishing and meaning. For example, we could focus our time on obscure and seemingly useless areas of scientific research. Indeed, this may be to return to the ideal of scientific inquiry that has been lost in an era obsessed with the market value of research. So let me make two new points that I believe provide some reason to doubt our ability to find new ground for human achievement in a world of rampant automation.

First, it is difficult to contain the rise of automating technologies in a way that ensures that it only displaces forms of work that are ill-suited to human flourishing and meaning. In fact, there is every reason to think that the opposite might be true. Following Moravec's paradox, it could well be the case that the kinds of activities that are most readily susceptible to automation are the ones from which we derive most meaning and satisfaction. If we think, broadly, about the domains of activity that are most commonly associated with flourishing and meaning—the Good, the True, and the Beautiful—we already see evidence for the encroachment of automation. For example, many basic moral problems[33]—disease, suffering, inequality—are caused by human imperfections and could be addressed through better automated systems. Much of the excitement around self-driving cars stems from the belief that they can reduce the carnage on our roads that is caused by irresponsible human drivers. Removing humans from the loop could make the world a better—or at least safer—place for all. This logic also applies to the decision to use automated systems for disease diagnostics or criminal sentencing, and to deciding how to distribute other social goods and services like healthcare. This is not to say that the current crop of automated systems are necessarily making the world a better place—there are well-documented problems of bias and unintended consequences associated with their use.[34] It is, however, to say that there is a growing will and desire to use automating technologies to solve basic moral problems, which will mean that this aspect of the good life is likely to be reduced in scope by the development of such technologies.

The same goes for the pursuit of knowledge and the discovery of truth. Science is currently the major pathway to truth and it is increasingly being undertaken with the assistance of machines. I gave some examples of this in Chapter 1 when I described the ADAM and EVE robot scientists created by research teams in the United Kingdom. This is just the tip of a very large iceberg. Science is now, and increasingly, a big data enterprise in which large teams of human researchers rely on machines to interpret, process, and make sense of the data they use in their theories. The room for individual achievement has been greatly downsized, and the capacity for individuals to actually make a difference to discovery has been attenuated by the increasing complexity of the inquiries and the need for machine assistance.

This leaves only the Beautiful as a potential domain of activity for human flourishing. Even there we see the encroachment of automation, with many robot artists and musicians being created in recent years.[35] That said, there may be less cause for concern here than in the other two domains. There is an infinite number of artworks that can be created, and the value of one does not diminish the value or importance of another. I can write a play and a machine can write a play, and they will, more than likely, be different enough that my achievement in writing the play is not undermined by the machine's achievement. The same is not true in relation to science and morality. To use an old cliché, if Shakespeare had never been born, we would never have had the wonders of *Hamlet, Othello,* and *Macbeth;* if Einstein had never been born, someone else would have come up with the theories of special and general relativity.[36] It might be fun to replicate someone else's scientific or moral achievements, but it's not quite the same thing being the first to do so. So we have to ask ourselves whether a world in which the Beautiful is our main source of flourishing and meaning is enough. That's the kind of world we could be heading for with the rise of automating technologies.

The second point I would make is that even if it is true, in principle, that there are other domains of activity that are conducive to our flourishing and meaning, and that these domains could be opened up to us by automating technologies, we have to ask how practically feasible it is for us to access those domains. It could be that other features of automating technologies distract us from, or undermine our ability to engage in, the kinds of activities we need if we are to live truly flourishing and meaningful lives. Some of the arguments discussed below suggest that this may indeed be the case. Consequently, optimism about the possibility of finding new terrains of fulfillment might be difficult to sustain in practice.

That's the severance problem. It is the most basic and fundamental of the problems discussed in this chapter. The four remaining problems complement and elaborate upon it.

The Attention Problem

The second argument for pessimism focuses on the problem of distraction and attentional manipulation. The gist of the argument is this: the technological infrastructure that we have created over the past half century is an infrastructure that is designed to absorb our attention.[37] Social media and digital content platforms—including the obvious culprits like Facebook, Twitter, YouTube, Google, as well as a plethora of other apps and services—are predominantly built on advertising models. They do not charge for their services. Instead, they sell their users' attention (and personal data) to advertisers. To do this they have to manipulate and control attention for their benefit. This undermines the human ability to live a flourishing and meaningful life because both the content of and capacity for attention is integral to both.

The logic of this argument works in the following manner (the numbering continues from the previous argument in this chapter):

(4) Attention is integral to the good life: our capacity to pay attention to the right things, for extended periods of time, largely determines how flourishing and meaningful our lives are.

(5) Automating technologies (a) undermine our capacity to pay attention for extended periods and (b) focus our attention on the wrong things.

(6) Therefore, automating technologies undermine our capacity to live flourishing and meaningful lives.

This argument is interesting because it takes direct aim at the unspoken assumption underlying the anti-work ideology that I defended in the previous chapter, namely, that freedom from work creates an opportunity to pursue activities that are more conducive to our flourishing. This argument says that this will not happen because our digital technologies will distract from those higher pursuits. Let's consider the premises in more detail.

Premise (4) is common sense. We all live in a stream of consciousness. This stream of consciousness can be quite confusing and multilayered: we are constantly bombarded by stimuli from the external world that intrude upon this stream of consciousness, and thoughts bubble up from our subconscious minds on an irregular schedule. As I sit here typing these words, I am bombarded by the sounds of passing traffic, the flickering of the fluorescent light bulb above my head, the sensation of the keyboard clacking beneath my fingers, the thoughts of the conversation I had yesterday with my friend. These are eddies in my stream of consciousness. But I am only dimly aware of some of them. My conscious experience is layered and differentiated.

Some experiences take center stage, others fade into the background. What's really important to me right now are the words that I am typing and the thoughts of what I want to type next. These are part of my focused conscious awareness. They are where my attention lies.

Attention is integral to the good life for a number of reasons. What occupies our attention has a significant influence on the quality of our lives. This is true for any theory of flourishing and meaning that includes a subjective component. If my attention is taken up with thoughts of doom and gloom, or experiences of pain, anxiety, and sadness, I cannot flourish. The most wonderful things could be happening in the world around me—people could be curing cancer, creating breathtaking works of art, and making new scientific discoveries—and I might even be partially responsible for those outcomes, but if my faculty of attention is so distorted and disrupted that I do not realize this, then my life will not be good.[38] This is a long-standing insight. The ancient philosophy of Stoicism, for example, argues that managing your attention—focusing on what is within your control and ignoring what is not—is essential to flourishing. This idea has also found support in more recent times in psychology and behavioral science. Several studies in the psychology of well-being suggest that attention is what matters most. In her 2009 book *Rapt*, the science journalist Winifred Gallagher recounts her realization that attention was integral to well-being after her cancer diagnosis. This led her to investigate the scientific literature on the importance of attention, and to conclude that the "skillful management of attention" was the sine qua non of the good life.[39]

But this is to focus purely on the *content* of our attention. Another reason why attention is so important has to do with the *capacity* to pay attention for sustained periods of time. This is, of course, a central idea in Buddhist mindfulness meditation, which is now regularly touted as key to managing the stresses and strains of modern life.[40] A regular mindfulness practice builds up one's capacity to pay attention to the present moment (in a non-judgmental way). And there is more to the capacity for sustained attention than that. Sustained focus helps to develop skills and abilities that are essential for achievement, and is often rewarded by intense feelings of pleasure and satisfaction. The psychologist Mihaly Csikszentmihalyi is famous for his pioneering studies on this feeling, which he called "flow."[41] In a series of studies, he showed that people report the highest levels of happiness and well-being when they are deeply absorbed in tasks that push their capacities to their limits. Flow is not possible without a strong capacity for sustained attention.

All of this suggests that the case for premise (4) is strong. What about premise (5)? Why think that automating technologies are undermining our capacity to pay attention and getting us to pay attention to things that are less conducive to flourishing and meaning? In some sense, this is just an obvious feature of our current predicament. To repeat an example from earlier, walk down any busy high street and you will be greeted by swarms of people gazing intently into the screens of their smartphones, flitting from social media app to social media app, and occasionally looking up in order to avoid walking into one another. There is significant financial incentive for the companies who control these devices and services to keep people intently focused on them. It is how they make their money. They are willing to invest significant amounts of time and labor into perfecting the art. Well-known tricks and techniques from behavioral science are leveraged to maximize the amount of time people spend on devices and services. The pleasing yet irregular ping of the latest Facebook or email notification—with its attendant promise of some fresh stimulus / reward—is like a modern-day version of the one-armed bandit machine: the actual rewards are few, but they are infrequent and pleasant enough to keep us checking in. This is partly because the services provide ongoing feedback for our activities, often dressed up in the guise of social interaction (likes, retweets, comments, leaderboards, etc.), all of which has a natural appeal to the human mind.[42]

To suggest that technology has not captured our attention would, then, fly in the face of everyday experience. But has it captured our attention in destructive and counterproductive ways? That might be less obvious, but the indications are certainly there. For one thing, the kinds of attention that it captures are noted to be remarkably shallow and fragmented in nature.[43] Opening your Facebook or Twitter feed is like drinking from a fire hose. There is a never-ending stream of new content, new notifications, and new possibilities, all of which are competing for your attention. It is difficult to stay focused on any one thing for an extended period of time: there's always some potentially better bit of digital content a click away. One of my favorite illustrations of this problem—though undoubtedly niche and slightly dated—comes from the comedy sketch show *Portlandia,* where one of the main characters gets trapped in a "technology loop," constantly flitting back and forth between new emails, cat videos, Facebook updates, listicles, Netflix shows, and never settling on a single thing. I have lost many days of my life on such technology loops. What's more, even if we do pay attention to something for more than a few seconds, the kinds of things we are paying attention to are not conducive to well-being and flourishing. The social interactions online are often minimal and shallow (likes, upvotes) and frequently encourage anxiety since people tend to share successes and hide failures. The ever-present gaze of advertisers compounds the situation because their goal is to identify or create needs / wants, and so to promise us better versions of ourselves. Living in the moment, being absorbed and happy in what you do, is not allowed. This is to say nothing of the negative political consequences of this attention capture, which manifests itself in increased polarization, the spread of fake news and conspiracy theories, and the hijacking of the public space.

So I think a good argument can be made for the claim that technology is capturing our attention in destructive ways—ways that ultimately undermine our capacity to live flourishing and meaningful lives. That said, there are two important objections to this argument.

The first is that although I have framed this argument as a critique of automating technologies, you could argue that those technologies have little to do with the problem. It is the internet, and smartphones and digital content providers in particular, that are doing the damage. Robotics and AI are not the issue. This objection is seductive but misleading. While it is true that robotics and AI are not *necessary* for the problem of attention capture, they are likely to exacerbate and deepen it. This is not due to the intrinsic properties of those technologies but rather due to how they are and will be leveraged for the foreseeable future. It will be companies that are heavily invested in the attention economy that will implement these technologies in the most immediately impactful ways. We see this already. Digital surveillance and machine learning are central to how social media platforms hone the addictive potential of their services, and most of the social robots and AI assistants that have been marketed in recent years (including Google's Assistant and Amazon's Alexa) are made by the major players in this system of "surveillance capitalism."[44] There is a very good reason for this: the impressive machine learning programs at the heart of these advances in AI depend upon widescale surveillance and attention capture for their success. Future automating technologies can only avoid this problem if there is some radical change in both technical and social systems, of the sort to be discussed in later chapters.

The second objection is that although the picture painted seems bleak for attention in the modern age, it is surely the case that other social institutions have tried to capture our attention in the past—for example, religion and the state—and that the current system of attention capture is not necessarily any worse than those historical precursors.[45] There is something to this objection. It is certainly true that we should avoid status quo bias when evaluating new features of our technological world.[46] Nevertheless, there seem to be two features of the current environment that make it appreciably worse than its historical precursors: (i) the technology enables far more pervasive and finely tuned forms of attention capture, and (ii) there is, prima facie, much less reason to think that advertising content is conducive to the good life than content provided by religions and the state. To be clear on point (ii), I am not in the least bit religious or statist in my philosophical leanings—as I hope to make clear in later chapters—but whatever you like to say about both institutions, they did at least try to present a particular model of the good life to their subjects, telling them about their vision of the Good, the True, and the Beautiful. Advertising does not seem to do this: it fosters need and anxiety, without trying to make well-supported claims about what is good, true, or beautiful.

The Opacity Problem

The third argument for pessimism focuses on the problem of opacity. This requires a bit of setup. Think, for a moment, about what it might have been like to live in an ancient society, one that lacked the insights of modern science, and believed that the natural world was controlled by unseen gods and goddesses. In such a society, you might frequently resort to bizarre ritual sacrifices and celebrations in an effort to make sense of what was happening and to give some illusion of control.[47]

You might resort to such practices for an obvious reason: the world is complex and unpredictable, and you would want to have some power over it. We see this desire everywhere in human culture and history. Humans grasp, desperately, at any perceived correlation between what we do and what happens to us. It gives us a sense of direction and purpose. The behavioral psychologist B. F. Skinner demonstrated that such desperate grasping at correlation was not even unique to humans. In a series of experiments performed on pigeons in controlled experimental environments, he showed that even they will resort to ritual dances and contortions if they think it might result in the experimenter providing them with a reward.[48]

The struggles of our animist ancestors and the pigeons in Skinner's boxes are illustrations of the problem of opacity—of what happens when the world is deeply mysterious and seemingly enchanted, when the world is blanketed by a veil of ignorance, and when things just happen to us and we don't really know why. To be clear, this problem of opacity doesn't arise only in relation to our understanding of the natural world. The social world can also be opaque. Bureaucratic systems can be mysterious and labyrinthine: think about the plight of Josef K. in Kafka's novel *The Trial*. The motivations of our friends and colleagues can seem perverse, dark, and Machiavellian. We undoubtedly have a better intuitive grasp of what they are up to than we do of fluid dynamics, but the problem of opacity can still rear its ugly head in the familiar world of friendships. We always see through a glass, darkly.

Although opacity is a persistent problem, what I want to suggest here is that automating technologies are likely to exacerbate the problem of opacity, making both the natural, and particularly the social, worlds more difficult to understand. This will significantly undermine our capacity to live flourishing and meaningful lives. The argument works like this:

(7) The more opaque the natural and social worlds are, the less capacity we have to live flourishing and meaningful lives.

(8) Automating technologies make the natural and the social worlds more opaque.

(9) Therefore, automating technologies undermine our capacity to live flourishing and meaningful lives.

There is a lot to this argument. Let's start with premise (7). The claim being made there is not that a total absence of opacity is required for flourishing and meaning. The natural world was quite opaque to our animist ancestors, but I have no doubt that at least some of them lived good lives. Furthermore, I doubt that the total absence of opacity is feasible: there will probably always be some mystery to reality; some brute facts that remain unexplained and unaccounted for.[49] The claim is, rather, that reducing opacity is important and critical to our flourishing. Over the past few centuries, particularly since the dawn of the scientific revolution, we have opened a chink of light in the veil of ignorance. We have acquired more *understanding* of our world. This understanding is important to the good life, and any possibility of it decreasing as a result of automating technologies should be disturbing.

There are two reasons for this. The first is that understanding typically goes hand in hand with an enhanced control of the world, which in turn allows us to bring about the changes to the world that are conducive to flourishing and meaning. The correlation isn't perfect—we understand how and why the sun will become a white dwarf in seven billion years, but there is little we can do about it right now—but it generally holds true. Once we understand how crops grow we can develop refined breeding and fertilization techniques that can feed billions.[50] Once we understand how disease occurs and spreads, we can control it and cure it. Understanding enables us to build a platform for developing our capacities for achieving the Good, the True, and the Beautiful. The second reason is that understanding is itself a good—something that makes our lives better, irrespective of the ends to which it is put. Understanding is different from knowledge. Understanding unites and explains. Before Newton, we knew that billiard balls collided with one another in particular ways, that objects fell to Earth in particular patterns, and that the planets followed particular arcs through the sky. After Newton, we united all these discrete observations under a single explanatory framework. At last, we understood.

There are several different accounts of why it is that understanding is so central to the good life.[51] Some are purely subjective in nature. Linda Zagzebski, for example, argues that understanding is valuable because it increases the "conscious transparency" of the world: once we understand we are a little more comfortable in our skins, seeing and grasping things we didn't before, and so more satisfied with our lives.[52] Other theories cash out the value of understanding in terms of how it fuses the subjective and objective. In other words, understanding creates a connection between the world inside your head and the world outside your head that is intrinsically valuable. This can seem mysterious, particularly when people explain this idea in terms of the "deep mirroring" between the subjective and the objective, but there are more readily comprehensible theories too. For instance, Duncan Pritchard argues that the value of understanding lies predominantly in the fact that understanding is a kind of achievement, specifically a *cognitive achievement*.[53] When you understand things, you have overcome a cognitive impediment and demonstrated cognitive competency. This makes understanding part and parcel of the more general, "achievementist" theories of meaning that were discussed earlier. I do not have any dog in the fight about how we should categorize the good of understanding. For my purposes, it suffices that understanding is valuable and part of what it takes to live a flourishing and meaningful life.

This brings us to premise (8) of the argument. Why should we think that automating technologies are undermining the capacity for understanding? There are several mechanisms at play. Some of the mechanisms are social-cultural in nature, some are technological, and some are a product of the mismatch between human cognition and machine intelligence.[54] Automating systems are often introduced to manage complexity in efficient ways. This was a major theme in Chapter 1 of this book. The rise of digital surveillance and big data has led to the formation of large, dynamically updated datasets that are used in a variety of research and policy settings. Real-time traffic-management systems, for example, enable public sector workers to address traffic problems in major urban centers. These systems rely on networks of data-collecting devices that are too large and complex for human data managers to make sense of by themselves. They require the assistance of data-mining algorithms to parse and organize the information and package it in a way that helps humans. This might give the impression that the automating systems increase, rather than decrease, understanding, but this is not the case. Data-mining tools present outputs and recommendations to human users—traffic is too high on Street X, reduce the problem by diverting traffic to Street Y—without necessarily explaining the logic or rationale behind those recommendations. This is true in other domains too. The use of predictive policing or sentencing algorithms, for example, helps police officers and judges to manage complex data streams, and to make decisions on the basis of ready-to-use recommendations, but they do so without providing detailed explanations of why.[55] You are also likely to be familiar with this phenomenon. You have probably been recommended some product or service by an algorithm, or been nudged to do something by such a system without knowing exactly why. The systems help to manage complexity, but do so in a way that provides us with actionable information, not deep understanding. They introduce a layer of opacity between the human user and the underlying phenomena. This may benefit the human user in certain ways, but blocks them from understanding. Some advocates of big data actually celebrate this. Mayer-Schonberger and Cukier, for example, argue that one of the benefits of big data-assisted science is that it will replace causal understanding with correlative knowledge—a prospect that has, unsurprisingly, met with less enthusiasm from advocates of traditional scientific inquiry.[56]

Jenna Burrell argues that there are three main causes of this automated opacity.[57] The first is that many automated systems are deliberately designed to be opaque in order to protect intellectual property rights. The companies that create them want to profit from doing so, and they fear that they cannot do so if the source code is public knowledge. The legal and political systems in many countries are complicit in facilitating this kind of *intentional* opacity. The second cause of opacity is digital / technological illiteracy amongst those who both use and are affected by the systems. Even if source codes were made public, relatively few people have the technical competency needed to understand them.[58] This is compounded by certain psychological biases that encourage people to reduce their understanding of automated processes. For example, there is a well-known automation bias that tends to creep in whenever people use seemingly well-functioning automated systems. To get a sense of what this is like, ask yourself the question: How many times have you second-guessed Google Maps' routing algorithm? Automation bias of this sort can lead to terrible injustices when people are negatively affected by recommendations from automated systems, but this is oftentimes a result of the lack of understanding of how these systems operate, and an unwillingness to challenge the perceived wisdom of the algorithm.[59] This makes some sense: understanding is cognitively costly—it wouldn't be an achievement if it weren't—and people have an innate tendency to reduce their cognitive burden: if a machine can do all the hard work, why should I bother?[60] This can lead to a positive feedback cycle wherein people start off by deferring to the machine out of convenience but then end up being unable to challenge it due to reduced cognitive capacity.[61] The third cause of automated opacity is *intrinsic* to the technology itself. Some automated systems are just exceptionally difficult, maybe even impossible, to reverse-engineer. Machine learning systems that rely on neural networks have become very good at solving certain kinds of problems—for example, facial recognition and voice recognition—but they do so in a highly opaque, non-interpretable fashion. This problem of technical opacity is further compounded by the fact that many automated systems are grafted together from other bits of code, and interact with other algorithms in complex and unpredictable ways.[62]

All of this leads me to conclude that premise (8) is well supported and hence that automated opacity could pose a serious impediment to flourishing and meaning. But you could resist this conclusion. You could argue that premise (8) is not as compelling as it seems because we could overcome the problem of automated opacity. We could dismantle the laws that facilitate and encourage intentional opacity; we could change our educational curriculums to ensure digital literacy; and we could introduce regulations / prohibitions on using systems that are intrinsically opaque. Indeed, there are some efforts in this regard already. There are attempts to teach programming in primary and secondary schools; and there is much discussion of explainable automated decision-making as a result of the EU's new General Data Protection Regulation.[63] But despite these efforts, I think there are reasons to remain pessimistic. Dismantling the legal framework that facilitates opacity will require a significant amount of collective will, and implementing an educational program that will genuinely help people to understand automated systems would be incredibly challenging. Our current efforts at teaching civic awareness or mathematical literacy are, after all, woefully inadequate. Furthermore, when it comes to regulating away the intrinsic opacity of certain technical systems, I fear that the horse has already bolted: these systems are out there already and being used to productive ends; to prohibit their use may require sacrificing the benefits they bring. In previous work, I argued that this may be one of the tragic tradeoffs we face in the automated future: do we want the most efficient and effective automated systems or do we want the most comprehensible ones?[64]

You could also object that I vastly overstate the impact of automated opacity on understanding. The social and natural worlds may become somewhat more opaque through automation, but we will have plenty of opportunities for understanding. We can still understand our friends and families, and enjoy our interactions with them. What's more, all the understanding that was brought to us by past human inquiries will still be available to us, and there is some good to be found in accessing them again. I can learn how the Pythagorean theorem was derived and benefit from this understanding without necessarily needing to understand how modern-day computers are proving conjectures that have resisted proof for centuries.[65] But I argue that there would be something tragic in this. The same issue that I discussed in relation to the severance problem rears its head: we would nevertheless be cut off from new domains and new frontiers of understanding. Our role in making sense of the world around us may come to an end. All we will be left to do is to make sense of ourselves.

The Autonomy Problem

The fourth argument for pessimism focuses on the impact of automating technologies on autonomy / freedom.[66] I already noted the importance of autonomy / freedom in Chapter 3 when I discussed the dominating influence problem in the workplace. To reiterate what I said there: autonomy and freedom are central goods in modern liberal societies. Protecting and respecting autonomy is often claimed to be the first step in ensuring the legitimacy of liberal institutions of governance.[67]

This might make it sound like autonomy is an intrinsic good, something that is good in and of itself, irrespective of the uses to which it is put. If taken to an extreme, this position can have some disturbing implications. It could be taken to suggest that there is some good in an autonomously chosen act, even if the act itself is bad.[68] Better to rule in hell than serve in heaven and all that. But you don't have to take it to this extreme to accept the importance of autonomy. It is possible to take a more instrumentalist perspective, arguing that autonomy is not intrinsically good but is worth protecting because it serves other goods, particularly the goods of individual well-being and flourishing. The argument would be that people are more likely to flourish if they are in control of their own lives.[69]

Irrespective of the view you take, autonomy is generally agreed to be a good and to be something that plays a key role in a flourishing and meaningful existence. Indeed, addressing the impact of the loss of autonomy on meaning is thought to be a key challenge for those who deny its existence: If we have no freedom to choose our own path in life, then doesn't this add an air of futility or nihilism to our existence? What is the point in trying to achieve anything, or understand anything, if we don't have the freedom to pursue these ends in the first place?[70] If this is right, it helps to motivate the following argument:

> (10) Individual autonomy plays an important role in a flourishing and meaningful existence.
> (11) Automating technologies undermine the capacity for individual autonomy.
> (12) Therefore, automating technologies undermine the capacity to live a flourishing and meaningful existence.

I take it that no more needs to be said in defense of premise (10). This makes (11) the sticking point. Why should we think that automating technologies undermine autonomy? To answer that we will need to delve deeper into the nature of autonomy. Autonomy is the capacity for self-governance. Much has been written about what exactly is required in order to be a true self-governor. Here, I adopt a conception of autonomy that was first introduced and defended by the legal philosopher Joseph Raz. He said:

> If a person is to be maker or author of his own life then he must have the mental abilities to form intentions of a sufficiently complex kind, and plan their execution. These include min-

imum rationality, the ability to comprehend the means required
to realize his goals, the mental faculties necessary to plan
actions, etc. For a person to enjoy an autonomous life he must
actually use these faculties to choose what life to have. There
must in other words be adequate options available for him to
choose from. Finally, his choice must be free from coercion and
manipulation by others, he must be independent.[71]

This quoted passage identifies three conditions of autonomy: (i) the capacity
for rationality, specifically the capacity to form and execute complex intentions; (ii) the presence of an adequate range of options to choose between
when exercising this capacity; and (iii) the absence of interference, manipulation, and coercion by others (to which we could also add the absence of
"domination," in line with the argument from Chapter 3). We can call these
three conditions the *rationality, optionality,* and *independence* conditions for
short. In conjunction, these conditions give us a test we can deploy to assess the impact of automating technologies on autonomy. Instead of asking
the general, and vague, question about whether or not they affect autonomy,
we can ask the more precise question about whether automating technologies negatively impact on the three conditions.

I argue that they can do so, particularly when we think about their impact on the optionality and independence conditions. I discount the rationality condition because it seems unlikely that automating technologies
could completely undermine our capacity to plan and execute complex
intentions—though if we follow the arguments of technology critics such as
Nicholas Carr, they could degenerate our cognitive capacities to such an extent that we lose some of that ability.[72] Carr's pessimism notwithstanding I
think it is much more plausible to suppose that automating technologies will
be used to limit the range of options available to us and affect the independence of our decision-making.

Let's consider the limitation of options first. David Krakauer, whom I
mentioned earlier in this chapter, has expressed some fears about this, specifically in relation to the widespread deployment of AI decision-support
tools. He is concerned about AI "recommender" systems that block us from
exploring an adequate range of options.[73] We are fed recommendations by

such systems on a daily basis. When I go shopping on Amazon, I am immediately presented with a list of recommended products; when I go to watch a movie on Netflix, I am fed different menus of options with titles like "currently trending," "films with a strong female lead," and so on; and when I am trying to find my way around a strange city, Google Maps tells me which route to take, and which routes have a similar ETA. This is just a small sample of recommender systems. As noted above, similar systems are also widely deployed in business and government.

These systems could certainly have a negative impact on the optionality condition because they all work by designing the "choice architecture" in which we select our preferred options.[74] One major concern about this is that the range of options made available to us through such recommender systems might be quite limited, and not adequate to our preferred self-conception. The options might be more reflective of the needs and interests of the corporations who control the recommender systems. In extreme cases, the choice architecture might be so limited as to give us only one "live" option to choose from. Google Maps sometimes has this effect, due to the way in which it highlights a preferred route. In even more extreme cases, the system might block us completely from making a choice among available options and simply make the choice for us. This is, in many ways, the apotheosis of all automating technologies: obviating the need for human activity.

It is important, however, not to overstate the negative impact of automating technologies on the optionality condition. There are ways in which AI recommender systems could help to promote autonomy by filtering and pre-selecting options. Having a range of valuable options is no good by itself: you have to be able to search through those options and exercise judgment in selecting the ones you prefer. Too many options could actually hinder us from doing this. I could be presented with ten million randomly arranged movies on Netflix and quickly get overwhelmed. I might get stuck in the choice architecture, hovering between all the possibilities, like a modern-day version of Buridan's Ass. The psychologist Barry Schwartz calls this the "paradox of choice," and he and others have examined it in a series of experimental studies. Some of these studies suggest that it has a significant impact on our capacity to choose; others suggest it has a more modest effect.[75] Either way, AI recommender systems could help to overcome the paradox of choice by limiting our options and making it easier for us to navigate through the choice architecture. In addition to this, we should also be wary of status quo bias when it comes to assessing the impact of AI systems on our choice architectures. We must remember that governments, religions, and other cultural institutions have long played a role in limiting our options. If you grew up in mid-twentieth-century Ireland (my home country), when the Catholic Church was intimately interwoven with the machinery of state, you would be impressed (and frustrated) by the energy spent on limiting your access to contraception, pornography, and various forms of healthcare that were thought to encourage "loose" morals. AI recommender systems are nothing dramatically new in this regard. Where they differ is in who controls them, how ubiquitous they are, and how selective they can be in constructing our choice architectures.

This might be why the most significant impact of automating technologies is likely to be on the independence condition. The widespread deployment of such technologies, even if ostensibly used to assist us, creates new opportunities for manipulation, coercion, and domination in our lives. Automating technologies could be used to "brainwash" us into accepting a certain set of values and beliefs, thereby manipulating our choices; they could be used to coerce us into doing things against our will (for example, by telling us to stand up and get some exercise or risk losing access to health insurance or government-funded healthcare),[76] or they could introduce a new form of domination—domination by tech company or even AI itself—into our lives.

On the problem of automated manipulation, Karen Yeung has recently argued that a distinctive feature of AI decision-support tools is their capacity for "hypernudging."[77] Nudging is a concept that was first introduced into behavioral science and policy by Richard Thaler and Cass Sunstein.[78] Thaler and Sunstein were aware (and in some cases directly involved) in behavioral science experiments suggesting that people did not always behave rationally or in ways that served their long-term interests. They had innate biases and cognitive heuristics that encouraged them to act against those long-term interests. Thaler and Sunstein used the term "nudge" to describe practices whereby these innate biases could be overcome by gently pushing people in the right direction. For example, they noticed that most people don't save enough money for their retirement; but that they could be nudged in the direction of doing so by making retirement savings plans opt-out rather than opt-in.

Automated decision-support systems seem to engage in similar nudge-like practices: they highlight certain options and make them more salient and attractive, while suppressing and ignoring others. Thaler and Sunstein would argue that this is acceptable because, if done right, nudging is autonomy preserving: it always allows people to choose a non-preferred option (for example, not save for retirement); it just makes it less likely that they will do so. Not everyone is impressed by this logic, with many arguing that nudging is a form of freedom-undermining manipulation. Whatever the truth of this in relation to traditional nudging, Yeung provides support for this skepticism in the case of automation by arguing that automated nudging is like nudging on steroids. In traditional cases of nudging, a policy maker can design a choice architecture that biases people toward making certain decisions, but this design will usually be updated and changed quite slowly. Furthermore, the same choice of architecture will be imposed on many people at the same time. This gives people the chance to learn how the system works and to develop and share strategies for avoiding or circumventing its biases. Automated nudging systems are different because they can be individualized and updated in real time. This means that the choice architecture may not be stable enough for people to develop resistance strategies. This is the problem of hypernudging.[79]

What about the problem of automated domination? Recall from the previous chapter that domination arises where there is some agent—a master or dominus—that has authority over your life, and to whom you must ingratiate yourself in order to live a trouble-free existence. This master may never actually interfere with or manipulate your choices; the fact that they could (and could be imbued with the authority to do so) is enough. Hoye and Monaghan have recently argued that the systems of mass surveillance that are required for automating technologies introduce a new mode of domination into our lives.[80] The net result of the widespread deployment of these technologies is that we live in a digital panopticon, all watched over by machines of loving grace, waiting to nudge us back on track if we ever step out of line. They thus enclose and constrain our space of autonomy, without us even realizing.

Again, it is important not to overstate the problem here. Humans have a long and checkered history in manipulating, coercing, and dominating one another. The problem with automated systems is that they may overwhelm our natural forms of resistance to these types of interference: there are already so many of them and they operate in forms and at timescales that are not readily comprehensible to beings like us. They have started to, and will probably continue to, pervade our lives. If we remove one source of automated manipulation, we may be quickly confronted with another, like an automated hydra. Furthermore, the growth of these systems may help to centralize power in the hands of those who control them, thereby consolidating and exacerbating the problems of inequality that were outlined in Chapter 3. So, although we shouldn't exaggerate, we shouldn't be complacent either. The erosion of autonomy is a major reason to be pessimistic about the automated future.

The Agency Problem

The fifth argument for pessimism is a distillation of the preceding arguments. Each of the preceding arguments identifies some feature or features of automating technologies that threatens our flourishing and meaning—some mechanism that blocks us or undermines us in our pursuit of the good life. These features include their power to sever the connection between what we do and what happens to us; their power to distract us from what really matters; their power to render the world more opaque to our understanding; and their power to undermine our autonomy. Each of these features points toward a common effect of automating technologies on human beings: a tendency to undermine our (moral) "agency" and to accentuate our moral "patiency." This tendency is another reason for automated pessimism.[81]

The conceptual vocabulary at play in this argument is important and needs to be understood. Moral philosophers often contrast moral agents with moral patients.[82] An agent is someone with the capacity for autonomous action, that is, with the ability to pursue goals, to execute complex intentions, and select among options, in a free and independent manner. A "moral" agent is someone with that capacity who is specifically able to (a) recognize and act upon moral reasons for action, and (b) take responsibility for their moral failures and successes.[83] A moral patient is different. A moral patient is someone who is a subject of moral concern.[84] They have moral status, which implies that they can be harmed and benefitted by what is done to them, and they may also be owed duties and obligations. One and the same person can be a moral agent and a moral patient. For example, most adult human beings are both: they are subjects of moral concern, but can also act upon moral reasons and take responsibility for their actions. The two properties can also pull apart. Most people would say that young children are moral patients—they are subjects of moral concern and we owe duties to them—but not moral agents—we don't (yet) hold them to account for their actions. Similarly, although this is surprisingly controversial, most people would now agree that non-human animals can be moral patients but not moral agents.[85]

The common view among philosophers is that agency and patiency are properties that you either have or you don't. They are "all or none." This is true in a sense: if you have the capacity to be a moral agent, then, barring some disabling accident, this capacity is not going to be taken away from you. But at the same time, it is very clear that these properties can wax and wane in their expression over the course of a human lifetime: sometimes we are more patient-like than agent-like (for example, in early childhood) and sometimes we are more agent-like than patient-like (for example, when occupying a parental role). To be clear, the waxing and waning applies primarily to the property of agency, rather than to that of patiency. Unless we lose the capacity to suffer and feel pain, we will probably always count as moral patients, at least in some minimal sense.[86] But the property of agency is more like a skill that can be highly cultivated or not. An analogy might help. I can play the piano: I learned as a child; I still remember basic scales and pieces; and I can, if given the time, read music. Consequently, you could say that I have the property of being a piano player. The problem is that I haven't played the piano in a very long time: the skill lies dormant and would need to be rekindled. I think the same can be true of our moral agency. The ability to recognize, appreciate, and take responsibility for moral actions is something that needs to be cultivated and can atrophy in the absence of continued practice.[87]

This is significant because moral agency is central to the good life. A moral patient can experience many of the joys of life, but to actually participate in them, achieve them, and take responsibility for them, agency is crucial. Objective list theories of well-being often focus on developing agency-related capacities, for example, health, practical reason, and education; and objective-hybridist theories of meaning state that the capacity to change the world through your actions (actions for which you are responsible) is essential if you are to contribute to the Good, the True, and the Beautiful. There are other reasons for cherishing moral agency too: it is central to a virtue-ethical model of the good life; it is a grounding presumption of liberal democratic states; and the history of moral progress can be understood as the history of recognizing the moral agency of others, particularly women and those of other races / nationalities.[88]

The problem with automating technologies is that they suppress our agency. By severing the connection between what we do and what happens to us, by distracting us from projects and tasks of significant concern, by making the world less comprehensible to creatures like us, and by nudging or interfering with our autonomy, they bring our patiency-like properties to the fore and encourage us to neglect our agency-like skills. If these problems were limited in scope, or if we only had to confront them one at a time, then the problem might be manageable, but dealing with them all together, across large swathes of human activity, is the real problem. This is not to deny that automating technologies can do wonderful things for us: they can provide us with cheaper and better goods, and faster, safer, and more efficient services. But if this comes at the cost of agency, we might need to rethink the bargain.

This is where the depiction of humanity's future in the movie *Wall:E* is pertinent once again. It may be hyperbolic and satirical, but if you want a sense of what things might be like in a world in which our agency is completely suppressed, look no further.

Table 4.2 The Five Threats of Automating Technology

Problem	Description	Relevance
The Severance Problem	By obviating or reducing the need for human activity, automating technologies sever the connection between what we do and what happens to us and in the world around us.	Some "significant" connection between human activity and what happens is necessary on most objectivist theories of flourishing and meaning. • Automating technologies pose a particular problem for human achievement • As automation proceeds across multiple domains of human activity, the problem becomes more severe
The Attention Problem	Many (if not most) automating technologies are created as part of the attention economy and try to capture our attention for commercial purposes and / or distract us from other more valuable things.	What we pay attention to determines our subjective well-being and the capacity for attention is essential for goal achievement, mastery, etc.
The Opacity Problem	Automating technologies render the world more opaque. They make discoveries in data and do things to us that are not readily comprehensible due to (a) rules and norms that protect the technology from scrutiny, (b) technical illiteracy, and (c) intrinsic complexity / non-interpretability of the technology.	Understanding is crucial for *instrumental* reasons: i.e., enabling us to plan activities that are conducive to flourishing and meaning; it is also *intrinsically* valuable: i.e., helps us feel more at home in the world, and is itself a kind of achievement.
The Autonomy Problem	Automating technologies threaten autonomy by limiting or filtering the options with which we are confronted and by introducing new, and more difficult to manage, forms of manipulation, coercion, or domination into our lives.	Autonomy might be an intrinsic good (i.e., worth protecting in its own right); it might also be an instrumental good (i.e., people are more likely to attain states of well-being/flourishing if left to their own devices); or it might be an axiological catalyst, i.e., make good things better.
The Agency Problem	By doing things for us and encouraging us to replace human effort with machine effort, automating technologies suppress our moral agency and accentuate our moral patiency.	Moral agency is central to objectivist theories of flourishing and meaning: you need to actively participate in the world and not just be a passive recipient of benefits. It is also key to virtue-ethical theories of the good life, central to liberal democratic governance, and a key marker of moral progress.

Whither Humanity? Evolving Out of the Cognitive Niche

Throughout this chapter, I have tried to be honest and upfront about the threats that automating technologies pose for human flourishing and meaning. I have tried to do so in a systematic and comprehensive fashion. Despite this, I have overlooked some obvious critiques of automating technologies. For example, I have overlooked the concerns of people like Nick Bostrom, Roman Yampolskiy, and Olle Haggström, who argue that superintelligent forms of AI could pose an existential threat to humanity.[89] They could become so smart and so powerful that one small misstep in their design could result in catastrophic harm to humans. This view has influenced some key figures in the tech industry too, such as Elon Musk and Jaan Tallinn. If this doomsaying turns out to be correct, then it would obviously have an impact on human flourishing and meaning. If the superintelligent AI turns us all into paperclips—to use a colorful thought experiment that is popular among contributors to the debate on existential risk from AI—then you can say goodbye to the good life.

Why have I ignored their arguments? I do so for two main reasons. First, I have previously expressed doubt about some of the epistemic principles underpinning this doomsaying school of thought. In brief, I argue that it could be very difficult to determine whether or not the view is correct, given the kinds of argumentative speculation its proponents are willing to entertain. Second, given that the view is extreme and depends on the possibility of creating a superintelligent machine, it seems worthwhile to explore threats to flourishing and meaning that are more immediate and arise at much lower levels of machine competence. The arguments I have outlined in this chapter do exactly that. They apply to many existing technologies and, even when they do call for speculation about future developments, do not require levels of machine competence that are significantly greater than what we currently see. In many cases, they just require more of it.

The other obvious critique that I have overlooked is the political one. To be sure, some of my arguments have a political backdrop and involve politically charged concepts—such as autonomy, opacity, and agency—but they have not singled out what many people perceive to be the biggest problem with the rise of automating technologies, namely, that they reallocate power by centralizing and enhancing the influence of technology companies over our lives. This is, no doubt, a very serious concern. Who gets to rule and who controls the corridors (or networks) of power are important questions, and there are legitimate concerns one can have about the rising power of tech companies. Whose interests do they serve? Do they manipulate and undermine democratic processes? Do they enable a new form of technocratic dictatorship? Do they discriminate against and foster intolerance toward certain groups of people? It is important to consider these questions. I haven't made them the central focus of my arguments in this chapter for the simple reason that I think they are peripheral to the question of human flourishing and meaning. That might sound like a controversial claim, so let me clarify. My view is that societies need *some* governance structure, and this governance structure will tend to distribute power to some set of individuals and organizations. This is true even in small, tribe-like or family-like societies. This distribution of power is necessary and often good because it brings a measure of stability to society. Consequently, unless one wants to live in a libertarian / anarchist state (and I will discuss this desire in Chapter 7), the mere fact that some group has significant power in society is not, in and of itself, a problem. What matters is how they exercise that power, more precisely how they translate it into effects on individual flourishing and well-being, and how they are held to account for those effects. I have been focusing my attention on those effects in this chapter. To the extent that the political questions connect with that focus, I have not ignored them (for example, I discussed concerns about the centralization of power when examining autonomy, above), but because I think it is how power gets translated into effects on lives that really matters when it comes to flourishing and meaning, I also think the broader political questions are peripheral to my concerns.

Assuming that my characterization of the threats to flourishing and autonomy is accurate, what does it all mean? The simple answer is that it means we need to work to mitigate and minimize these threats: to try to ensure that automating technologies help rather than hinder our flourishing. This is going to be easier said than done. It's too late to head off some of the threats identified above: they have already become entrenched. Addressing others would require calling a halt to current trajectories in technological development and dismantling the institutions that make them possible. None of this is impossible, but it is challenging. Furthermore, and in line with my argument about work and automation in Chapters 2 and 3, given the kinds of effort involved, perhaps we would be better off channeling our energies into more radical social reforms, not just trying to preserve our current way of life?

That's what I want to consider in the remainder of this book by sketching and evaluating two possible post-work utopias. To set up the second half of the book, I want to close with one last metaphor for understanding the problems identified in this chapter. The metaphor comes from work in evolutionary psychology. This work is scientifically contentious and open to critique (as all scientific work is). I use it here not because I wish to defend its scientific accuracy, but because it provides a useful way to think about where we have come from and where we are going.

One of the questions asked by proponents of evolutionary psychology concerns the origins of modern human beings. How did we evolve to become the kinds of creatures we are? In evolutionary theory, organisms evolve to fill niches in their ecologies. Once upon a time, all creatures lived in or about the sea. There was, however, a living to be made on land. So the ancestors of modern plants and insects (first) and modern mammals and reptiles (later) made their way onto land to exploit the available niches. It turned out there was also a living to be made in the air, so the ancestors of modern insects and, later, birds found a way to do that too.

What niche did modern humans evolve to fill? Steven Pinker and others have argued that humans evolved to fill the "cognitive niche."[90] Most creatures have a limited, hardwired repertoire of behaviors. If their environment changes dramatically, they usually suffer and die as a result. A big brain, with a flexible capacity to solve complex problems, was an obvious niche that was waiting to be filled. The ancestors of modern humans filled it. They developed extraordinary problem-solving capacities as a result of enlarged frontal lobes and improved capacities for cooperation and coordination in groups. They developed complex cultural rituals and institutions for transmitting that problem-solving knowledge from generation to generation.[91] They no longer had to wait for their genes to play catch up. They could escape, to some extent, from the constraints of evolutionary time. Much of what is central to our flourishing and meaning flows from this evolutionary development. The mechanisms of flourishing highlighted in this chapter—achievement, focus, understanding, autonomy, and agency—are all made possible by our cognitive systems. Furthermore, it is these very same systems—coupled with the impressive institutional framework we have developed around science, technology, and innovation—that enables the development of automating technologies.

But this is where things get interesting, and somewhat paradoxical. Cognition has always been a costly enterprise. Our brains consume huge amounts of energy—more than a quarter of our daily intake of calories—and it is always tempting to minimize that cost by outsourcing cognitive labor to others. This is one reason why we create automating technologies. Until now, our occupation of the cognitive niche has never really been threatened. This is starting to change. With the increasingly impressive gains in artificial intel-

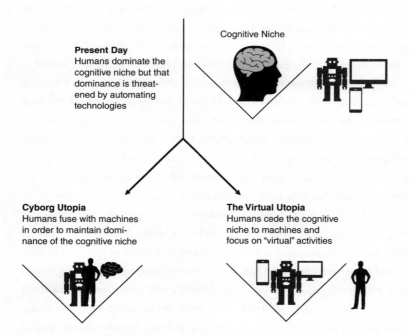

Figure 4.2 The Cognitive Niche and the Two Futures

ligence and robotics, our dominance of the cognitive niche is no longer guaranteed. We are slowly being pushed out.

We must, consequently, confront a fundamental existential question: do we want in or out? Do we wish to cede the cognitive niche to smart machines and find flourishing and meaning elsewhere? Or do we want to push back and try to retain our dominance? In the second half of this book I will consider both possibilities. I will start with some general reflections on utopian projects in Chapter 5, and follow this with a detailed investigation of two distinctive utopian visions for humanity in Chapters 6 and 7 (the Cyborg and Virtual Utopias, respectively).

PART TWO
‗‗‗‗‗‗‗‗‗‗‗‗

Utopia

Proposition 3: One way to manage our relationship with technology would be to build a Cyborg Utopia, but it's not clear how practical or utopian this would really be: Integrating ourselves with technology, so that we become cyborgs, might be one way to regress the march toward human obsolescence outside of work. Doing so may have many advantages, but will also carry many practical and ethical risks that make it less desirable than it first appears.

Proposition 4: Another way to manage our relationship with technology would be to build a Virtual Utopia, and this is more practical and utopian than it is commonly assumed: instead of integrating ourselves with machines in an effort to maintain our relevance in the "real" world, we could retreat to "virtual" worlds that are created and sustained by the technological infrastructure that we have built. At first glance, this seems tantamount to giving up, but there are compelling philosophical and practical reasons for favoring this approach.

CHAPTER 5

In Search of Utopia

TO THIS POINT, I have argued that we should embrace the idea of a post-work future, albeit with some degree of caution. Such a future could be utopian *if we get it right*. But what exactly does it mean to get it right? How can the future be utopian? This chapter provides an answer to that question, starting with a cautionary tale.

When his Italian girlfriend left him for someone "younger but more mature," David Bramwell decided to go on a quest. He had long sensed that there was something shallow, incomplete, and feckless about his life. He wanted to change that. He had been reading about "intentional communities"— small-scale societies built around a set of shared values—for several years. In an effort to find a modern-day utopia, he decided to visit as many as he could in a twelve-month period. His journey—amusingly recounted in his book *The No. 9 Bus to Utopia*—took him from the windswept coast of Scotland to the sun-drenched cliffs of California. Along the way he encountered a diverse cast of characters, including aging hippies, free-love practitioners, spiritual healers, burned-out businessmen, cult-like gurus, and more.[1]

Did he find what he was looking for? It's not clear. Many of his experiences were less than ideal—his trip to a fly-infested BDSM camp in the Czech Republic being the obvious nadir—and there is a general sense of disappointment permeating the book: the utopian ideals of the different communities seem underwhelming in practice. Nevertheless, one modern-day utopia does get a glowing review: Esalen, a hot-spring retreat in Big Sur, California. Esalen rose to prominence in the 1950s and 1960s when it became a retreat for writers like Jack Kerouac, Hunter S. Thompson, and Henry Miller, and when its owner, Michael Murphy, decided to turn it into a center for the "development of human potentialities."[2] Nowadays, Esalen is an expensive luxury resort, with hot tubs overlooking the Pacific Ocean and more spirituality, self-improvement, and yoga classes than you might care to take. Bramwell describes his hot-tub soaking experiences there with fondness: "I soon found my perfect daily routine; a morning soak in the hot tubs before breakfast, another before lunch and then I'd settle there in the evening when the sky swelled under the weight of the stars and the Milky Way snaked its thin cloud across the night sky."[3]

But he also finds that this modern-day utopia has its dark side. One of the aged hippies wandering the woods warns Bramwell that his quest for utopia is misguided and that he shouldn't become too attached to the luxury of Esalen: "Enjoy Esalen's beauty, David, and move on. Don't become a 'bliss junkie.' Otherwise you might end up like half the old bastards who used to teach here . . . All this beauty and pleasure on tap? Nothing to fight for? . . . They drank themselves to death."[4]

The aged hippy's words of warning make an interesting point. The idea of "pleasure on tap," though initially seductive, strikes many people as being anti-utopian. It is certainly a long way from what one finds in famous utopian works of fiction and philosophy. Plato's *Republic*—usually identified as the first utopian work in Western philosophy[5]—argues that the ideal society is one with a rigid, caste-like, militarized governance structure. Everyone has their assigned place and role, and they must learn to live with this. There is little time for idle pleasures. Thomas More's famous work *Utopia*—the first to actually use the word "utopia"[6]—also depicts a rigid, highly organized and categorized, semi-feudal society, albeit one with technological enhancements (artificial incubators and advanced weapons of war) that ease some of life's burdens. Luxury and pleasure on tap are not obvious features of either of these works.

But if pleasure on tap is not the essence of a utopia, then what exactly is? The previous chapter gave some sense of what a future post-work utopia is not. The five threats that automation poses to human flourishing and meaning give some indication of the pitfalls to be avoided (or at the very least minimized) if we are to create an ideal world. But there has to be more to a utopia than avoiding the negative. There must be some positive vision too. What is this?

Defining Utopia

First things first, let's clarify the meaning of the word itself. A utopia is an ideal society. Indeed, in everyday parlance, "utopia" is usually synonymous with *the* ideal society—the society, out of all the possible societies that could exist, that is the best. In philosophical and academic parlance, "utopia" has a more precise meaning. It is a particular type of ideal society, usually one that is better than the current reality but still practically attainable.[7] One of the most widely discussed academic studies of utopianism in literary and cultural history is J. C. Davis's 1981 book *Utopia and the Ideal Society*.[8] In this book, Davis sets out a typology of ideal societies, arguing that there are actually five distinct forms, of which a utopia is but one. First, there is the Cockaygne, a surreally bounteous society with no scarcity and all the food and resources we desire, completely devoid of social institutions (the name comes from the medieval poem "Cockaygne," which is about the land of plenty).[9] Second, there is the Arcadia, which is a sufficient but not excessively bounteous society, devoid of all institutions apart from the family, where humans live in harmony with the natural world. Third, there is the Perfect Moral Commonwealth, which is a society governed by universally agreed upon institutions and managed by humans who have perfected themselves (namely, conquered their inner demons and allowed their better natures to thrive, usually through religious training). Fourth, there is the Millennium, which is a society that is rescued from human imperfection by divine intervention (and corresponds, roughly, to the typical Christian understanding of the ideal society). And finally, there is the Utopia, which is a society in which socio-technical institutions have been improved and help to rescue humans from their own flaws and imperfections (without divine assistance).

Davis uses this typology to exhaustively categorize the English literature on ideal societies. I pass no judgment on whether it succeeds in that particular aim. What I do pass judgment on is its ability to illustrate the distinctive takes on what the ideal society looks like and to suggest that it may be more confusing than illuminating to lump them all together under the label of a "utopia." Furthermore, I use it to highlight how, of all our imaginings about the ideal society, the truly utopian imaginings might be the ones that are closest to our present reality. They require the least fanciful speculation about the future of the world and our place within it, and do not depend for their success on some supernatural savior. They focus on practically attainable technological and sociological reform.

This doesn't mean that a utopia is not a radical improvement on the current social order. In most utopian fictions and writings, the potential for radical improvement is key. Christopher Yorke captures this style of utopian thinking in his definition of the concept of a utopia, which I propose to use throughout the remainder of this book:

> *Utopia* = "Any prospectively achievable scheme of radical social-political improvement which would, if installed, leave every affected party better off and none worse while respecting the rights of all."[10]

This definition packs a lot of important ideas into a small space. First, it clearly stipulates that a utopia must be "prospectively achievable," which means that it must be practically and technically possible for us to realize it. A purely speculative, pie-in-the-sky ideal society is no good. Second, it states that the change in the ordering of the world would need to be "radical" in order to count as utopian. As Yorke put it in conversation with me, imagining the current world with one small improvement, such as everyone getting a free ice-cream on Sundays, wouldn't be enough for it to count as a utopia.[11] There needs to be some radical break from the current reality. Third, Yorke's definition also clearly stipulates that a utopia cannot be achieved on the backs of others; it must respect everyone's rights and leave them better off. This addresses one of the big worries about utopian projects (discussed in more detail below), which is that they often justify great suffering on the road to the imagined utopia. That said, Yorke's definition might go too far in saying that everyone must be made better off by the change. It's probably very difficult to prove or ensure that this is the case, however valuable it might be as an aspiration. Respecting their rights—that is, ensuring that they can participate in, challenge, and be compensated by the utopian project—seems far more important and practically attainable.

Utopias as Possible Worlds

There is a way of enriching our understanding of utopian thinking that, although it takes some time to set out, will pay dividends when we consider what it might take to create a genuine utopia. This enriched understanding comes from thinking about utopias as possible worlds.

"Possible worlds" are widely discussed in philosophical circles. Very roughly, a possible world is any logically coherent and describable world. Philosophers think about this in terms of lists of propositions that describe how the world operates and functions. As long as that list of propositions is sensible and contains no contradictions or absurdities, the world described is possible. The number of possible worlds is infinite: there is an infinite number of ways to vary the list of propositions that describe a world and remain logically consistent. Our actual world—the one we live in right now—is but one of those logically possible worlds. There are other possible worlds, very similar and very close to our own that differ in minor ways (for example, worlds in which I am right-handed, not left-handed, or in which I was born a day later). These are physically or technically possible worlds. There are other worlds that are very different and which may not be physically possible, at least given what we currently know about the laws of physics (for example, worlds in which we can travel faster than the speed of light or teleport around the solar system). Some philosophers think that all possible worlds actually exist; most disagree but still think that it is useful to think about different possible worlds in order to better understand the nature and function of different objects and properties.[12]

I believe that thinking about different possible worlds is especially useful when it comes to thinking about the future of humanity. I think it is useful because our future is essentially a landscape of different possible worlds. We, in the present, are like explorers setting out toward a horizon of future possible worlds. Which world we will end up in depends on many variables, including which technologies get developed and when.[13] If we develop superintelligent AI, then our future is going to be very different from what it will be if we do not invent it. The same goes for whether we invent interstellar space travel or not.

The job of the futurist is the job of figuring out which pathway we are going to take through the landscape of possible future worlds. Which possible world is more likely? More technically feasible? And what will that world look like in its totality? Answering these questions is not an easy task. Futurists often fall into the trap of narrow thinking. It is relatively easy for them to describe a possible future if they just imagine one or two changes to the list of propositions that describe the present reality. But the likelihood is that any one change, particularly if it concerns something major like the development of superintelligent AI, will cause hundreds or thousands of other, difficult to anticipate, small changes to that possible world. Can you imagine all of these (or at least a significant chunk of them) in rich detail? This is something that the best futurists must do. It is also something I must do throughout the remainder of this book. I must imagine and evaluate the different possible futures toward which we could be heading, in rich and plausible detail.

I think the "possible worlds" concept is also useful when thinking about utopianism. This is especially true when it is paired with Yorke's definition of a utopia.[14] Utopian theory is concerned primarily with sketching out the different possible ways in which the social-normative order could be radically altered so as to maximize human flourishing and meaning. In other words, it's about taking some of the key features of the present world—its institutions, its citizens, its technologies—and imagining how they could be reformed, innovated, and improved to form a radically better world. The closer the imagined possible world is to our own, the more practically attainable it will be (the easier it will be to get from here to there); the more different it is, the more difficult it will be. For a utopian vision to meet the conditions set down by Yorke, it must strike a balance between radical improvement and practical attainment, and there must be a path from our pre-

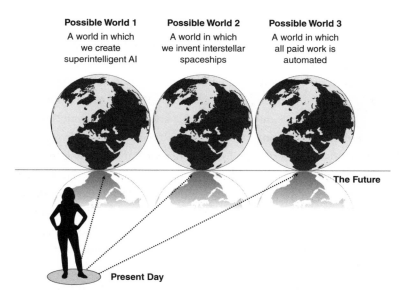

Figure 5.1 Futurism and Possible Worlds

sent world to that world that improves things significantly, but doesn't trample over the rights of others.

For the remainder of this book, I will be adopting this "possible worlds" way of thinking about post-work utopias. I will be imagining two significant changes to our present world, specifically relating to its technological infra-structure. I will then try to describe and evaluate the practicality of these changes, as well as the knock-on effects they will have on human flourishing and meaning. This method might sound quite highfalutin, particularly when it is dressed up in the language of possible worlds, but it is not. It is very down-to-earth and tractable.

Here is one way to think about it. In his book *The Geography of Morals*, the philosopher Owen Flanagan points out that our present world is already subdivided into different possible moral / axiological worlds.[15] Our evolu-tionary history means that all humans share a common foundation for our moral systems: there is a limited range of things that we care about, and a limited range of things that are conducive to our flourishing. However, the limits that this common foundation puts on the possible moral orderings of society are not that strenuous. You can see this by simply taking a look around. The world is fragmented into different countries, societies, tribes, and cults. These groupings often have different moral codes and different ways of ranking and prioritizing values. Some of these societies have settled into less than ideal "evaluative equilibria," that is to say, their moral codes and ways of prioritizing values are not conducive to human flourishing and meaning. Other societies are highly unstable and prone to revolution and decay. Nevertheless, by casting a wide net around the world, we can see some of the radical possibilities that get hidden when we limit ourselves to a specific culturally embedded vision of what is "ideal" or "preferred." This broader perspective is particularly valuable when we consider the clashes, collisions, and inconsistencies between different, present and future, possible worlds. Perhaps societies that seem alien to our own would actually constitute a significant moral improvement? Perhaps we should consider shifting our moral equilibrium to theirs?

One of the examples that Flanagan uses to illustrate this idea is the different moral equilibria currently associated with anger in different parts of the world.[16] Although most cultures seem to agree that anger, when taken to an extreme, is bad, some believe that certain forms of anger are good. In Western liberal cultures, for example, righteous anger is usually seen as a good. It is a justified response to the injustices of the world. It motivates right action—revenge, retribution, reform—and it is an important catalyst for moral improvement. Buddhist cultures (as well as the more ancient traditions of Stoicism and Taoism) see things rather differently. They see anger as something that is necessarily bad and that ought to be extirpated from our way of life. They have no truck with those who claim that this is impossible. They say that it is possible through a combination of reason, discipline and meditation. And they claim that much of the alleged good that is associated with righteous anger can be achieved in its absence. By evaluating the arguments in favor of each of these possible moral worlds, by scrutinizing them in accordance with the universal laws of reason, and by measuring them against the core beliefs and practices of the respective societies, we can start to see the wisdom in shifting from one equilibrium to another. What was once absurd might suddenly seem desirable. Flanagan follows this methodology in his book, and although he doesn't offer a ringing endorsement of the Buddhist approach to anger, he thinks a strong case can be made for thinking that Western liberal societies should move closer to it in the landscape of possible moral worlds.[17]

This example provides a useful model for thinking about the Cyborg and Virtual utopias that will be discussed in Chapters 6 and 7. These utopias represent different possible moral worlds—worlds with values and priorities that are somewhat different from our own. As you read about these possible worlds, you may find that some of your current values (values associated with human agency and autonomy, for example) are being de-prioritized or extirpated. At first glance, this may make the world seem antithetical to any utopian aspirations. But it is important to keep an open mind and consider the possibility that this may not be the case. There may be good reasons for dropping or de-prioritizing something we currently hold dear. Indeed, this is an obvious lesson to be learned from Chapter 3. In that chapter, I argued that although Western liberal societies currently place much value on work and the work ethic, they are wrong to do so: a possible world without work could be much better than the one we currently live in. You may have thought that idea was absurd at first, but hopefully, after you read through my arguments, you saw that there was some wisdom to it. The same holds true going forward. Different possible post-work utopias might seem a little strange or unusual at first glance, but this doesn't mean they are not credible and plausible utopias. We have to open ourselves up to a broader landscape of moral possibility.

To summarize, a utopia is a possible, but practically achievable, world that represents a radical (moral) improvement over the current world. When imagining and evaluating potential future utopias, we need to avoid narrow-mindedness and parochialism and consider the possibility that some elements of our existing understanding of flourishing and meaning will need to be extirpated or reimagined in a utopia. In other words, the landscape of possible future utopias might be wider than we initially suppose.

Three Additional Criteria for Post-Work Utopias

So far so good. We have a clearer conception of what a utopia is and how to explore the landscape of possible post-work utopias. Are there any other considerations or constraints that we should bear in mind while doing this?

There are three: (i) we need to avoid the temptation to use violence and understand the allure of negative utopianism; (ii) we need to ensure that our envisaged utopia maintains a balance between stability and dynamism; and (iii) we need to bridge the cultural gap between our present world and any possible future utopia. Let's consider all three constraints in a little more detail.

Avoiding Violence and the Negative Utopia

To understand the first constraint, it is worth looking at the work of Karl Popper, who was one of the most famous mid-twentieth-century critics of utopianism. Popper had two concerns about utopian thinking. The first was that utopian projects tend to lead to violence and authoritarianism; the second was that we would be much better off if we abandoned utopianism and adopted a form of negative utilitarianism instead.[18]

Popper's first concern stemmed, in part, from his definition of "utopianism." In one of his key essays on the phenomenon, he says that utopianism is the political philosophy according to which "we must first attempt to become as clear as possible about our ultimate political ends and only afterwards can we begin to determine the means which may best help us to realise this state."[19] It is important to note that this understanding of utopianism is quite distinct from Yorke's definition of a utopia that was adopted above. Popper is focused on the political movement that is invested in utopian reforms; Yorke is focused on the actual goal of this political movement (the utopian society to which they aspire). The two things are, obviously, connected, and it is worth considering why Popper thinks that utopianism, so defined, tends to lead to violence, but they are also conceptually distinct and this should be remembered.

The main reason that utopianism tends toward violence is that utopian political projects are, according to Popper, built around particular blueprints of the ideal society. They assume that there is some ideal *telos* or end state for human society (for example, the Platonic republic or the Marxist commune) and that we ought to do whatever it takes to get to that end state. We can't let any obstacles stand in our way. This kind of thinking naturally encourages violence. This seems to be confirmed by the historical evidence. Popper pays particular attention to the consequences of fascism and communism in his critique. But Popper wants to go beyond historical evidence in making his case. He wants to argue that an impulse to violence is inherent to all utopian movements, not just an accident of history. It is the natural consequence of three fundamental features of how human societies work: *plurality, conflict,* and *irrationality.* "Plurality" is the fact that different groups of humans have different blueprints for the ideal society (meaning, different groups have different conceptions of utopia). "Conflict" is the fact that, on at least some occasions (and perhaps many), these different groups, and their different utopian visions, come into direct conflict. It is, therefore, not possible for the groups to live in harmony with one another. "Irrationality" is the fact that it is not always possible for these disharmonious groups to resolve their conflicts by rational means; oftentimes violence is the only way to eliminate the conflict. Combined, these three features of society point to an inherent tendency toward violence in utopian thought. Only by denying the truth of one or more of these features can you overcome this tendency.

Is Popper right? Plurality and conflict seem like uncontroversial facts: it seems obviously true that people have different conceptions of the ideal society and that these conceptions can conflict. Think about the conflict between communists and anarcho-capitalists or between secular humanists and radical Islamists. They each have different, incompatible visions of what the ideal society should be. That said, plurality and conflict by themselves need not lead to violence. If there were some objective hierarchy of value that could be agreed upon by all, it may be possible to resolve the apparent conflicts by rational argument. But this is exactly what Popper disputes with his point about irrationality. He argues that human values are not subject to scientific investigation and analysis. This means they are not open to the same kind of objective (or intersubjective) agreement as scientific facts. As Popper puts it, "since we cannot determine the ultimate ends of political action scientifically, or by purely rational methods, differences of opinion concerning what the ideal state should look like cannot always be smoothed out by the method of argument."[20]

This might sound reasonable, but it is a surprisingly self-defeating claim for Popper to make. After all, what is Popper trying to do with his argument against utopianism? He is trying to resolve our utopian conflict through rational argument: by arguing that we should avoid the allure of utopianism because of its tendency to violence. Popper concedes that this is what he is doing, but he denies that it is self-defeating by saying that a rational argument is not completely out of bounds in the political arena. He thinks it may be possible to secure some kind of consensus or coordination on a utopian project in the short term. He just thinks the problem of irrational conflict will rear its head again in the long term because our values and priorities will shift over time. What seemed desirable to one group of people at a particular historical moment might not seem desirable to another group at a later moment. He himself is happy to live with the possibility of future shifts, but he thinks that will be anathema to the present-day utopian. After all, they think their blueprint for the ideal society is the correct one. They don't want future generations coming in and ruining everything. So, Popper argues, they will have a natural tendency to stamp out any alternative views, and to engage in propaganda wars (and other nefarious practices) in order to annihilate any opposing ideologies. This will lead to a great deal of authoritarian oppression and violence.

I have set Popper's concerns about violence and oppression out in some detail because I think they should give any prospective utopian, like myself, some pause for thought. If we are to promote post-work utopianism, we would be well advised to consider the potential violence that it may encourage and the costs that may accrue on the journey from here to there. Admittedly, this is something that I already tried to head off by adopting Yorke's definition of "utopia," which stipulates that we cannot achieve a utopia by trampling on the rights of others or by sacrificing them to the greater good. But stipulations are cheap. This doesn't make Popper's claims about pluralism, conflict, and irrationality any less pertinent.

That said, there are some problems with Popper's argument that make his critique of utopian thinking less compelling than it first appears. One problem is that Popper is probably guilty of overextending the definition of violence in his critique and as a consequence misdiagnosing one of the main problems with utopian political projects. As Aldous Huxley famously said to George Orwell, after the publication of the latter's novel *1984*,[21] what is going to be truly insidious about utopian projects is not that they use violence to enforce their preferred vision but that they use techniques of mind control to get you to agree with their vision. This is still a problem—and one that should weigh against the alleged utopianism of a particular political project—but I don't think it is a problem that stems from violence. It is a problem that stems from the need to protect freedom of thought and autonomy, both of which were discussed in Chapter 4 and raised as serious concerns about the impact of automation on human flourishing. The other problem with Popper's concern about violence is that his definition of utopianism is itself deeply misleading insofar as it assumes that utopianism is always built around a clear and precise specification of what the ideal society should look like. Most modern utopian thought rejects this notion. There is no precise blueprint for an ideal society. Rather, the ideal society is one that allows for dynamism and change over time. I discuss this in more detail below.

What about Popper's second critique of utopianism? This is not so much a critique as it is an argument for an alternative form of utopianism, and again it is worth considering because it might be thought to give additional guidance on how to think about building an ideal society. Although dismissive of utopian projects, Popper thinks there is some role for idealism in the political sphere. Popper has an optimistic bent when it comes to the future of human society. From whence does this optimism spring? It springs from Popper's belief that society should not aim at realizing optimal states of happiness and well-being in the future (as seems to be entailed by utopianism); rather, he thinks society should try to eliminate "concrete evils" in the here and now (that is, society should adopt a form of negative utilitarianism). The elimination of such evils is all we need for political idealism to flourish.

You might wonder whether this "elimination of concrete evils" strategy is substantially different from the utopianism that Popper critiques. After all, both seem to be concerned with making the world a radically better place. But he argues that it is very different, for largely epistemic reasons, two of which figure prominently in his writings: (i) We have better knowledge / understanding of what it takes to eliminate concrete evils because we have direct and immediate acquaintance with them; we only know ideal situations through, often vague, imaginings; (ii) There is far greater intersubjective agreement about the most serious concrete evils than there is about what is ideal.

There is something to be said for both of these reasons. Concrete evils do indeed exist in the here and now. They are not merely hypothetical or imagined. There are people suffering from war, disease, starvation, displacement, and so on. And even if we ourselves are not suffering, we can easily gain epistemic access to the suffering of others (if we are willing to expose ourselves to it) through media and first-hand accounts. No one has similarly direct acquaintance with what it would be like to live in an ideal society. Furthermore, it does seem broadly true that people agree on the major concrete evils that exist in the world today.

That said, there are still problems with seeing this as an alternative to utopian thinking, or indeed as a serious constraint on utopian thinking. For one thing, the distance between the elimination of evils and the realization of ideals is shorter than Popper seems to think. Identifying a concrete evil often requires, by necessary implication, an agreement on an ideal. In other words, if X is a concrete evil, then not-X (or the opposite of X or denial of X) is going to be a necessary element in any blueprint for an ideal society. If you draw together enough not-Xs, you will probably come up with something that looks an awful lot like a utopian political project. Traditional medieval conceptions of the ideal society—such as the land of Cockaygne—are largely built up in this way. We are asked to imagine a world without the deprivations of the current world—no scarcity of food, drink, sex, sociality, knowledge, and so on. Similarly, when imagining the ideal automated society, we are asked to imagine a world without the restrictions and drudgery of current existence.

That's not to say that there is no conceptual or practical distinction between the elimination of concrete evils and the realization of ideals. If we take it that great physical pain is a concrete evil, then the opposite of this (the ideal state) would be something like great physical pleasure / joy. It might seem like in identifying the concrete evil, you (necessarily) develop a conception of the ideal. Nevertheless, trying to eliminate great physical pain, does not, by itself, mean that you are trying to bring about great physical pleasure. There is presumably an intermediate state of being—one in which pain is absent—that you can bring about without achieving the ideal. This is illustrated in the diagram below. Popper could argue that his political project is about aiming for these intermediate states, and he could argue that this makes it distinct from a utopian project.

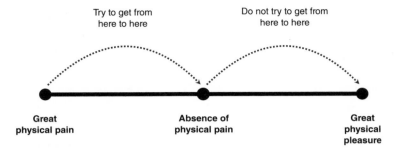

Figure 5.2 Popper's Negative Utilitarianism

But this then leads to another problem. If aiming for these intermediate states is what we should be doing in order to avoid the sins of utopianism, it is unlikely to succeed. After all, aiming for the intermediate state is still vulnerable to the same concerns about conflict, plurality, irrationality, and dynamic changes in values that concerned Popper when looking at utopianism. Contrary to what Popper claims, there does not seem to be widespread agreement on the correct hierarchy of concrete evils that need to be addressed by society today. Just as there are incompatible hierarchies of value that thwart utopian projects, so too are there incompatible hierarchies of disvalue that thwart negative utilitarian projects. Different groups often disagree about what deserves priority. Should we be alleviating malaria and hunger in the developing world? Or should we be campaigning for the end of global capitalism? Both views have their advocates. Furthermore, what counts as a concrete evil shifts over time. Once upon a time bullying and sexual harassment wouldn't have got a look-in when it came to identifying society's greatest challenges; nowadays they are front and center. This is a good thing, but it shows how easily priorities can shift, even at the negative end of the spectrum.

This doesn't mean that Popper's counsel to avoid thinking about hypothetical ideal states and instead focus on eliminating concrete evils is bad advice. It just means that it's best to understand Popper's negative utilitarianism as a kind of utopian project itself, not something that is distinct from utopianism. By focusing on eliminating successive waves of concrete evils, a

Popperian can progressively "asymptote" toward an ideal society without ever setting out a precise description of what that ideal should look like. They might stumble toward a utopia, without knowing exactly what they are looking for. In fact, this might be a very good way to think about making a post-work utopia practically attainable. This is something worth bearing in mind when evaluating the different utopian visions discussed in the next two chapters.

So, in sum, Popper's critique of utopianism shouldn't dissuade us from undertaking the utopian quest. It should just be viewed as providing additional guidance on how we are to undertake that quest.

The Problem of Stability and Dynamism

As mentioned in the above, utopias are sometimes thought to represent stable end points for society. The idea is often that we are in the midst of a struggle right now, but if we persevere with the utopian project we will eventually reach the utopian ideal and then the struggle will be over. Society will settle into a stable, perpetual equilibrium. The Marxist utopian project clearly illustrates this mode of thinking. According to Marx, all pre-communist societies are characterized by repetitive cycles of conflict and revolution. Each system of production (such as feudalism and capitalism) contains the seedbed of its own destruction: there are tensions and contradictions embedded within them that will eventually lead to breakdown.[22] The profit-maximizing depredations of the capitalist will push the workers to breaking point and there will be a revolution. This cycle of revolution will, however, reach an end once the communist utopia is achieved. At that point, an ideal, stable equilibrium will arise. This new world will not be vulnerable to the same kinds of contradictions.

Everything I have said so far about what a utopia would look like seems to presuppose a similar view. And it's easy to see why the elimination of conflict and the achievement of stability are attractive to utopians. Conflict seems to be an obvious source of misery and suffering—the very antithesis of an ideal society. Revolutionaries might be energized by conflict and societal breakdown, but only because they see them as precursors to something better. If life was nothing but conflict and revolution, they would get sick of it pretty soon. Thomas Hobbes captured this most eloquently in his famous discussion of the perpetual war of all against all that would arise in the absence of stabilizing government, arguing that in such a world there would be no place for "Industry," "Culture of the Earth," "Navigation," "Building," "Knowledge," "Arts," "Letters" and "Society," and that the "life of man" would be "solitary, poore, nasty, brutish and short."[23] Immanuel Kant, in his most utopian work, "To Perpetual Peace," also thought that humanity should aspire to a stable end state.[24] In that essay, he acknowledges the role that war and conflict have played in human (read: European) expansion and innovation, but hopes that once we have expanded to fill all territory on earth, we will be rationally compelled to make peace with one another, and to live together in harmony.

But stability can also have a dark side, one that is antithetical to utopian aspirations. Without some sense of unease with the present reality, and without some goals and aspirations for improvement, it seems like we would have little reason to get out of bed in the morning. If a utopia was truly a stable end point of social development, then it would be pretty boring. In his famous essay "The End of History," the political theorist Francis Fukuyama captured this sense of apathy pretty well. Writing in the aftermath of the Cold War and the fall of the Berlin Wall, he argued that the end of the conflict between Western liberal democracy and Soviet communism represented the "end of history," a stable equilibrium that would persist for the foreseeable future. Far from welcoming this, Fukuyama sounded depressed:

> The end of history will be a very sad time. The struggle for recognition, the willingness to risk one's life for a purely abstract goal, the worldwide ideological struggle that called forth daring, courage, imagination and idealism, will be replaced by economic calculation, the endless solving of technical problems, environmental concerns, and the satisfaction of sophisticated consumer demands. In the post-historical period there will be neither art nor philosophy, just the perpetual caretaking of the museum of human history.[25]

The last sentence is particularly evocative. Not only does it directly echo and contradict Hobbes's concerns about perpetual conflict, its image of a once proud and dynamic humanity reduced to mere caretaking is quite haunting.

Fukuyama, of course, was famously sneered at for his claim that history had reached some stable end point with the collapse of the Soviet Union. The intervening years suggest that there is plenty of fight left in humanity yet. Still, his fear about the apathy-inducing nature of stability is worth taking seriously. It has cropped up several times in this book already. One of the major fears people have about the end of work is that it will leave us with nothing to do. One of the terrifying things about the *Wall:E* dystopia is how it reduces us to apathetic, fat, and lazy beings. To return for a moment to David Bramwell's experiences at the luxury resort of Esalen, the advice that we should avoid becoming bliss junkies seems to be well taken. There needs to be some larger goal to which we aspire and from which we can derive meaning and purpose.[26]

So stability is attractive but it also has its dark side. How do we resolve this apparent paradox and what does it mean for the utopian project? The answer is straightforward. We need to achieve stability in the right areas—a reduction of conflict, deprivation, and suffering—while maintaining dynamism in others—innovation, discovery, development. As Ian Crawford puts it, we want to achieve a society that is "an exciting place in which to live; a civilisation which is at peace with itself, but whose history is still open."[27] How exactly we go about doing that is a question whose answer I postpone for the time being, but it is worth noting that this idea—that a utopian vision should not assume a stable end point for society—has long featured in utopian thought. Oscar Wilde said as much: "A map of the world that does not include utopia is not even worth glancing at, for it leaves out the one country at which humanity is always landing. And when humanity lands there, it looks out, and, seeing a better country, sets sail. Progress is the realisation of utopias."[28] As did H. G. Wells in his discussion of "modern" utopias: "the Modern Utopia must be not static but kinetic, must shape not as a permanent state but as a hopeful stage leading to a long ascent of stages."[29]

Christopher Yorke emphasizes this idea by calling for a sharp distinction between what he calls "blueprint" and "horizonal" models of utopian thinking:[30]

> *Blueprint Utopianism:* This is a type of utopianism that focuses on achieving some stable, ideal end state for humanity.

Horizonal Utopianism: This is a type of utopianism that focuses on
constantly shifting horizons of desire for humanity. It is premised on
the idea that there is no single, ideal blueprint that represents a stable
end state for humanity. Utopia is, rather, always just over the horizon:
it is something we aim for but never quite achieve.

The former is, of course, similar to the model of utopianism that Popper cri-
tiqued; the latter is similar to the one he endorsed (or that I argued he could
be interpreted as endorsing). It should be obvious from what I have said here
that I too favor the horizonal model. It avoids the pitfalls associated with stability and apathy. It also helps to avoid the Popperian fear of violence and
the trampling on the rights of others. It is usually only when people are trying
to implement a very specific vision of the ideal society that they feel justified in sacrificing a few lambs to the slaughter. They know that once they
attain the ideal the conflict will end. If there is no single, stable ideal to be
achieved, if the struggle will go on indefinitely, this justification for violence
is less readily available.

In subsequent chapters I will be using this horizonal model of utopia to
evaluate the Cyborg and Virtual visions of the future. In other words, I will
be checking to see whether either of these particular visions allows for an
expanding horizon of possibility.

Transformative Change and the Problem of the Cultural Gap

The last constraint we need to bear in mind before we start evaluating
different post-work utopias has to do with how radical a break from the
present reality the envisaged utopia actually is. To this point, I have been
assuming that the quest for utopia makes sense—that it is possible to rationally compare and evaluate possible worlds to see whether they deserve to
be called utopias. But this could be called into question. It could be that
some possible worlds are beyond our ken and that we can never satisfacto-
rily evaluate their utopian potential. Consider the following thought experiment, taken from L. A. Paul's book *Transformative Experience:*

> Imagine that you have the chance to become a vampire. With one
> swift, painless bite, you'll be permanently transformed into an

elegant and fabulous creature of the night. As a member of the undead, your life will be completely different. You'll experience a range of intense, revelatory new sense experiences, you'll gain immortal strength, speed and power, and you'll look fantastic in everything you wear. You'll also need to drink blood and avoid sunlight.[31]

Should you want to become a vampire? Paul argues that there is no way to make a rationally informed choice about this. The reason for this is that you are missing an essential bit of knowledge: what would it actually be like to be a vampire? What would the lived, day-to-day experience be like? Sure, you could rely on testimony from all your friends who have made the switch, but until you have walked a mile in a vampire's shoes, you won't really know what it is like.[32]

To be clear, the vampire example is just for laughs. Paul's point is more serious. She argues that we face this kind of decision-making dilemma many times over the course of our lives. Decisions about whom to marry, whether to take a new job in a new city, and whether to have children all depend, critically, on experiential knowledge of what it would actually be like to live with those decisions. Since we cannot have that experiential knowledge until after the decision is made, we cannot make a rational choice. We cannot rationally evaluate and compare our possible futures.

Paul possibly goes too far in her skepticism of rational choice in these cases,[33] but she is right that there is sometimes too much *epistemic distance* between where we are now and where we are being asked to imagine we might be in the future. Imagine a world in which humans no longer experienced pain. Imagine a world in which there was no such thing as gender or sex. Imagine a world of total material abundance and no scarcity. Can we really imagine these things? Can we rationally compare these possible worlds to our own? Christopher Yorke refers to this as the problem of the "cultural gap" and he thinks it is an important constraint on utopian theorizing.[34] When there is too much epistemic distance to be traveled, it may not be possible to evaluate and recognize the utopian potential of a particular model of society.

You might think that we can solve this problem by simply stipulating—as we already did—that in order to count as a utopia a prospective ideal society must be rationally intelligible. But this is easier said than done. Sometimes it is hard to tell whether a utopian vision is too epistemically distant until you start to probe its details. It is particularly hard to avoid this problem when evaluating techno-utopian visions. Imagining future trends in technological innovation oftentimes lends itself to fanciful speculation. You take a particular technology, for example, artificial intelligence, and imagine what would happen if its development was taken to some extreme, like superintelligence. This particular imaginative journey might seem sensible and rationally intelligible. But when you start to consider all the other changes that this would entail—for other technologies and for cultural norms and values—what seemed rationally intelligible might soon slip outside the realm of rational comparison.

My sense is that we shouldn't overstate the problem of the cultural gap. There is a significant cultural gap between Buddhist attitudes toward anger and Western liberal attitudes, but rational cross-comparison is not impossible, as noted above when discussing Owen Flanagan's able cross-comparison of the two. It just takes a lot of hard work to bridge the gap.

But we shouldn't be insensitive to the problem either. Sometimes our speculation may go too far and we'll need to exercise some imaginative restraint to make the utopian quest a fruitful one.

Conclusion: The Utopian Scorecard

Let's draw together the various strands of this chapter before moving on. The goal of this chapter was to provide a better map of the territory to be explored over the next two chapters, both of which consider in more detail the possible post-work utopias to which we may wish to aspire. To briefly recap, I've suggested that we follow Christopher Yorke and define a utopia as a prospective, rationally achievable society that represents a radical improvement over our current society. I've further suggested that we think about the search for utopia in terms of a landscape of different possible moral worlds: we are trying to isolate and describe possible future worlds and then evaluate their utopian potential.

In the remaining chapters, I will be doing this with two possible future worlds: a world in which humans maintain their dominance of the cognitive niche through cyborgization (the Cyborg Utopia) and a world in which humans cede the cognitive niche to automating technologies and retreat to the virtual (the Virtual Utopia). As I evaluate these possible worlds, I will be keeping the following considerations in mind:

(a) If these visions are truly utopian, they will resolve or mitigate the five problems of automation that were discussed in Chapter 4 (severance, opacity, distraction, autonomy, and agency). This does not mean that they have to perfectly preserve our existing attitude to meaning and flourishing—we have to be open to more diverse moral possibilities—but if they are going to shift from these attitudes, this needs to be explained and justified.

(b) If these visions are truly utopian they will pay attention to the problems of violence and conflict; they will not justify great violence and conflict for the sake of realizing the utopian project. (We should also leave open the possibility that the utopian project should be conceived of in negative terms, namely, the progressive elimination of evils as opposed to the realization of some ideal.)

(c) If these visions are truly utopian, they will try to maintain the right balance between stability and dynamism; they will not be too fixed or rigid in how they conceive of the ideal society; they will leave open a horizon of possibility.

(d) If these visions are truly utopian, they will not require us to traverse too much epistemic distance between our current world and the world we are being asked to imagine, meaning, they will be rationally intelligible to creatures like us.

Combined, these considerations provide us with a "utopian scorecard"—a tool for evaluating and comparing the respective utopian visions. We'll keep it in our pockets and refer to it from time to time as we proceed.

CHAPTER 6

The Cyborg Utopia

NEIL HARBISSON IS AN ARTIST. Unlike most artists his preferred medium of expression is not a canvas or other external artifact. It is his body. He likes to experiment with it, using technology to transform how he sees and interprets the world. If you ever meet him, he cuts quite a figure. Diminutive, with blond hair in a bowl-like haircut, the most noticeable thing about him is the antenna that protrudes from the back of his head, and arcs over the top of his skull. This antenna is not an ornament. It is an implant, embedded in his skull. It is the reason why Harbisson refers to himself as a "cyborg artist."[1]

Harbisson was born in Belfast, Northern Ireland, but grew up in Barcelona, Spain.[2] Early on, he was diagnosed with an extreme form of color blindness. He sees the world in a dull grayscale. His antenna allows him to perceive color in a different way.[3] It is connected to a chip that converts color sensory data to sound. As he describes it, "it detects the light's hue and converts it into a frequency that I can hear as a note." He hears in color—a technologically induced form of synesthesia. When he visits an art gallery he remembers it as an aural experience as much as a visual one. He says that he likes "listening to Warhol and Rothko because their paintings produce clear notes," but "can't listen to Da Vinci or Velázquez because they use closely related tones—they sound like the soundtrack for a horror film."[4]

Harbisson's implant does not simply compensate for his congenital color blindness. It allows him to do things that a normal human cannot. He can hear infrared and ultraviolet colors that humans cannot see. He can receive data from all over the world, not just in his immediate environment. He can make and receive phone calls directly to his skull. Harbisson has also now moved beyond his original antenna and is creating new cyborg implants that further extend and develop his capacities, including a device that allows him to communicate through vibrating chips with another human being, and a "solar crown" that allows him to feel the passage of time during the course of a day.

Harbisson takes his cyborg status very seriously. He is a campaigner for cyborg rights. In 2004, his application for a British passport was rejected on the grounds that he should have taken off his antenna before taking his passport photo. He argued that the antenna was part of who he was and should not be removed. He was successful. In 2010, he co-founded the Cyborg Foundation to defend and promote cyborg rights. In 2017, he co-founded the Transpecies Society, which tries to raise awareness of people, like him, who have "non-human identities," and supports the right to redesign one's body through technology. Speaking in 2014, Harbisson summed up his view on his cyborg identity: "I've been a cyborg for 10 years now. I don't feel like I am using technology, or wearing technology. I feel like I am technology. I don't think of my antenna as a device—it's a body part."[5]

Harbisson is not a lone voice in the wilderness. There are many others who self-identify as cyborgs. Harbisson's artistic collaborator Moon Ribas is implanted with an RFID (radio-frequency identification) chip that vibrates every time there is an earthquake somewhere on earth. It allows her to feel more connected to the world in which we live. The Canadian engineer Steve Mann also claims cyborg status. He has worn an "eyecam," which is now directly implanted into his skull, since the early 1980s. This not only allows him to record his daily interactions, it also augments his natural vision with infrared and heat detection. And then there is Kevin Warwick, an academic researcher leading what he himself calls "the cyborg revolution." Warwick is a pioneer in the field of brain-computer interfaces. He was one of the first people to have an RFID chip implanted in his body to allow him to open doors and turn on lights and heaters. In 2002, he attained widespread notoriety for having an electrode array implanted directly into his brain. Thanks to the wonders of the internet, this electrode array allowed Warwick, located in Columbia University, New York, to remotely control a robot arm in the University of Reading, UK. The stunt earned Warwick the nickname "Captain Cyborg," and was an important proof of concept. Since then, further developments in brain-computer interfaces have refined and expanded the cyborgian potential of this technology.[6]

This is just a small sample of the wannabe cyborgs. There are countless other bio-hackers and "grinders" who experiment with chip implants and cyborg enhancements in their basements and backyards. Many of these self-experimenters conceive of what they are doing as something that is explicitly utopian, as a way of expanding our moral horizons and exploring a new possibility space. Some of them think it essential that we do this. They think we have become trapped in a suboptimal moral equilibrium and that what is holding us back is our evolved, biological hardware. We need an upgrade if we are to have any chance of radically improving our lot. This is how the bio-hacker Tim Cannon explains his efforts to the journalist Mark O'Connell, saying that humans "just don't have the hardware to be ethical, to be the things we say we want to be. The hardware we do have is really great for, you know, cracking open skulls on the African savannah, but not much use for the world we live in now. We need to change the hardware."[7]

What is most interesting about this comment is how Cannon's way of framing and motivating his cyborg project is similar to the framing I proposed at the end of Chapter 4. As you recall, I argued there that humans evolved to fill the cognitive niche but that our dominance of this niche is now under threat as a result of advances in automating technology. I also suggested that this prompted something of an existential crisis for humanity. So much of our existing sense of what it takes to live a flourishing and meaningful life is dependent on cognitive dominance. That's now under siege. The world we have created is one in which machine cognition is in the ascendancy. We are no longer optimized, if we ever were,[8] for the future. We must either do something to change our hardware and thereby maintain and extend our cognitive dominance, or give up and try something else. Wannabe cyborgs favor the first option. In the remainder of this chapter I want to consider whether their strategy offers a credible path to utopia. In doing so, I will defend the third of the four propositions set out in the introductory chapter:

> **Proposition 3:** One way to manage our relationship with technology
> would be to build a Cyborg Utopia, but it's not clear how practical or
> utopian this would really be: integrating ourselves with technology,
> so that we become cyborgs, might be one way to regress the march
> toward human obsolescence outside of work. Doing so may have
> many advantages but will also carry many practical and ethical risks
> that make it less desirable than it first appears.

What Is a Cyborg Anyway?

To understand the Cyborg Utopia, we need to get a clearer handle on what a cyborg is. The word "cyborg" is a neologism that was coined by the polymath Manfred E. Clynes and the pharmacologist Nathan S. Kline in September of 1960. It is a portmanteau that combines the words "cybernetic" and "organism" into an attractive, two-syllable package.[9]

The coining of the term has an interesting backstory. Clynes and Kline published their famous article about the cyborg in the journal of the American Rocket Society. Three years previously the Soviets had launched the first successful earth-orbiting satellites (*Sputnik 1* and *2*) thereby kickstarting the Space Race. The Americans had to clamber to make up lost ground. The best and brightest scientific talent was marshalled to the cause. Clynes and Kline answered the call. But instead of offering practical proposals for getting people into space, they offered a more abstract, conceptual perspective. They looked at the biological challenge of spaceflight. The problem, as they saw it, was that humans were not biologically adapted to space. They could not breathe outside the earth's atmosphere, and once beyond the earth's magnetic sphere they would be bombarded by nasty solar radiation. What could be done to solve the problem? The standard engineering approach was to create mini-environments in space that are relatively congenial to human beings. Hence, the oxygen-filled spaceship and the hyperprotective spacesuit. Such technologies would suffice for short-term compatibility between fragile human biological tissue and the harsh environment of space, but they would provide a precarious and short-term solution at best.[10] If we ever wanted to do more in space—if we wanted to travel to the farthest reaches of our solar system (and beyond)—a different approach would be needed. We would have to alter our physiology through the creation of technological implants, substitutes. and extensions of our innate biology.[11] What should we call a human being that was technologically enhanced so as to adapt to the environment of space? Clynes and Klines favored the term "cyborg."

From this origin, the term "cyborg" has taken on a life of its own. It is now deeply embedded in popular culture, providing the name for a terrible series of films starring Jean-Claude Van Damme, as well as, in abbreviated form, the name for one of the chief villains of the *Star Trek* universe (the Borg). The term is also influential in academia, featuring prominently in biotech, philosophy, and humanities disciplines. Some academic uses of the term stray, considerably, from the idea of the cyborg as a scientific and technological reprogramming of the human. Indeed, some academic commentators claim that "we are all cyborgs now," that we were "always already" cyborgs, and that we as a species are "natural-born" cyborgs.[12] It's just part of who we are.

How can we make sense of this? David Gunkel argues that we can make sense of it by realizing that when people use the term "cyborg" they are not always talking about the same thing.[13] At least, not exactly. There are two distinct conventional uses[14] of the term that are must be kept in mind:

Technical Cyborgs: These are cyborgs in the original Clynes and Kline sense, and in the sense in which Neil Harbisson describes himself as a cyborg, namely, they are literal fusions between humans and technology. This typically requires the incorporation of technology into human biological tissue in order to form a single functional hybrid system (the cyborg).

Conceptual / Metaphorical Cyborgs: These are cyborgs in the sense preferred by proponents of the extended mind thesis like Andy Clark (discussed in more detail later in this chapter). They arise from close partnerships between humans and technical / cognitive artifacts in their environments, such that the humans and the artifacts can be thought of as forming a single extended system.

The gist of the distinction is that technical cyborgs have some technology directly implanted into or grafted onto their biological tissue, whereas as conceptual cyborgs do not—they maintain *some* independent ontological identity. The line between the two is, however, blurry. Would Neil Harbisson be less of a cyborg if his antenna wasn't implanted in his head but, instead, he carried it around in his hand at all times? Presumably this wouldn't make a big difference to the overall functionality of the device—he would still be able to hear the colors—but it might make a difference to how we categorize him. If we favor the technical sense of the term "cyborg," we would probably reject his cyborg status. Conversely, if we favor the conceptual sense of the term, we might still classify him as a cyborg. The importance of these classificatory issues becomes more obvious, below, when we consider the utopian potential of different interpretations of the Cyborg Utopia. For now, I want to address a preliminary question: how feasible is it for humans to become cyborgs in the technical or conceptual sense?

The feasibility of any project is dependent on what the end goal is. Is it feasible to send humans to Mars? Yes, if all you care about is getting their bodies there. We could launch that mission within the next six months if we put our minds to it. No, if you want to get them there safely and enable them to live on Mars for an indefinite period of time, and if you want them to be able to return to Earth if they choose. That's going to take some more time. So what is the end goal of the cyborg utopian project? It's hard to say. All wannabe cyborgs want to achieve some tight interface between humans and machines. They don't want machines to be mere tools that we use to accomplish our goals; they want the machines to be part of who we are. Beyond that general aspiration, people probably have different end goals in mind. Neil Harbisson sounds like he is happy to just tinker with technological implants and create new forms of experience and modes of interaction. Tim Cannon sounds like he wants to reboot humanity in its entirety—to achieve some maximally enlightened, machine-like state of being. Harbisson's cyborg project seems pretty feasible right now; Cannon's seems like more of a stretch—at least in the short-to-medium term.

For the purposes of this chapter, the end goals, and hence the feasibility of the cyborg project, hinge quite considerably on the utopian aspirations of the cyborgians. What exactly is it that they think we can get by blending ourselves with machines? What radically improved possible world are they trying to bring about? We'll have to take this on a case-by-case basis, looking at the various utopian goals underlying different pro-cyborg arguments, and then assessing the feasibility of attaining them. Nevertheless, we can still say something quite general about the feasibility of the conceptual or technical pathways to cyborg status.

Let's focus first on the conceptual pathway. As noted in Chapter 4, humans already make extensive use of technological artifacts in their daily environments. These artifacts range from the humble pen and paper to more sophisticated smart phones and watches. We are constantly interacting with and relying upon these artifacts. This constant interaction is what leads people like Andy Clark to claim that we are "natural-born" cyborgs.[15] As our technological development continues apace, it seems obvious that the scale and scope of these interactions is going to grow. That's largely what this book has been about to this point. The tricky thing is determining when these interactions are genuinely cyborgian in nature. As was also noted in Chapter 4, sometimes our relationships with technological artifacts are *competitive* and *dependent*. They do things *to* us and *for* us. They are not part of us. For cyborgian status, it seems like there must be some interdependency and complementarity.

So how can we test for that? Philosophers have been thinking about this for a while and developed a number of markers of complementarity. The philosophers Andy Clark and David Chalmers, for example, in their defense of the extended mind hypothesis, argue that a human can be said to form an extended mind with a technological artifact if there is a high degree of *trust* between the human and the artifact, if there is a high degree of *reliance* on the artifact, if the artifact is readily *accessible,* and if the human *endorses* the role that the artifact plays in their mental / cognitive life.[16] The problem with these criteria, however, is that they look like *dependency* conditions, not *interdependency* or *complementarity* conditions. They allow us to determine when a human is heavily dependent on a technological artifact; they do not allow us to determine whether the human and the artifact form a single extended system. A more promising approach, and one that does not involve any commitment to the controversial metaphysics of the extended mind, is suggested by Orestis Palermos.[17] He uses dynamical systems theory to assess when and whether two systems can be said to form a single extended system:

> *Extended System* = For two initially independent systems, A and B, to give rise to a single overall extended (or "coupled") system, C, there must be nonlinear interactions (via feedback loops) between the sub-components / parts of A and B.

His claim is that when you have these nonlinear interactions, the coupled systems will have properties that the two previously independent systems lacked: it will be neither human nor machine but some blend of both. Furthermore, once the systems become coupled in this way it will no longer be meaningful to decompose the overall system (C) into the subsystems. You won't be able to say that A contributed this effect to C, and B contributed this effect. A and B will have become so interdependent that such distinctions no longer make sense.

This is a bit too abstract. To make it more concrete, imagine a case where someone is trying to perform a cognitive task with the help of a technological artifact.[18] Suppose you are trying to remember your friend's phone number and you look it up in the phonebook stored on your phone. Does this give rise to a nonlinear interaction between yourself and the smartphone? No. The interaction is linear. The phone provides you with the information that you then use to make the phone call. There is no back-and-forth. Conversely, when you use a service like Google Maps to navigate an environment, there is some back-and-forth. Your movements affect the data picked up by the mapping algorithm, which then changes your representation on the screen. This tells you whether you are closer to your destination or not. Through continuous feedback and updating, you can eventually arrive at this destination. There is some complementarity and interdependency here. To give another example, there is also clearly some genuine complementarity between Neil Harbisson and his antenna (even though he may also be a technical cyborg, not merely a conceptual one). His movements affect the light rays received by the antenna, which in turn affect the colors he hears. Neither Harbisson nor the antenna by itself hears in color; it's the combination of the two that hears in color. When Harbisson uses this data to create paintings of his own—ones that represent the color soundscape that he hears—there is an even greater nonlinear interdependency.

This dynamical systems approach is more promising than Clark and Chalmers's one because it identifies cases of genuine human-machine complementarity, not dependency. That said, by itself, the approach is too binary, and possibly over-inclusive. Although you could say that I am a (conceptual) cyborg when I use Google Maps, I certainly don't feel like that much of a cyborg when I do. The interdependency between myself and the app quickly dissolves when I stop using it. I then return to my original biological form. There's nothing cyborgian about me. But we can account for this by clarifying that there are degrees of nonlinear interdependence. There is no simple threshold of interdependence beyond which someone counts as a cyborg. Rather, people who form complementary relationships with technology can slowly morph into conceptual cyborgs the more complementary relationships they form.

Richard Heersmink offers a useful, if complicated, way of thinking about this. He argues that the degrees of integration and complementarity that are relevant to this process are arrayed along a number of distinct dimensions, each of which concerns the type of interaction that the human has with a technological artifact (which he refers to as a technological "scaffold" in the quote below):

> The dimensions of this spectrum include the kind and intensity of information flow between the agent and scaffold, the accessibility of the scaffold, the durability of the coupling between the agent and the scaffold, the amount of trust the user puts into the information the scaffold provides, the degree of transparency-in-use, the ease with which the information can be interpreted, the amount of personalization, and the amount of cognitive transformation.[19]

There is obviously some overlap between these dimensions and the criteria suggested by Clark and Chalmers, but by focusing on the type of information flow, coupling, transparency, personalization, and cognitive transformation, Heersmink's framework also captures the need for interdependency. Following his approach, it's easy to see why I don't feel much like a cyborg when I use Google Maps. Although it is quite accessible and personalized (depending on how I use it), and I put a lot of trust in it, it doesn't score highly when it comes to the intensity of information flow, the amount of cognitive transformation it entails, and the durability of the coupling. Neil Harbisson's antenna, on the other hand, scores highly on all dimensions.

The bottom line then is that the conceptual path to cyborg status is quite feasible. We do make widespread use of technological artifacts in our everyday lives and we always will. Nevertheless, whether we attain cyborg status by following this pathway depends on the degree of complementarity between ourselves and the technological artifacts we use to navigate and make sense of the world. The more complementarity, the more cyborg-like we become.

What about the technical path to cyborg status? Remember that this requires the direct fusion of biology and machine. As such, the distinction between the technical and conceptual cyborg is, as already suggested, itself also really a matter of degree. We can easily just say that technical cyborgs are people who lie on the extreme end of the integration spectrum: they have bound the fate of their biological systems to technical systems. Indeed, Neil Harbisson would again seem to be a perfect example of this. His antenna is not just an artifact with which he forms an interdependent feedback relationship; it is something directly fused to his body. They are bound together, at least for the time being. The close integration of two systems does not have to be irreversible for it to count as an instance of technical cyborgization, though this may be important when it comes to evaluating its utopian potential, as we shall see below.

Harbisson, and the others like him, are thus a proof of concept. They show us that it is possible to become a technical cyborg. That said, there are clearly limitations to the degree of technological integration that is possible nowadays. Harbisson is an eloquent spokesperson for the cyborg revolution, but he is hardly the radical leap forward in human evolution Tim Cannon desires. To get a better sense of what some of the current possibilities and limitations might be, we need to consider the different methods and means of becoming a technical cyborg. The aforementioned Kevin Warwick describes three pathways to cyborgization that are currently being developed:[20]

> *Cultured Brain in a Robot:* This involves taking a lab-cultured network of biological brain cells (usually taken from rodents, but possibly from humans) and connecting them to an electrode array that enables them

to send and receive signals to the outside world. Initial experiments on this technique suggest that it is possible for the cultured network of brain cells to control robotic bodies and to learn and develop behaviors in response to environmental stimuli. At the moment, the lab-cultured networks of brain cells are relatively small, and the behavioral repertoires limited, but in time there is the genuine possibility of growing a human-size brain in a lab and having it embedded in a robotic body for which it is the command center.[21] Such an entity would clearly be a technical cyborg.

Brain-Computer Interfaces (BCIs), Implants, and Prosthetics: This typically involves the use of electrode arrays to monitor electrical activity from nerve cells. This electrical activity is then decoded into something that can control another electrical device (for example, a mouse cursor on a computer screen or a robotic arm). Some of these devices are just wearables (for example, skull caps). Some are more invasive implants and prosthetics (for example, Deep Brain Stimulators). Some only send and receive signals in one direction (for example, from the brain to an electrical device); some are bidirectional and involve genuine feedback between the user and the device (from the device to the brain and back again). Warwick was himself one of the first people to test a bidirectional BCI that involved a microelectrode array that was directly implanted into his nerve cells. This was in the experiment I mentioned earlier in which he controlled a robotic arm in Reading, UK, from Columbia University, New York. BCIs of various types have become more widespread in recent years. Deep Brain Stimulators (DBSs), for example, are implanted in hundreds of thousands of Parkinson's patients, and are now being used for other psychiatric disorders. Similar devices include cochlear implants and artificial retinae. Although there are some differences between these technologies, they all share the same basic idea: signals being sent directly from our brain cells to some technological artifact (and back).

Other Non-Neural Implants and Prosthetics: This is a catch-all category. It covers any implants and prosthetics that do not involve direct brain-to-device communication. Implanting an RFID chip under the skin is a classic example of this. The RFID chip communicates directly with external devices. There is no signal being passed by the RFID chip through your nerve cells to the external device or vice versa. You wave your hand in front of a sensor and the RFID chip implanted beneath the skin can open a door (or something like that). It's the chip itself that does the work. Indeed, it's not even clear what the real advantage of implanting the chip is. Wearing it on the surface of the skin would have a similar effect, though if the chip can vibrate or send other signals into human tissues (as is the case with Moon Ribas's earthquake-sensing RFID chip), then there may be some phenomeno-logical gain. Other examples could include subdermal magnetic implants (which can be used to manipulate and respond to electro-magnetic waves) or prosthetics that do not directly replace or integrate with some biological system. Neil Harbisson's antenna would fit within this category. It doesn't communicate directly with Harbisson's brain cells. It just detects light waves in his environment and transduces them into a sound that he can hear around his head.

To Warwick's three approaches, a fourth could be added:

Biomedical Enhancement Techniques: This involves the use of pharma-cology and psychopharmacology to improve cognition, mood, dexterity (and other human capacities), as well as the use of genetic engineering methods to similar effect. While these might not seem like methods of technical cyborgization—since they don't involve the fusion or integration of humans and machines—I think it is still correct to classify them as such. For one thing they are partly founded on a technologized and mechanized understanding of human biology— namely. they see the body as a machine that can be tinkered with and optimized. For another, they can complement and support the other technical methods of cyborgization. As such they can contribute to the overarching mission of rebooting the hardware of humanity.

This is not an exhaustive list but it gives a sense of the major methods of technical cyborgization that are now open to us. How impressive are they?

How far down the road to full human-machine hybrids do they take us? The most fanciful method—the lab-grown brain that develops in such a way that it controls a robot body—would get us pretty far. But we are still some way from growing a full human brain in the lab, and it's not clear that the resulting cyborg would be a genuine human-machine hybrid as opposed to some successor species (more on this idea later in this chapter). Also, it doesn't provide an immediate, practically achievable route to cyborg status for any of us; it only provides that for future generations. The other methods offer more hope in the immediate future and could be used in tandem with one another. They make it possible for already-born humans to become technical cyborgs in the course of their lifetime. But how significant this transition is depends on how integrated the systems are and how many functions they can perform. At the moment there are technological limits to how small electrode arrays can be and how many brain cells they can interact with. We can use BCIs to simulate, augment, and restore certain basic functions (like hearing, sight, movement). But it's going to require further advances in nanotechnology if we are to obtain true synergy between human and machine systems. Nevertheless, people like Warwick are bullish about the long-term potential for BCIs. He, for example, thinks they will eventually advance to the point that humans will be able to think about and see the world in the same way as machines.[22]

If he is right, then in the long-term a full hardware reboot of humanity is possible through technical cyborgization. If he isn't, then even in the short term, advances in human-machine integration are still possible, and these advances will open us up to new ways of interacting with and understanding the world, as they already have for people like Neil Harbisson and Moon Ribas. The question we must ask now is, does this offer the potential for a post-work utopia?

The Case for the Cyborg Utopia

It's time to take out your "utopian scorecard" (introduced at the end of the last chapter). I am now going to evaluate the utopian prospects of the cyborg revolution. I will do this in two stages. First, I will present five arguments in favor of the Cyborg Utopia. When combined, these arguments paint what I believe to be a compelling picture of what life might be like in such a possible world. Then, I will present six objections to the Cyborg Utopia that make it seem less attractive. I will conclude that the Cyborg Utopia—tantalizing and seductive though it may be—is not the utopia we are looking for. Let's start with the five arguments in favor of cyborgization.

The Conservation and Extension Argument

The first argument in favor of the Cyborg Utopia might seem a little odd. It claims that by pursuing cyborgization we get to preserve and extend much of what we currently value in the world. The reason why this might seem odd is that it is an inherently *conservative* view. Utopianism is supposed to be about radical improvements from our current position. It is supposed to be about exploring the more exotic outer-reaches of the landscape of moral possibilities. To turn around and offer a *conservative* argument in favor of a utopian project seems downright perverse. But you must remember that the radicalism of a utopian project needs to be tempered by its rational intelligibility. The problem of the cultural gap rears its head if we are too radical. There cannot be too much distance between where we are now and the future we are being asked to imagine. If there is, then we won't be able to make sense of the utopian project. So the radicalism of utopianism must be counterbalanced by some degree of conservatism—something that keeps us grounded in the present reality.

But it's not just any old conservatism that is needed.[23] It is conservatism of a particular type. Some forms of conservatism are opposed to all radical change. These forms of conservatism favor stability and order for their own sake, usually because change is uncertain and difficult.[24] While there might be some wisdom to taking such a precautionary approach to technological developments, this inherently precautionary understanding of conservatism faces two problems. First, it must confront the problem of rapid change elsewhere in society. There is no point preserving certain ways of life or institutional orders if they are being rendered obsolete or unnecessary by other technological developments. For example, preserving and maintaining the telegraph network in a world of email and other forms of media-rich instant communication is obtuse, not wise. Second, there must be some deeper justification for any precaution. Specifically, there must be some values that guide you when you decide what needs to be preserved and what needs to be changed. In the case of email vs. telegraph, it is probably fair to say that what really matters is the value of human communication. We want humans to be able to communicate with one another, in a frictionless manner, because communication is intrinsically valuable, as well as something that can enable other human goods (such as social coordination and interpersonal relationships). When we think clearly about the values that are at stake, we see that making the shift to the new form of communication is probably, on balance, the right thing to do, even though it has, of course, had some undesirable side effects (constant availability, spam mail, etc.): the cheaper, frictionless forms of communication enable more of the goods of communication to flourish. When you focus on the underlying justifying values in this way, it becomes clear that protecting them may require some change from the current status quo. Blanket precautionary conservatism makes no sense.

The telegraph vs. email example does, however, point the way to the kind of conservatism that is worth taking seriously, namely, "evaluative conservatism." This is a form of conservatism that tries to conserve existing sources of value in the face of threatened change. Evaluative conservatism was first articulated by the philosopher G. A. Cohen.[25] Cohen used it to argue that we should, on at least some occasions, hold on to existing sources of value even if we were being promised something (potentially or definitely) better. For example, I have an old and battered copy of J. R. R. Tolkien's *The Lord of the Rings.* I bought it when I was eleven years old and spent about six months reading it. I have very strong memories of this time in my life and my reactions to the book. I have read the same edition at least two more times since then. The cover has been scotch-taped back on a few times. It is severely sundamaged, and the cover art has faded quite considerably. Nevertheless, I am inordinately fond of this particular edition of the book.[26] Now suppose someone came along and offered me an exchange. I could trade in my battered old copy for a brand-spanking-new deluxe hardback edition, richly illustrated and signed by all the cast members from *The Lord of the Rings* films. This deluxe edition is worth far more, on the open market, than my old paperback, and is guaranteed not to crumble and fall apart. I will be able to pass it on to my children, and they'll be able to pass it on to their children, and so on. The only catch is that I have to trade in my old copy to get it. I cannot have both. Should I make the exchange?

Cohen argues that even if the new edition is better, I would be well within my rights to hold on to the old edition because it is an existing source of value to which I am deeply attached. This is true even though the story that both books contain is the exact same—word for word. The deep attachment that I have to the old edition, and the role it has taken on in my life, justifies my conservatism. Cohen argues that the same evaluative conservatism applies to decisions in which you are asked to forgo an existing relationship for a new (and objectively better) one, or in which you are asked to give up a beloved family pet for a new (and objectively better) one.[27]

While these examples are compelling—no one wants to imagine trading in their beloved pet for a new one—they may go too far. It makes sense to want to conserve existing sources and sustainers of value, but only up to a point. Values should not be understood in discrete terms. Particular sources and sustainers of value are always parts of larger systems or sets of values. As discussed in Chapter 4, there is no single thing that is conducive to a meaningful and flourishing life. There are, rather, several plural sources of meaning and flourishing. Sometimes these different sources will need to be traded off against each other. You might have to surrender one source of value in order to maintain another. Holding on to my old battered copy of *The Lord of the Rings* makes sense if all I am being offered is a newer, fancier copy. But what if the trade I'm being offered is something else? What if I'm being asked to hand over my copy or risk getting shot in the head? In that case, I will probably hold on to my life (an obvious source of value for me) rather than the book. Furthermore, even in those cases in which evaluative conservatism is compelling, you may need to consider radical changes to your life in order to hold on to what you value. Thus, somewhat paradoxically, radical change may be the very thing you need in order to be a consistent evaluative conservative.[28]

This brings us back to the conservative argument for the Cyborg Utopia. There is a "set of values that undergirds and permeates our current way of life."[29] We can call this our evaluative equilibrium. This is the possible moral world into which we have settled. Some aspects of this evaluative equilibrium are negative. In Chapter 3, I argued that our valorization of work and the work ethic is, on balance, negative. But some aspects are positive and are threatened by advances in automation. In Chapter 4, I identified some key values that are under threat (connection with the external world, attention, understanding, autonomy, agency). The conservative case for the Cyborg Utopia hinges on the idea that by integrating ourselves with machines, directly or indirectly, we can stave off these unwelcome threats to our evaluative equilibrium. By becoming more machine-like, we can stop automating technologies from severing our connection to sources of objective value, we can continue to understand and concentrate on external sources of value, and we can maintain our autonomy and agency in the face of rampant automation. If done right, cyborgization will mean that we no longer need to fret about machines making all the important scientific discoveries, or solving the important distributive moral problems. Through technological augmentation and enhancement we can prevent ourselves from losing touch with our current sources and sustainers of value.

Of course, cyborgization is not the only way to conserve our current evaluative equilibrium. Consider the strategy favored by technological pessimists and neo-Luddites. They also tend to be evaluative conservatives, but they favor resistance, rejection, or regulation of new technologies.[30] They want to stop the advancing tide of technological growth in order to maintain our present way of life. Proponents of the Cyborg Utopia clearly see things differently. They don't long for some pre-digital, pre-AI golden age of humanity. Such a thing never existed. They want to race with the machines, not against them. This doesn't mean that they are naive, techno-optimists—the conservative argument is rooted in the techno-pessimism set out in Chapter 4—it just means that they see the advantages of greater human-machine complementarity alongside the disadvantages. They think that going all in on the cyborg revolution will allow them to ensure that the advantages outweigh the disadvantages. Indeed, as a strategy they think it has at least three major benefits when compared to techno-pessimism and neo-Luddism.

First, in addition to fending off the five threats discussed in Chapter 4, pursuing the Cyborg Utopia maintains another of the key advantages to our present way of life: its relative pluralism. Nurturing agency and autonomy is a way of nurturing pluralism. It allows each individual to develop the capacities they need to pursue their own vision of the good life. It does not impose a single, univocal blueprint for the good life on them. Preserving pluralism of this sort is one of the criteria of success that is listed on our utopian score-card. It's a way of avoiding the conflict and violence that Popper warned was implicit in blueprint models of utopia. Consequently, by conserving agency and autonomy, the Cyborg Utopia can conserve pluralism. Techno-pessimism and neo-Luddism cannot do this because they deliberately disable some visions of the good life.

Second, the Cyborg Utopia is, arguably, a more realistic conservative strategy than the neo-Luddite one. Of course, "realism" is a vague concept. There are probably several dimensions to realism, and, as I will argue below, the Cyborg Utopia may score lowly on some of them. But when considered in the grand sweep of history, it provides more hope than the neo-Luddite solution. It is hard to reverse the tide of progress at a societal level. Generations of technologically displaced workers are a testament to that. If a technology has some perceived advantage, it is almost impossible to prevent it from being pursued or realized. Individual resistance has limited utility. Legal bans and restrictions can work for a time, but they require considerable ongoing effort to maintain. This is particularly true if the bans or restrictions would have to work on a global scale—which is almost certain to be the case if we are dealing with automating technologies. If one country bans cyborg technologies, another country is likely to welcome them, because of the competitive advantages they could bring at an economic and (alas) military level. Alleged exceptions to this—such as the various treaties on nuclear weapons and bans on human cloning—tend to prove the rule. It has been exceptionally hard to stop countries from developing nuclear weapons if they see some advantage in doing so. And the many bans on human cloning that one can find around the world (including under the EU Charter of Fundamental Rights), haven't stopped us from pursuing other kinds of cloning—including the cloning of human tissues and body parts—or other advances in human biotech, including genetic engineering. The reluctance to invest much time and effort in human cloning stems more from the fact that there are few, if any, perceived advantages to cloning humans. Things will be different with cyborg technologies, most of which are currently being researched and developed with government support. It will be hard to hold back the tide at a societal level. Better then to embrace increased cyborgiza-tion. This doesn't mean that everyone must be forced to become a cyborg. Individuals should have the choice to do with their lives as they see fit—just as people nowadays can reject the advantages of industrial society and live hermit-like lives of self-sustainability. This is what the pluralistic ethos is all about. It just means that society as a whole will not block those who wish to become cyborgs and can put in place supports for enabling them to do so.

Finally, and perhaps most importantly, favoring the Cyborg Utopia over the neo-Luddite solution doesn't just conserve what we value about our cur-rent way of life. It also allows us to extend and develop those values, that is, to pursue augmented understanding, agency, and autonomy to their tech-nological limits. This will open us up to radically improved possibilities in living. So the conservative advantage of cyborgization is nicely balanced with its radical utopian potential.

Overcoming Humanity and the Horizon of Possibility

The second argument in favor of the Cyborg Utopia takes up this idea of radical possibility. It claims that pursuing cyborgization will allow us to re-alize an improved model of the good life. As you recall from Chapter 4, whether we live a good life or not is dependent on the satisfaction of internal and external conditions of meaning and flourishing. To flourish I must be subjectively satisfied by what I do and develop objective capacities that en-able me to do so; to find meaning I must be subjectively fulfilled by the achievement of projects of objective value (the Good, the True, and the Beautiful). What prevents us from realizing those conditions of flourishing and meaning?

The answer is always some kind of limitation within ourselves or our en-vironments. If I am depressed or melancholy, I may be incapable of appre-ciating the beauty of the world around me. If I am selfish and ridden with social anxieties, I may be incapable of directing my attention to solving the world's problems. If I am dull-witted or unimaginative, I may be incapable of knowing and understanding the world around me. Even if I am none of these things—if I am, per impossibile, an optimized human being—there are still limits imposed by my innate biology that prevent me from pursuing some projects and some states of existence. My mind has evolved to manage a limited amount of information. I can understand the "middle world"[31] of medium-sized objects moving a relatively slow speeds. I cannot really wrap my head around the microscopic world of atoms and quarks; or the macroscopic world of superclusters, dark energy, and light years. Machines can easily rotate, analyze, and decompose multidimensional spaces into their principal components. I cannot.

The claim then is that cyborgization, particularly when understood as part and parcel of an enhancement project, is a way of removing these obstacles to greater flourishing and meaning. By fusing ourselves with machines, we can enhance our biological capacities and overcome our limitations. Of course, you could argue that this is what technology always does and that there is no need for cyborg technologies to overcome the obstacles to greater flourishing and meaning.[32] A simple tool like a hand ax helps to overcome the limitations of the human hand. You could argue that automating technologies do something similar. They are tools that help us to overcome internal and external obstacles to goal fulfillment. With their assistance, we can do the things we would otherwise be incapable of doing.

But I hope I have already convinced you of the error in this style of thinking. It is certainly true that automating technologies help us to overcome obstacles. The problem is that they remove those obstacles by removing us from the picture. They do not facilitate meaningful human participation in the process. The logical apotheosis of automation is the world of *Wall:E*—a world in which we are the well-fed and distracted beneficiaries of machines. The Cyborg Utopia is different because it builds human participation in from the start.

But how many obstacles can we expect the process of cyborgization to remove? Will it really enable greater flourishing and meaning anytime soon? Well, it is already doing this to some extent. Neuroprosthetics and brain-computer interfaces allow those who have lost some functionality (or never had it in the first place) to overcome the limitations this might impose. And it is not just about replacing lost functions. It is also about adding new ones, overcoming limitations, and opening up new ways of living the good life. Neil Harbisson's antenna enables a whole new form of aesthetic experience and production. Moon Ribas's earthquake monitoring chip enables a new form of ethical awareness and empathetic connection. Kevin Warwick's neural implant enables new forms of action at a distance. The possibilities here are staggering, particularly if the various methods of cyborgization are pursued in tandem: new forms of interpersonal communication and intimacy will be possible; new forms of action and embodiment will be realized; new enhanced moods and experiential awareness will become the norm. Cyborgization will open us up to new ways of living the good life that we never realized were there.

You could criticize this argument for the Cyborg Utopia as an attempt to sketch a blueprint for an ideal mode of existence. This would be a mistake. This argument is not claiming that if we overcome the limitations of human biological form we will realize some optimal end state. It should be clear from what I have just said that we don't know exactly where the process of cyborgization will lead us. Some people have speculated about there being some *telos* or omega point or attractor state to which these developments will all lead. For example, Ted Chu, in his book *Human Purpose and Transhuman Potential,* thinks that the technologies of human enhancement and cyborgization will one day cause us to evolve into a cosmic being (CoBe).[33] He thinks it is the purpose of humans living today to facilitate this evolution. In saying this, Chu echoes and updates the arguments of Pierre Teilhard de Chardin from *The Phenomenon of Man.*[34] But it is a mistake to assume that the arc of cyborgization is bending toward some ideal end state. It is clear that there are tendencies within technological development that are highly negative and may deflect us from any ideal state, and there are multiple ways in which the process of cyborgization could play out. It all depends on what we choose to emphasize, and on what is technologically possible, at any given moment.

This is why I think it is better to think of this argument in terms of a horizonal model of utopianism. It is always tempting to conceive of horizons in physical / geographic terms. We push out into new physical territory, explorers and frontiers people that we are, always searching for new and better ways of life. But horizons need not be geographical in nature. We can think of them in more abstract terms. The human body, with its biological limitations, constitutes a horizon of sorts. It constrains what it possible for beings like us. The Cyborg Utopia is about exploring that horizon and seeing what lies beyond. There is no fixed destination; there is an unfolding landscape of possible cyborg forms.

Thinking about the Cyborg Utopia in these terms has the advantage of addressing the Popperian fear that people will simply be sacrificed in order to achieve the ideal end state of a perfectly enhanced cyborg human. If there is no such state, then there is no good reason to sacrifice others. Furthermore, it has the advantage of maintaining the right balance between dynamism and stasis. It provides us with an endlessly fascinating project for humanity—a project of persistent self-transcendence—that can save us from the dusty archives of the museum of history.

Cyborgs in Space

The third argument for the Cyborg Utopia takes us right back to the very origins of the word "cyborg." Clynes and Kline's lexical innovation was prompted by the desire to get humans into space. And, indeed, space exploration has long featured in utopian thought. The quintessential post-work utopia is, in many ways, the world of the United Federation of Planets, as depicted in TV show *Star Trek*.[35] It is a world of material abundance: there are replicators that can create any physical object at the touch of a button. It is a world of pleasure on tap: virtual playgrounds (holodecks) that will cater to our every whim and desire. It is also a world in which the economic need for work has been obviated: we are repeatedly told that money no longer exists in the Federation.[36] Nevertheless, the residents of the Federation do not rest on their laurels and become the engorged pleasure junkies that we see in *Wall:E*. They continue to dedicate themselves to a project of great significance: the continued exploration of space—the final frontier.

This is not to say that the message of *Star Trek* is unremittingly utopian. There is plenty of danger lurking in the farther reaches of space, and life in the Federation is less than ideal (for example, there is still rampant careerism and noticeable power elites). Still, there is something about this vision of space exploration that appeals to the utopian instinct. As Christopher Yorke observes, getting off-planet provides rich opportunities for utopian imaginings. If cyborgization could make it easier for us to explore space, then it might contribute to utopian world-building.[37]

But to prove this, you need to establish two things: (i) you need to show that space exploration really is utopian in nature; and (ii) you need to show that cyborgization helps in the process of space exploration. The former of these is tricky. You have to move beyond vague aspirations and science fictional musings to something more concrete and philosophically plausible. I think there are three arguments that allow you to do this.

The first is simply to reapply the "horizonal" argument from the previous subsection. In keeping with the idea that having an open horizon is a good thing, it seems obvious to say that space exploration keeps our horizons open. The horizon on this occasion is genuinely geographical, not abstract. Space is unimaginably vast. There is no meaningful limit to its exploratory depths (though there may be technical and biological limits to how much we can explore—more on this in a moment). Space is thus the ultimate arena in which to act out the neverending march to the horizon of possibility. It complements the march to the horizons of biological possibility that is inherent in the Cyborg Utopia. Indeed, there is a very real sense in which both horizonal marches must be undertaken in tandem. If we want to explore the outer reaches of space, then we will probably need to explore the outer reaches of human form. And if we want to be motivated to explore those biological horizons, we will probably need to move beyond the planet earth. Staying put may only foster satiety and idleness. As Christopher Yorke puts it: "In the barest physical sense, but also in an important psychological one, the abandonment of space exploration is the acceptance of a fixed horizon for humankind."[38]

The second argument for thinking that space exploration is genuinely utopian is Ian Crawford's "intellectual" case for space exploration.[39] This argument maintains that space exploration allows for the continual advancement of human knowledge and creativity. This could be viewed as a continuation of the preceding line of argument, namely, as a plea to keep open the horizons of human knowledge and creativity. That interpretation of the argument is respectable, and Crawford himself explicitly couches the argument in terms of the need to ensure an "open" future for humanity. But it can also be viewed as a standalone argument that has nothing to do with the need to keep our horizons open. If you recall from Chapter 4, the pursuit of the Good, the True, and the Beautiful (projects of objective value and significance) are usually taken to be integral to the good life. Crawford's intellectual case for space exploration can be understood as an attempt to ensure ongoing human pursuit of the Good, the True, and the Beautiful. To see how this works, we need to go into the details of the argument itself.

Crawford defends three main claims. The first is that space exploration will enable new forms of scientific investigation and progress. This claim is partly based on history—space exploration has enabled scientific advances in the past—and partly on plausible predictions of what would be possible if we did journey through space. Crawford identifies four types of scientific inquiry that would be made possible by space exploration: (i) physical and astrophysical studies conducted using spaceships as observing platforms; (ii) astrophysical studies of the wide variety of stars and their circumstellar environments; (iii) geological and other studies of planetary bodies; and (iv) astrobiological and exobiological studies of habitable planets. Other scientists might ask, "why not let robots do all this?" After all, that's how we advance scientific knowledge of space at the moment. In response, Crawford, argues that in situ observation and measurement are going to be far more precise in many cases, and essential in some, particularly in the search for life on other planets (we cannot penetrate the atmospheres of such planets from a distance). This might, however, be a weak argument since improvements in robotics will overcome some of the limitations to which Crawford appeals.[40] Nevertheless, and in keeping with the motivating premise of this chapter, if we want to ensure continued human flourishing, handing things over to machines may not be the best way to go even if they are more effective explorers of space. We need to be involved in these projects of discovery too.

Crawford's second claim is that space exploration will have a positive impact on artistic expression. Crawford is a fan of Karl Popper's three-world theory. According to this theory, humans sit at the intersection of three worlds: (a) World One, which is the world of physical objects and events; (b) World Two, which is the world of mental states and events; and (c) World Three, which is the world of human knowledge and representations (theories, concepts, models of reality, etc.). The worlds interact with and relate to one another through a series of feedback loops.[41] Crawford argues that art belongs to World Three (the world of human representations) but is an expression of the kinds of human subjectivity (World Two) that result from human observations / responses to the physical world (World One). Artistic expression is made possible when human subjectivity (World Two) speaks through the manipulation of physical objects and materials (World One) to create new artifacts and representations (World Three). The argument that Crawford makes is that space exploration will position humans within new physical landscapes, which will prompt new observations and subjective reactions, which will in turn prompt new forms of artistic expression. He also argues that this will lead to a "cosmicizing" of the human mind—an enlargement of perspective—which will add a new dimension to our artistic endeavors. Even without Popper's theoretical overlay, this argument makes sense. Art has always been, at least in part, a response to the world that we inhabit (though it can also be an anticipation of the worlds we may inhabit), and if space exploration brings us into contact with new experiences and new realities, we can expect our artistic endeavors to respond appropriately.

Crawford's third claim is that space exploration will prompt new developments in philosophy, particularly moral and political philosophy. Why so? Because interstellar exploration will prompt new forms of human association—for example, interstellar economies and colonies—that will require their own political rules and institutions. Establishing those institutions and working out their operations will provide lots of opportunities for philosophers and lawyers. It will also allow for new experiments in living, that is, the construction of new possible moral worlds. Similarly, interstellar exploration will throw open new ethical challenges and questions, such as the ethics of terraforming, multigenerational starships, planetary colonization, the relationship between humans and machines, the duty to continue and diversify life, and the relationship between humans and other (potential) moral subjects, such as alien life. Philosophers are already starting to explore some these issues, but one can imagine that the intellectual excitement would increase greatly if we embarked on an ambitious program of space exploration.[42]

Taken together, I think Crawford's three claims make for a strong intellectual case in favor of space exploration: it's a way of continuing to pursue the Good, the True, and the Beautiful. And since the intellectual possibilities he raises would constitute a radical break from what is currently possible, there is reason to see this as a strongly utopian argument.

This brings me to the final argument for thinking that space exploration is utopian. This is the argument from the "ethic of life."[43] The most plausible way to run this argument is to point out that humans have an interest in their continued survival as a species. From the utopian point of view, any project that is committed to radical improvements in the human condition requires the continued survival of humanity as a species.[44] Granting this, a reasonably strong case can be made in favor of the utopian need for space exploration. If we continue to stay on earth, we are likely to face a number of survival-threatening risks, including resource depletion, meteor strike, and the eventual burnout of the sun.[45] Exploring space is a way of addressing these risks. We can escape the limitations of our home planet and develop technologies that mitigate those risks. If humanity is to survive and thrive in the long term, then it looks like we must, as space entrepreneur Elon Musk argues, become a multi-planetary species. There is also the related argument, from Nick Bostrom, that a failure to explore and colonize space is a wasted opportunity for our species. This rests on the utilitarian presumption that by colonizing space we could greatly increase the number of sentient human beings who live pleasurable / valuable lives. So we should get started on the project of exploring space as soon as possible.[46]

There is also a less plausible way of running the "ethic of life" argument. This rests on the belief that we have some strong interest in (or possibly duty to) ensure the continued survival of all living things. Christopher Ketcham argues for this view on the basis that we are the only species that knows that it is alive and, hence, we have a stewardship duty toward all other living things.[47] If you accept that, the same essential argument for space exploration can carry through, only this time we're not just trying to ensure our survival, we're trying to ensure the survival of life more generally. This will no doubt seem like an odd and counterintuitive idea. It's very hard to imagine that we have some duty to ensure the survival of, say, the E. coli bacterium. But there is an advantage to broadening our survival interest beyond our current species boundary: the process of space exploration may, itself, lead to our descendants branching off into post-human species.[48] This could happen if colonizing groups populate different planets and form isolated breeding groups (facing different selection pressures). Or it could happen through deliberate and directed technological intervention into human biology. Either way it might be wise to conceive of our survival interest in non-human terms.

This brings us neatly back to the merits of the Cyborg Utopia. I have presented three arguments for thinking that space exploration is utopian in nature, but none of these arguments has appealed, specifically, to the need for cyborgization. This is the necessary second half of the argument that I alluded to earlier on. Fortunately, it is relatively easy to tack this on to what I have just said. Anyone with an interest in space exploration will know that humans, as they are currently constituted, are not well equipped for space travel. There is considerable biological incompatibility between humans and space. We have evolved to survive and thrive in a certain set of habitats and ecosystems—environments that are not too hot and not too cold. The Earth provides us with these. On Earth, we are shielded from solar radiation by the magnetic sphere. We have symbiotic relationships with bacteria and other organisms. An Earth-bound existence is convenient for beings like us. Space is different. We have not evolved to live there. It is a much harsher environment, not congenial to our flourishing. If we go there, we would have to live in highly protective and restrictive spaces that we create for ourselves. If there is life on other planets, we could be exposed to new biological threats and diseases.

These are the kinds of concerns that motivated Clynes and Kline's original argument in favor of cyborgization. If we want to be part of the space exploration process—if we don't simply wish to cede that territory to automating technologies as well—then it seems like we will have to, at some point, commit to reforming our biological constitution to make it more robust. This could be achieved through genetic and biological manipulation, and through closer integration with machines (cyborgization). This is one area where being a purely conceptual cyborg probably wouldn't cut it. Some deeper integration will be required. That integration could be undertaken slowly and incrementally. There is no need to get to space immediately. As with many utopian projects, we can view this as a long-term commitment. The job for the next few generations can be to build up the technological capacity needed for exploring the furthest reaches of space. This goes for all space-related technology, not just cyborg technologies. Jeff Bezos, one of the leading private investors in space technology through his company Blue

Origin, articulates this point. In an interview with Christopher Davenport, author of the book *The Space Barons*, Bezos argues that his job—and the job of other space enthusiasts—is to build some of the technological infrastructure that will enable future generations to do more inventive and dramatic things in space.[49] In saying this, he points out that Amazon benefitted greatly from the digital and computing infrastructure that was put in place by researchers and developers from the 1940s through to the mid-1990s. Without that infrastructure he and all the other internet giants would not have been able to do what they have done. The goal now is to build the infrastructure for turning us into a multi-planetary species. Cyborgization is an essential part of that infrastructure.

The Collective Afterlife Argument

The fourth argument for the Cyborg Utopia picks up the "ethic of life" baton from the preceding argument. This can be developed into an independent argument in favor of the Cyborg Utopia. I have done this at considerable length in some previous work, focusing in particular on the value of creating a cyborg successor species.[50] Here, I will offer a summary of that argument that focuses on the value of cyborgizing our own species.

The argument is premised on an idea that was originally developed by the philosopher Samuel Scheffler in his book *Death and the Afterlife*.[51] Scheffler's claim is that the "collective afterlife" is an important source and sustainer of meaning in our present lives. In saying this, Scheffler works with a wholly secular conception of the collective afterlife. His vision of the collective afterlife focuses on of the lives of all those who will continue to live (on earth or elsewhere in the universe) after we die. It is not about our continued survival in some heavenly realm.

Scheffler is adamant that the fact that there is going to be a collective afterlife, or at the very least *our belief* that there is going to be one, plays an important role in our individual flourishing and meaning. If we were convinced that there was never going to be a collective afterlife, then our lives would be very different. We would be depressed and filled with existential angst. More than that, much of what we currently do just wouldn't make sense (or wouldn't be as valuable) without a commitment to the collective afterlife. Why dedicate yourself to curing cancer if there aren't going to be any future generations who will need the cure? Why make significant scientific discoveries or create great works of art, if no one will be around to appreciate them? Sure, these things may have some intrinsic value, and you might derive some satisfaction from doing them, but they take on an added aura of significance if there is going to be a collective afterlife. Scheffler defends this with two interesting thought experiments. One of them asks you to imagine how you might feel if you know that you will live a long and normal human life but that thirty days after you die all human life will be destroyed in some catastrophic event ("The Doomsday Thought Experiment").The second asks you to imagine how you might feel if you know that the human species is collectively infertile and slowly going extinct ("The Collective Infertility Thought Experiment").[52]

Both scenarios, according to Scheffler, would provoke the same reaction: you would feel pretty awful as a result. You would think twice about the value of the life you are currently living. That said, the thought experiments reveal different things. The first reveals that there is a significant non-experiential aspect to how you value your life. In other words, the value of your life isn't determined solely by what you experience within your life; it is also determined by things that you will never experience (specifically what happens to those in the collective afterlife). Furthermore, it suggests that there is a conservative element to how we value the collective afterlife. In other words, part of the reason why we have an interest in the collective afterlife is because things that we currently value will continue to be valued there. This is consistent with the evaluative conservatism that I developed earlier in this chapter. The second thought experiment also reveals these things but goes on to suggest that your interest in the collective afterlife is not purely selfish. You don't just care about the collective afterlives of your family, friends, and relatives (though you probably do care about them); you care about the fate of humanity more generally. As Scheffler himself puts it, our understanding of what makes life worth living, and what is conducive to our meaning and flourishing "relies on an implicit understanding of . . . a life as itself occupying a place in an ongoing chain of lives and generations."[53]

I find this persuasive. I believe that the collective afterlife does play an important role in how we find meaning and value in our present lives, and I believe that this can be leveraged into an argument in favor of the Cyborg Utopia. That argument states that the cyborgization of the human species provides a way of ensuring that there is a collective afterlife, and that this way of ensuring a collective afterlife might be better than the traditional biological method. In more formal terms:[54]

(1) The collective afterlife is an important source and sustainer of value and meaning in our lives.

(2) We have reason to pursue projects that have a greater probability of supporting or maintaining that which provides our lives with value and meaning.

(3) Therefore, we have reason to pursue projects that have a greater probability of ensuring that there is a collective afterlife.

(4) The cyborgization of our species has a greater probability of ensuring that there is a collective afterlife that sustains the conditions needed for meaning and value than the creation of traditional biological offspring.

(5) Therefore, we have reason to pursue the cyborgization of our species.

I'll assume that the first half of this argument (1–3) is relatively uncontroversial. You may not accept the collective afterlife thesis, of course, but I've outlined the rationale for it already, so if you do, and if you accept the arguments from preceding chapters concerning the need for humans to flourish and find meaning in their lives, you should find it persuasive. It's the second half that is controversial, specifically premise (4). Why accept this?

The main reason is that the cyborgization of offspring offers more hope for the collective afterlife than does the creation of normal biological offspring, particularly in light of the threats of automation outlined in Chapter 4. Scheffler's thought experiments suggest that we don't want there to be no collective afterlife at all. That would be bad. But we don't want a collective afterlife at any cost either. If the choice was between extinction thirty days after I die, and a collective afterlife in which everyone was tortured from dawn to dusk for ninety years (pausing only briefly to procreate and ensure that there will be another generation to continue the torture), I think we might find the extinction option more attractive. By the same logic, if there is a choice between a collective afterlife in which our off-spring must accept their inferiority to machines and forgo any participation in projects of objective meaning and value, and a collective afterlife in which our offspring are technologically augmented so that they continue to par-ticipate in those projects, we would be right to prefer the latter. We want the best for our children, and a cyborgian existence would come with the advantages described in the three preceding arguments. It would conserve many of the values that we currently care about, and it would allow future generations to expand into new horizons of possibility.

This might suggest to you that this argument is redundant because it ends up relying on the previous arguments to support its crucial premise. This is only partly true, and it doesn't stop it from providing an independent reason to favor the Cyborg Utopia. The preceding arguments were all about what life would be like in the Cyborg Utopia and centered on the claim that this existence would score highly on the utopian scorecard. This argument is about life in the here and now. Scheffler's collective afterlife thesis is intended to show how our current lives derive meaning and value from the prospect of a collective afterlife. In other words, Scheffler isn't just concerned with the value of the collective afterlife for the people who will be living in it; he is concerned with its value for us, right now, living in its shadow. That's also key to the argument I am making. Committing ourselves to cyborgization of our species right now is a way of providing meaning and value to those of us who are alive today—who are a long way from achieving total human-machine integration. It gives us a utopian project around which to organize our present lives, threatened as they are by the rise of automating technolo-gies. And again, as with the space exploration argument, it's not necessary that the next generation achieve some high-level form of human-machine integration for this project to provide meaning. It's enough that we start along a pathway toward increased cyborgization.

Existential Robustness and Death

The final argument for the Cyborg Utopia is the most straightforward. It is that increased cyborgization will make us more existentially robust and, at the limit, possibly even allow us to escape the clutches of death. This is one of the main reasons why transhumanists are fond of cyborgization. They believe that by gradually replacing our feeble and febrile biological parts with silicon and metal, we will be able to control the process of aging. We can end voluntary death and achieve digital immortality. I wouldn't push the argument so far. I doubt that true immortality is an achievable or desirable goal. But enhancing our existential robustness, and perhaps greatly extending our lifespans, does strike me as a utopian aim, and something that could be assisted by greater cyborgization.

My position here is somewhat subtle. It is not that I think death is a great evil that eliminates all meaning from our lives and so must be conquered. Some people do believe this. In fact, as Iddo Landau notes in his book *Finding Meaning in an Imperfect World,* there are those who think that death renders all lives equally meaningless because it means that anything of value that we might have achieved in our lifetimes will, in the end, disappear from the world. This means that we are all caught in an existential blackhole. We can strut and fret all we like, but in the end it counts for naught. If you agree with this sentiment, then the urge to eliminate death through biotechnology should be strong. It's not just a utopian aim; it's an essential aim, one that is necessary if we are to make life meaningful in the first place.[55]

But, as I say, this is not what motivates my argument. I fully appreciate where this nihilistic fear comes from. In fact, as you'll have noticed, the collective afterlife thesis itself relies on a version of this fear—the fear that everything will disappear after we are dead. But I think this is subtly distinct from the fear that we won't be around to enjoy it. The collective afterlife thesis is motivated by the desire for some continuous overlapping chain of beings like us; it is not motivated by a desire for our indefinite existence along that chain. I do not think we should desire such an indefinite existence. There are two main reasons for this.

The first is that I think the classic Epicurean arguments against the badness of death are, at least somewhat, persuasive.[56] The fact that death is a state of nonbeing in which we will not suffer, and it is, broadly, similar in nature to the state of non-being that preceded our births, gives us some reason to think that death is not as terrible as people claim. This doesn't mean that death is good and something to be welcomed with open arms. Nor does it mean that the process of dying cannot be bad, since someone could suffer as they die. It just means that it is not a great evil that renders life meaningless.

The second reason is that an immortal existence, one in which death is truly eliminated, would also run the risk of meaninglessness. This is not for the oft-stated reason that immortality would be "tedious." This is a position that was popularized by the philosopher Bernard Williams in his article "The Makropulus Case: Reflections on the Tedium of Immortality."[57] He argued that having certain long-term projects and interests is essential to living a meaningful life. Not only that, these projects also shape your identity: they make you the unique person that you are. The problem with immortality is that you would finish these projects and have to revise them. You could only do this so many times while still retaining your unique identity. Inevitably, repetition and tedium would set in. Although I think Williams is on to something with this line of argument, I think he is wrong to be so critical of repetition—some of life's most rewarding pleasures are the ones that repeat (food, drink, sex, and so on). Furthermore, it is incorrect to assume that there is some upper limit to the amount of times we can change our long-term projects and interests and retain our sense of identity. There is no reason why our identities need to be so fixed and rooted. Your identity is defined by your beliefs, desires, memories, and dispositions. These mental states chain together over the course of your life. As long as there is some overlap and continuity between the links of the chain, you will have a continuous sense of identity. The fact that you might end up in a different place from where you started is of no consequence.

No, the real problem with immortality is that it will render our lives "weightless" and deprive our achievements of their significance. Aaron Smuts makes this case quite well. He points out that in a truly immortal existence you would eventually be able to achieve everything that is practically achievable—with enough time and effort anything that is possible will be done by everyone. This means that there is nothing special or unique about your achievements. Eventually all the other immortal beings will achieve them too. You will do everything, see everything, and experience everything that it is possible to experience—both good and ill. As for the things that aren't practically achievable, they will be an endless source of frustration.[58] Smuts argues that Jorge Luis Borges sums up the sad fate of the immortal being quite well in his short story "The Immortal." In that story, Borges notes that over an infinite lifetime "all things happen to all men" and so all actions become essentially unimportant and not worthy of respect, punishment, or awe. As he puts it: "Homer composed the Odyssey; given infinite time, with infinite circumstances and changes, it is impossible that the Odyssey should not be composed at least once. No one is someone; a single immortal man is all men."[59]

And yet I still claim that achieving greater existential robustness and life extension is a utopian aim. Why? The simple answer is that the problems of immortality lie at the extreme. Even if eliminating death entirely would not be desirable, it does not follow that extending our lives beyond their current limits is not desirable. At the very least, ensuring greater existential robustness is going to be essential if we are to achieve some of the other utopian aims described in this chapter, particularly the aim of space exploration. We cannot be so biologically vulnerable if that is one of our aspirations. Furthermore, irrespective of those projects, there is still something tragic about dying before one desires to die. To have one's life projects cut off while they are still in motion, to have one's relationships severed before they have reached some natural denouement, is less than ideal. As I was writing this chapter my sister died suddenly. She was forty-three years old and with a one-and-a-half-year-old son. She wanted to care for him and nurture him into adulthood. It's hard not to see something tragic about this. Her life was left unfinished. If we could stop this kind of thing from happening—or at least make it less likely—we would live in a radically better world.

There is no absolute guarantee that cyborgization would enable this. It is merely an assumption, albeit one with some grounding in reality. Our biological parts are vulnerable to disease and infection and are not easily replaceable or renewable, except by machine prosthetics. Machine parts themselves are less vulnerable and more easily replaceable. If we could minimize our reliance on biological parts and increase reliance on technological parts, there is some reason to believe that we could achieve greater existential robustness. This is going to depend on other complementary advances in medical science and biotechnology and, again, is likely to be a long-term project. There will be plenty of tragic and unfinished lives in the interim. Still, the project itself defines a utopian horizon toward which we can aim.

The Case against the Cyborg Utopia

When considered cumulatively, the five arguments just outlined provide a powerful case for the Cyborg Utopia. Pursuing the path of greater human-machine integration is a way of conserving and extending much of what we currently value, retaining a commitment to pluralism and diversity, whilst at the same time offering up several distinct utopian horizons toward which we can sail. This maintains a balance between stability and dynamism, and gives us some hope for a radically better future. It is a way to preserve what is best about humanity and yet still experiment in new ways of living.

I do not discount any of this. I find myself attracted to certain aspects of the Cyborg Utopia. Nevertheless, there is a darker side to that vision, one that suggests that hunkering down in the cognitive niche may not be the best response to the rise of automating technologies. I want to consider six problems with the vision now.

The Conservation of Work?

The first problem is that if the cyborg project succeeds in its conservative aims, it may have the unwelcome side effect of conserving one of the things we are trying to escape. This is an objection that probably occurred to you already, but let's spell it out. The conservative advantage of cyborgization lies in its ability to preserve and maintain our agency and sense of connection to the world around us. This is what automating technologies threaten and is what is integral to our flourishing and well-being. It is also, however, the very same thing that makes the automation of work possible.

Recall from Chapter 3 that one of the major arguments of this book is that the automation of work is desirable. Work is structurally bad: it undermines our freedom, compromises our well-being, and sustains systemic inequalities. It would be good if we could escape it. The rise of automating technologies can disrupt the negative equilibrium into which we have settled. It offers up the potential of a new, radically better post-work world. One of the goals of the second half of this book is to see if we can do something to facilitate this post-work possibility, whilst at the same time staving off the threats of automation. But it may not be possible to do that. It may be that we have to pick and choose, as figure 6.1 illustrates.

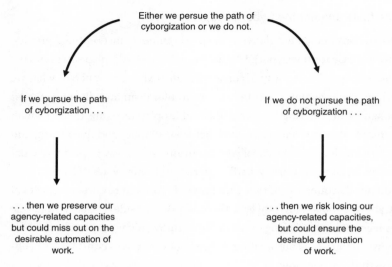

Either we persue the path of cyborgization or we do not.

If we pursue the path of cyborgization . . .

If we do not pursue the path of cyborgization . . .

. . . then we preserve our agency-related capacities but could miss out on the desirable automation of work.

. . . then we risk losing our agency-related capacities, but could ensure the desirable automation of work.

Figure 6.1 The Conservative Dilemma

Can we avoid the dilemma set out in figure 6.1? The defender of cyborgization might have something to offer. They might claim that cyborgization can make work more pleasant and meaningful, even if it is still a practical necessity. By enhancing individual ability and cognition, we could once again enhance the power of labor relative to capital. This might help to reverse some of the negative trends we currently see. Workers might be able to agitate for better pay and better rights if they are able to do things as cyborgs that machines cannot do on their own. It might also make work much easier and, if we include possible emotional and mood enhancements into the mix, more enjoyable.

There are, however, problems with this response. There is no guarantee that the advantages of cyborgization will be equally shared among all workers. Indeed, cyborgization could simply serve to reinforce and solidify the polarization of the workforce that was discussed in Chapter 3: most of the benefits, in terms of both the interesting work and the associated pay, will flow to the elite, creative workers who are best positioned to take advantage of cyborg technologies. Furthermore, the advantages of cyborgization themselves may be short-lived. Defenders of human-machine hybrids in the workplace often point to analogous cases of human-machine hybrids in board games to make their case. For example, Tyler Cowen, in his 2013 book *Average Is Over*, used the example human-computer partnerships in chess as a potential model for the future workplace; others have since followed suit.[60] Although Cowen didn't think that this would reverse the trend toward automation and inequality, he thought it provided one route to continued (elite) human participation in the workforce. It is noteworthy then that in 2017, a little over four years after Cowen's book was published, the human-machine partnerships in chess lost their advantage.[61] The latest crop of chess-playing computers are now outperforming them. A similar pattern is likely to be observed in other areas.

So the sad reality is that cyborgization is unlikely to get us out of the rut that we are in. It will simply delay the day that we need to consider the more radical possibility of a post-work future and, in the meantime, reinforce a negative culture of hyper-competitiveness in the labor market. In addition to expensive educations and endless self-promotion, people will now have to compete for cyborg implants to gain a foothold in the labor market. Furthermore, the one area where human-machine hybrids are most likely to maintain a long-term advantage over machines—although I am not even confident of this—is in the area of manual and physical work in an unpredictable environment. A human with an augmented exoskeleton, for example, is likely to be better (and cheaper) than a machine that is programmed to do the same thing. But unless there is some radical change in how we value and think about this form of work, this means many humans will be consigned to the less rewarding and less well-paid forms of work. We have to ask whether we are willing to risk this possibility for the other advantages of cyborgization.

The Enslavement Worry

A second major worry about the Cyborg Utopia concerns its impact on individual freedom. To this point, I have been selling the Cyborg Utopia on the promise that it will maintain agency and autonomy. By augmenting ourselves with technology, we can avoid the kinds overreliance and overdependency that concerned us in Chapter 4. But is this really true? In the rush to transcend our biological limitations, could we in fact undermine our freedom?

The journalist Mark O'Connell worries about this. O'Connell spent several years interviewing and shadowing some of the key figures in the modern transhumanist movement, including the basement biohacker Tim Cannon, whom I mentioned earlier in this chapter. O'Connell is disturbed by the faith these individuals place in liberatory powers of technology. He thinks their faith conceals a deep paradox. As he puts it, "transhumanism is a liberation movement advocating nothing less than a total emancipation from biology itself. There is another way of seeing this, an equal and opposite interpretation, which is that this apparent liberation would in reality be nothing less than a final and total enslavement to technology."[62]

There is merit to O'Connell's concern. To put it bluntly: in pursuing a process of increased cyborgization, there is a chance that we won't really liberate ourselves from anything, and we will simply swap our biological prison for a technological one. Think about it this way: In Chapter 4, I outlined various mechanisms through which automating technologies could undermine our agency and autonomy. I argued that these technologies could be used to dominate and manipulate our decision-making, make the world more opaque and less comprehensible to human reason, and control our attention and focus. With the exception of the methods of pharmacological and genetic enhancement, all the major methods of cyborgization are built off the back of integrating ourselves more deeply with very same kinds of technology. Why on earth should we think that this will free us from anything? It's like bringing the jack-booted guard who was patrolling the perimeter of your house inside and hoping that this will get him to change his mind. It's naively optimistic at best.

Although this is a serious problem for the Cyborg Utopia, it may be possible to dissolve the paradox to at least some extent. In fact, it could be argued that there is no real paradox here at all. What's happening is that proponents of cyborgization are trading one dimension of freedom off against another. Freedom, after all, is a very complex phenomenon. That should be clear from all the previous discussions of it in this book. There are several different theories of freedom, each of which identifies a distinct set of conditions of freedom. Examples of such conditions include the absence of interference, the absence of domination, the capacity for rational choice, the presence of an adequate range of valuable options, the ability to express your true self, and so on. If you view these conditions in the aggregate, and not as discrete and mutually incompatible theories (which they are not), then you start to see that each of these conditions defines a different dimension of freedom. You then arrive at a multidimensional model of what it means to be free.

This is important because when you have a multidimensional model in mind, you start to see that it may not be possible to optimize along all dimensions at the same time. To use an analogy, it may not be possible to have a fast and efficient decision-making system that is also meticulous in how it assesses and weighs evidence. The latter may necessarily take more time. You are either going to have to prioritize efficiency or meticulousness, or reach some compromise between them. The same could apply to freedom. It may not be possible to maximize our capacity to understand what we are doing, while at the same time minimizing external interference in our decision-making. It could be that maximizing understanding requires some degree of external interference (for example, through education and persuasion). Maybe this is paradoxical—because it reveals a tension at the heart of our theory of freedom—or maybe it is just being realistic about the multidimensional nature of freedom.[63]

Either way, it gives us a new way to understand what lies behind O'Connell's fear of technological enslavement. Wannabe cyborgs, particularly those of a transhumanist persuasion, are trying to minimize the biological constraints on our freedom and trying to allow us to explore new horizons of possibility beyond the human form. O'Connell (and others) worry that this opens us up to technological constraints on our freedom. It could be that there is a practically unavoidable tension here: it could be that minimizing biological constraints necessarily entails increasing technological constraints. You have to prioritize or compromise. That doesn't mean that if you pick biological freedom over technological freedom you are heading toward enslavement; it just means that you are favoring one dimension of freedom over another.

Of course, this doesn't help us all that much. It provides a more nuanced understanding of what it means to be free and highlights the hard choices we may have to make when it comes to freedom, but it doesn't allay the fear that in minimizing biological constraints we may open ourselves up to something much worse. As noted in Chapter 4, we are familiar with the biological constraints on freedom. We have lived with them for hundreds and thousands of years. We have developed resistance strategies to them. Are they really so bad that we want to trade them for a set of technological constraints? And even if they were, wouldn't that fly in the face of the main arguments presented this book? We are trying to find a way to stave off the threats of automation, not run to them with open arms.

There is a way to solve the problem though. Most of the fears of technological enslavement stem not from the technology itself but, rather, from (a) the sense that it is "other," meaning, not part of who we are; and / or (b) the fact that we do not *control* or *own* it, meaning, it is owned and controlled by third-party manufacturers and designers. The first of those worries can be addressed by ensuring that there is full biological and phenomenological integration with the technology—of the kind that many people with cyborg prosthetics and brain implants already report feeling.[64] Recall Neil Harbisson's statement from earlier in this chapter that he doesn't just *use* technology; he *is* technology. The second worry is more difficult to address. To use an analogy, people don't simply fret about the impact of social media on freedom because of how it changes our behavior but because those changes are induced / incentivized by others who own and control the technology (the companies that run those services or the hackers who hijack them). This means that the behavioral changes are not authentic to who we are and may not serve our own interests. There is reason to think that both of those concerns will apply to cyborg devices and implants too. The software in the systems that enable cyborgization of either the conceptual or technical kind can be programmed (and possibly even remotely controlled) by the manufacturers of these technologies. The technology can be hacked by third parties. Indeed, the susceptibility of such devices to hacks has already been established, leading some scholars to propose a new field of "neurosecurity" to respond to this threat.[65] A defender of the Cyborg Utopia might respond and say that the issue of who owns these technologies is just a readily changeable legal quirk: ownership rights are legal constructs, not something that inheres in the natural order. There is an easily attainable possible cyborg future in which external parties do not own cyborg implants. They might also say that the control problem is but a technical one: something that could be resolved (or at least minimized) by creating secure systems that are only accessible to (and programmable by) the individual that uses them. If we could address both of those problems, we could dissolve the paradox of transhumanism and maintain commitment to the Cyborg Utopia.

This is true, but I wouldn't hold my breath waiting for a solution. There are formidable difficulties with resolving both problems, particularly the control problem. Maybe through cyborgization we will each bootstrap our way to becoming highly competent programmers, and so won't need to rely on third-party intervention. And maybe we will create highly secure systems with minimal risk of hijacking, but there is every reason to suspect that this is going to be very difficult. There is a classic asymmetry involved in the conflict between security professionals and hackers.[66] The hacker only has to find one weak point in the system to make the hack; the security professional has to cover over all potential holes and create the perfect wall. No one has been able to do that yet. So if we care about our freedom, and don't want to open ourselves up to more severe forms of manipulation and control, we might be better off abandoning the ideal of cyborgization.

The Cultural Gap Problem

A third problem with the Cyborg Utopia is that, *in extremis,* it opens up too much of a cultural gap between the envisaged utopia and where we are now. As noted in Chapter 5, a utopia has to be a radical improvement on the current state of affairs, but it cannot be so radical that we cannot make sense of it. If we are asked to choose between living our current lives as embodied biological beings on Earth and an alternative life in which we live as beams of light chasing through the galaxy, it's unlikely that we'll really know what to make of that choice. It's too much of a transformative change. We lack the necessary information to judge whether that would be a radical improvement over what we currently have.

The Cyborg Utopia seems to suffer from this problem. In its more modest, and conservative, forms it is rationally intelligible. When Neil Harbisson describes his experiences with his Eyeborg antenna, they make a certain degree of sense to me. I haven't experienced what he has experienced, of course, but we share enough common ground for me to realize that he has extended his sensory engagement with the world in a very interesting way. I can also make sense of Kevin Warwick's experiences moving a robotic arm with a microchip implanted in his nerves. It's a little bit more alien to me than Harbisson's Eyeborg—I've never had a chip implanted in my hand but I have heard different sounds—but I can guess what it must have been like.

The problem is that as you start multiplying these differences, the cultural gap opens up more and more. If one of the goals of the Cyborg Utopia is to push back against the frontiers of human biology, and to transcend all our familiar limitations, then it could be that what I'm being asked to buy into is so different from what I am used to that I cannot really rationally assess the project. I cannot tell whether it would be a radical improvement. This is particularly true if one of the consequences of the Cyborg Revolution is that many of the things that seem valuable to me right now are replaced or reformed as a result of the technological transformations.

We can understand the problem more deeply if we consider some examples. Brett Frischmann and Evan Selinger, in their book *Re-engineering Humanity,* argue that modern forms of "techno-social engineering" have a dehumanizing effect. They use the term "techno-social engineering" as a catchall for behavior change / manipulation systems that use some novel technology but that are also filtered to us through social institutions (like the law). They are particularly concerned about the techno-social engineering that is enabled by modern automating devices. They argue that these technologies "program" us to act like simple machines, that is, to act in predictable, routine, and unreflective ways. This is dehumanizing because self-reflection, deliberation, and free will are key to the human condition.[67]

Frischmann and Selinger are so worried about this prospect that they go so far as to propose a test for determining whether or not humans are becoming like simple machines: the reverse Turing test.[68] Whereas Turing's original test was supposed to show us whether a machine was acting in a human-like way, the reverse Turing test is supposed to show us whether a human is acting in a machine-like way. Simple heuristics or rules of thumb can be used for this purpose. For example, humans are renowned for not following the rules of rational choice theory: they have various biases or quirks in their reasoning that deviate from this model. Machines, on the other hand, can follow these rules. So if a system of techno-social engineering results in humans more closely approximating the rules of rational choice theory, it suggests that we are becoming more machine like. Frischmann and Selinger propose other tests that can be used to reach similar conclusions. They are clear that they don't think that techno-social engineering will completely erode our humanity—they see the effects as being more situational and context specific—but they do think that the dehumanizing effects can aggregate in such a way that we might no longer be recognizably human as a result.

You may wonder, "Why does this matter?" The Cyborg Utopia is, after all, intentionally dehumanizing. It is about transcending human limitations. But while this is true, it's not about transcending them all. There are some aspects of the human condition that we would like to preserve. If cyborg technologies turn us into "simple" machines—as Frischmann and Selinger fear—then we may be losing touch with what it is we want to preserve. Being a simple machine might have some advantages, but those advantages would not be intelligible to creatures like us.

The same problem arises if we consider another example.[69] This one is more rooted in science fiction than fact. I mentioned earlier in this chapter that the seemingly utopian world of *Star Trek* also has its dark side. Perhaps the darkest side of all is represented by the Borg, an alien culture that has pushed cyborg technology to the extreme. They are a technologically advanced civilization in which organic entities (humans and other humanoid life-forms) have been cyborgized in such a way that cyborg implants connect each individual organic entity to a collective consciousness (or hive-mind). These collectives then roam the universe trying to assimilate other life-forms into the hivemind. The vision is dark because it seems to undermine some of our core values, particularly values associated with individuality and self-determination. A single Borg does not have any self-consciousness.

They do not think of themselves as individuals.[70] They refer to themselves in the first person plural, saying "we are Borg" not "I am Borg."

This is truly alien to us, and threatening, because so much of what we currently value about life flows from our sense of individuality. If we lose touch with that, we may lose too much to be able to evaluate what life might be like in such a world. That's not to say that pursuing greater cyborgization will necessarily lead to a Borg-like status, but there are features of current cyborg technologies, and tendencies among proponents of them, that tend in that direction. For example, direct brain-to-brain communication—without the inefficiencies of language—is a stated goal of Kevin Warwick, and greater connectivity and interpersonal connection are also features of Neil Harbisson and Moon Ribas's experiments with cyborgization. In the extreme, these developments could lead to the erosion of boundaries between self and other, and a collapse of the value system that has been built around individualism. The cultural gap between our world and these hypothetical cyborg worlds is like a chasm.

Are there ways for the Cyborg Utopia to avoid fears of the cultural gap? Possibly. Since the horizonal model of utopianism is deliberately open-ended, you could argue that it necessarily entails some risk of a cultural gap. It may always be that we end up somewhere very different from where we started out. That's part of what makes the horizonal approach so dynamic and exciting. But as long as the changes undertaken at each step in the journey toward the horizon are not too radical, then there is no real problem. Each individual or society that is being asked to contemplate those changes will be able to evaluate and make sense of them from where they are. They can determine whether it is in their interests or not. As long as we are not being asked to turn into Borg-like entities overnight, it's okay. Similarly, greater awareness of human history and cross-cultural studies of human values might help to put some of the fears described above into perspective. For example, Larry Siedentop, in his book *Inventing the Individual*, argues that the philosophy of individualism that was extolled in the preceding paragraphs is a relatively recent invention, something that evolved slowly over the past 1,000 years or so.[71] The ancient Greeks, he argues, did not really think of themselves as individuals; they thought of themselves as members of families or clans. Maybe our cyborg offspring will do something similar and be none the worse for it?

Maybe, but again, the mere fact that human value systems may be more malleable than we think does not mean that there is nothing to fear in losing touch with what we currently have. When I read Siedentop's descriptions of the value system of ancient Greece, where everyone was subordinate to a paterfamilias,[72] I am grateful that we no longer live in such a world. Looking forward to possible cyborg futures, I hope we won't return to it (or evolve toward something more extreme). In other words, even though you have to embrace some uncertainty about where we will end up, it still makes sense to try to guard against inversions of value that are too extreme. This suggests that we should proceed with caution when it comes to building a Cyborg Utopia.

Dystopias in Space

A fourth problem arises from the prospects of cyborgs in space. In the previous section I painted a rosy picture of the cyborg future in space. I argued that space exploration will allow us to push out against an ever-expanding horizon of possibility, contribute to the growth of knowledge, and ensure our continued survival. I also argued that cyborgization would help to mitigate against the biological risks of space exploration. But I ignored other potential risks in space. If we consider those risks, it may well be the case that space exploration is downright dystopian, not utopian.

One person who worries about this is Phil Torres. He argues that human exploration of space could lead to a catastrophic intergalactic conflict and that the risk of this is sufficiently high to counsel against the idea, no matter what benefits it might otherwise have. He puts it rather bluntly, saying that "every second of delayed colonization [of space] should be seen as immensely desirable, and the longer the delay, the better."[73]

Torres's reasoning is cut straight from the playbook of Blaise Pascal.[74] Pascal famously argued that skeptics should believe in God because even if the chances of God's existence were low, the possible gains from believing in him (if he existed) were so high, and the possible losses from not believing in him (if he existed) were so awful that it would be irrational not to do so. In other words, Pascal argued that there was a significant *risk asymmetry* between believing in God and not believing in God and only a fool would run that risk. This is true even if not believing in God has some temporary, earthly benefits.

In a similar vein, Torres argues that there is a significant risk asymmetry between colonizing space and staying on Earth. If we journey out into space, there's a chance that we will get embroiled in a catastrophic intergalactic war—a war that could wipe out all sentient life in the universe, never mind just here on Earth, or that could result in unimaginable amounts of suffering for sentient life. The chance of such a conflict might be very low, but as long as it is not negligible, it has to be factored into our plans. If we stay on Earth, we reduce that risk (although we could, of course, face other existential threats).

But why is Torres so convinced that there is a non-negligible risk of a catastrophic conflict in space? It all goes back to Thomas Hobbes. In *Leviathan*, Hobbes argued that humans tend to get into violent conflicts for three main reasons: (i) to compete for scarce resources; (ii) to protect themselves from threats to their safety; and (iii) to generate a reputation for violence that will keep threats at bay. In certain situations—for example, when there is a breakdown in social order—conflict ramps up and people get trapped in cycles of violence. The only way to address this problem, according to Hobbes, is to construct a "Leviathan"—a social institution that can keep the peace by monopolizing the use of force and enforcing rules that enable cooperation and coordination.

Keeping the peace on Earth is hard enough, but Torres argues that it will be nearly impossible in space. There are three reasons for this. First, human space colonies are likely to diversify and possibly even speciate from one another. The colonies on different planets will form isolated breeding communities. Over time, they will evolve apart and share neither genes nor culture. This means they could develop very different worldviews and values, and lose their shared interests and common humanity.[75] Second, the space environment itself will be so vast that it will be practically impossible to coordinate and enforce a common rulebook on an intergalactic scale. There will be significant communication time lags between the different colonies, and it won't be possible to maintain a single galactic police force to keep the peace. This will breed suspicion and uncertainty between the colonies, which will make the environment ripe for preemptive defensive strikes and other cycles of violence. Finally, these future space colonies could develop truly devastating cosmic weapons—ones that make our current weapons of mass destruction seem puny by comparison. Examples of such weaponry could include "planetoid bombs" that can be launched in the direction of rival colonies, self-replicating Von-Neumann machines equipped with weapons of mass destruction, gravitational waves that create black holes to suck up planets and asteroids, and weaponized particle super-colliders that create "vacuum bubbles" that destroy everything that they come into contact with.[76]

Torres may be somewhat fanciful in his thinking here.[77] His argument relies on a number of assumptions that can be questioned. For example, the distance between space colonies, coupled with their separate evolutionary trajectories could actually reduce the risk of conflict. Discrete isolated colonies may have less reason to be worried about one another. Good fences make for good neighbors, and what could make for a better fence than several light years of cold dark space? Similarly, the enhancing effects of cyborgization could include moral enhancement that suppresses our war-mongering instincts.[78] This is all speculative, of course, but probably no less speculative that Torres's speculation about weaponized particle colliders and gravitational waves.

Nevertheless, Torres isn't the only one who is worried about our future in space. The astrobiologist Charles Cockell, for example, believes that the harshness of space will provide a breeding ground for tyrannical governments.[79] His concerns have been echoed by the philosopher Koji Tachibana, who has argued that whatever the risk of Hobbesian conflict between different solar systems, there is a significant risk of Hobbesian conflict within specific space settlements.[80] And there is a deeper point here that is worth bearing in mind. The whole discussion about utopian prospects for cyborgs in space is premised on significant speculations about future technologies and the effect they will have on social order. When dealing with such speculations, you have to consider the good and the bad, and you have to accept that you may have no way in which to credibly weigh their relative probabilities.

The result is a sea of uncertainty. The question we have to ask is whether such a sea of uncertainty provides a credible basis for a utopian project. Can we really know if we want to take that plunge? I suspect that we cannot, and this strengthens the case for pursuing alternative, more credible, utopian projects.

Replaceability and the Lightness of Being a Cyborg

The fifth problem with the Cyborg Utopia has to do with the effect that the different pathways to cyborgization have on how we feel about and value our own lives. Most of the problems discussed to this point apply equally well to both technical and conceptual cyborgs. There are, however, some problems that are particularly acute for the conceptual cyborg (and vice versa). Let's consider this in a bit more detail.

As you recall, a conceptual cyborg is someone who does not directly fuse technological parts with their biological systems; instead they interact with technological artifacts in their environments in a highly interdependent way. The plausibility of the conceptual pathway to cyborgization is a function of how integrated the individual is with these external artifacts. People who are only loosely integrated with their artifacts—who are more dependent on them than interdependent—won't count as conceptual cyborgs. Nevertheless, even with this in mind, some of the problems discussed above would seem to be particularly problematic for the conceptual cyborg. For instance, the problems of enslavement and programming would seem to be particularly challenging if your route to cyborgization relies on externally located technologies. The impetus to treat those technologies as being legally part of who you are, and to remove the control and ownership of third parties, is likely to be less compelling than it is for technical cyborgs. This means conceptual cyborgs may face more of a struggle when it comes to balancing the good aspects of cyborgization against the bad. They may lose some of the associated goods of technical cyborgization. For instance, completely transcending the limitations of biological form and rebooting our hardware would not seem to be open to the conceptual cyborg. There could also be something phenomenologically and morally different about feeling a device to be part of who you are and not just a prop that you use to engage with the world around you.

Nevertheless, there are those who push back against this and argue that there is no important moral difference between internal (technical) and external (conceptual) forms of cyborgization. The philosopher Neil Levy, in his 2007 book *Neuroethics,* formulated something he called the "ethical parity thesis," which has this implication. In fact, Levy formulated two different versions of the parity thesis, both of which can be used to support this conclusion, albeit one is more modest than the other.[81]

> *Strong Parity:* Since the mind extends into the external environment, alterations of external props used for thinking are (*ceteris paribus*) ethically on a par with alterations of the brain.
>
> *Weak Parity:* Alterations of external props are (*ceteris paribus*) ethically on a par with alterations of the brain, to the precise extent to which our reasons for finding alterations of the brain problematic are transferable to alterations of the environment in which it is embedded.

The "strong parity thesis" depends on the "extended mind hypothesis," which holds that mental states can be *constituted* by a combination of brain states and features of the environment in which they are embedded. To use a simple example, the mental act of remembering to pick up the milk could, according to the extended mind hypothesis, be constituted by the combined activity of my eyes / brain decoding the visual information on the screen of my phone and the device itself displaying a reminder that I need to pick up the milk. The use of the word "constituted" is important here. The extended mind hypothesis doesn't merely claim that the mental state of remembering to pick up the milk is *caused by* or *dependent upon* my looking at the phone; it claims that it is emergent from and grounded in the combination of brain and smartphone. It's more complicated than that, of course, and as I noted above, proponents of the hypothesis like Andy Clark and David Chalmers don't allow just any external prop to form part of the mind; they have some criteria for determining whether an external prop really is part of the mind and not just something that plays a causal role in it.[82]

If you accept the strong parity thesis, then you might say there is no real difference between being a conceptual cyborg and being a technical cyborg. Both are equally utopian and equally compelling. There are, however, reasons to doubt the strong parity thesis. If you look back at Levy's formulation, given above, you'll see that it presents an enthymeme. It claims that because the mind is extended, external mental "realizers" (to use the jargon common in this debate) carry the same moral weight as internal mental realizers. But as Jan-Hendrik Heinrichs has pointed out, that inference can only be drawn if you accept another, hidden premise: that all contributors to mental processes are on a par when it comes to their value to the individual whose mind is in question.[83]

This hidden premise is false. Not all contributors to mental processes are morally equivalent. Some contributors could be redundant, trivial, or easily replaceable. You might use your smartphone to remember things. I could destroy your smartphone, thereby interfering with your extended mind. But you might have another smartphone with the exact same information recorded in it. In that case you will have suffered some short-term harm from the destruction, but to claim that it is on a par with, say, destroying your hippocampus, and thereby preventing you from ever remembering where you recorded the information about buying the milk, would seem extreme. So parity cannot be assumed, even if we accept the extended mind hypothesis.

The "weak parity thesis" corrects for this problem by making the reasons for thinking something is valuable part and parcel of the parity claim. Although not stated clearly, the weak thesis effectively says that (because of mental extension) the reasons for finding interferences with internal mental parts problematic transfer over to external mental parts, and vice versa. The weak thesis doesn't require a full commitment to the extended mind hypothesis, which many find implausible. It works with the more modest distributed / embodied theory of cognitive processes (which I discussed earlier in this chapter as well as in Chapter 4). An example of the weak thesis in practice can be illustrated by the now-familiar example of someone using a pen and paper to solve a mathematical puzzle. While in use, the pen and paper are critical to the resolution of the puzzle, so much so that it makes sense to say that the cognitive process of solving the puzzle is not confined to the brain but is rather shared between the brain and the two external props. They form a coupled dynamical system. The weak thesis then holds that if you would find it ethically problematic to disrupt someone's internal, math-solving, brain-module while they were trying to solve a problem, you should also find it problematic to do the same thing to their pen and paper when they are mid-solution (and vice versa). That sounds very plausible.

But even the weak thesis has its problems. Many will resist the idea that it is as serious to intervene with an external prop as it is to interfere with an internal process. Fiddling with someone's stationery doesn't seem to be the same thing as fiddling with their neocortex. So people have come up with criteria that suggest that there are still significant differences between an internally realized mental process and externally realized one. Examples include the degree of *functional integration* between an individual and their brain, the brain's involvement in *conscious reasoning,* and, perhaps most significantly, the *replaceability* of the brain vis-a-vis an external artifact. Each of these criteria provides a reason for worrying about the desirability of building a Cyborg Utopia, whether we follow the conceptual or technical pathway, because cyborgization involves replacing or integrating internal mental processes with technological artifacts. We can see this most clearly if we consider the replaceability criterion in a bit more detail.

Heinrichs is a fan of the replaceability criterion. He formulates it like this:

> *Replaceability Criterion:* "Generally, an irreplaceable contributor
> to one and the same cognitive process is, ceteris paribus, more
> important [that is, carries more value] than a replaceable one."[84]

Using this criterion, Heinrichs suggests that many internal brain parts are irreplaceable, and so their creation and destruction carry a lot of moral weight. Contrariwise, he argues that many external props that we use in mental processes are replaceable, and so their creation and destruction carry less weight. To give an example, suppose you have suffered from some traumatic brain injury that results in severe memory impairment. As a result, you rely on an electronic recording device to "remember" what has happened to you. Heinrichs's claim is that while destroying the electronic recording device would be bad for you, destroying the internal biological system that enabled the pre-accident version of you to form memories would be much worse. The former, at least, is replaceable.

That said, Heinrichs accepts that the distinction is not as categorical as we might like. There are some external props that could be classed as being relatively irreplaceable, which would imply that destroying them would do serious harm to an agent. However, he argues that such irreplaceability needs to be assessed over two different timescales. An external prop might be irreplaceable in the short term—when mid-activity—but not in the long term. Someone could steal a blind person's cane while they are walking home, thereby doing significant harm to them with respect to the performance of that activity, but the cane could be easily replaced in the long term. Similarly, taking away someone's external recording device while they are trying to remember something would be bad, but you could replace it with another, equally good, recording device.

Heinrichs's distinction between short- and long-term replaceability is intuitively appealing. Destroying something that is irreplaceable in both the short and long term would seem to be much worse than destroying something that is replaceable in the long term. Both are undoubtedly wrong, but they are not ethically on a par. But this raises a problem for the whole Cyborg Utopian project. If technology continues to advance, and if we develop more internal and external props that allow us to easily replace parts of our brains and bodies—if, in some sense, the component parts of all mental and biological processes are readily *fungible*—will that mean that there is something trivial about the destruction of the original biological parts? Here's where the replaceability criterion starts to get into trouble. If you accept that the ease of replaceability makes a moral difference, you start slipping down a slope to a world in which many of our commonsense moral beliefs lose traction. In a cyborg future, the destruction of limbs and brain parts could be greeted with just as much equanimity as the destruction of a smartphone because they can all be easily replaced by a functionally equivalent technological artifact. What effect would this have on our evaluative systems? What kind of moral world would we be creating if this became possible?

Science fiction provides some guidance. Richard Morgan's novel *Altered Carbon* (also a Netflix TV series) depicts a world of near-perfect biological fungibility. The basic premise of the book is that future humans develop a technology for uploading their minds to digital "stacks." These stacks preserve the identity ("soul") of the individual and can be transferred between different physical bodies, even after one of them has been killed. This has many social repercussions, one of which is that biological death—the destruction or fatal mutilation of the body—becomes a relatively trivial event. An inconvenience rather than a tragedy. As long as the stack is preserved, the individual can survive by being transplanted to another body. The triviality of biological form is explored in many ways in both the book and TV show. Violence is common. There are various clubs that allow people to destroy one another's bodies for sport. There is also considerable inequality when it comes to access to new bodies. The wealthy can afford to clone their preferred body types and routinely transfer between them; the poor have to rely on social distribution schemes, often ending up in the bodies of condemned prisoners. Bodies in general have become commodities: things to be ogled, prodded, bought, and sold.

The main focus of *Altered Carbon* is on the replaceability of the body. But what if we applied the same logic to the replaceability of the mind? What if we could swap out parts of our minds as readily as we swap out the batteries in an old remote control? Destroying a part of someone's mind is currently held to be a pretty serious moral offence. If I intentionally damaged the part of your brain that allowed you to remember faces, you'd hardly take it in your stride. But suppose that as soon as I destroyed the face-recognition part you could quickly replace it with another, functionally equivalent part. Would it be so bad then? This is a serious question for any proponent of the Cyborg Utopia. One possible consequence of cyborgization is that we achieve total mental and physical fungibility. But if we do achieve that, will we really have created a utopia? Or will it be a world where nothing really matters because everything is permissible, reformable, and revisable? In short, is there a danger that there might be an unbearable lightness of being in the Cyborg Utopia?

This concern is speculative and far-fetched. It could be that cyborg technologies never develop to the point that we attain total fungibility and so we never have to worry about it resulting in a kind of existential nihilism. But we could very easily achieve lesser forms of replaceability (for example, the replaceability of face recognition or the part of the brain that processes geographical / spatial information), and if we do that, we would still face important questions about the ethics of replaceability. We would still have to confront the possibility that actions we once deemed impermissible are now acceptable. Our current moral intuitions about right and wrong may not be trustworthy in a world of technological fungibility. That again adds to the cultural gap between the Cyborg Utopia and our current reality, and heightens our awareness of the risks entailed by embarking toward it.

Timelines and Other Risks

There is one final set of problems with the Cyborg Utopia that I wish to mention. Unlike the previous problems, these are about the practicalities, not the values, of cyborgization. One of these problems relates to the timeline of technological development. Recall that the Cyborg Utopia is being considered as a response to the five threats of automation outlined in Chapter 4. The idea is that by becoming more machine-like we can stave off these threats and build a more utopian future. But what if we can't? What if the technological breakthroughs required for fuller forms of cyborgization can only be achieved in the very long term? How do we deal with the intervening decades (or centuries) of automated immiseration?

There is already evidence to suggest that there is some timeline lag between automation and cyborgization. The developments in robotics and AI seem to be coming much faster than anticipated. People who claimed that self-driving cars would prove elusive or that real-time translation from one language to another were decades away look silly now. Meanwhile the opposite problem arises for philosophers and transhumanists who speculate about enhanced cyborg humans. They still await the technological breakthroughs that they have been so busy analyzing, criticizing, and defending.

This is not to say that greater cyborgization is technically impossible. There are clearly some impressive technological innovations in this space, some of which were described earlier in this chapter. But these innovations face a significant engineering challenge. They must find ways to integrate with human biology, and this carries significant health and other personal risks. These risks represent another practical hurdle for the Cyborg Utopia.

The human body is a complex, imperfectly understood system. Any attempt to graft something new into that system can have unintended consequences elsewhere. This is particularly true of the brain. Our best current theories of brain function suggest that although there is some functional specialization in particular regions of the brain, every system is interconnected, and adjustments to one system can have knock-on effects elsewhere. We already see this with pharmacological interventions in the brain (like anti-depressants) and the various side effects they are known to have.

It could be that cyborg interventions can be engineered to be more targeted and less vulnerable to this problem of side effects, but this is still a practical challenge. Opening up the body and implanting a prosthetic runs the risk of infection and disease. We have to ask whether we want to run that risk. It could well be that for any problem we might face, externalized, automating solutions are going to be more convenient and safer than internalized, cyborg solution. Nicholas Agar makes this point rather well with the following thought experiment:[85]

> The Pyramid Builders: Suppose you are a pharaoh building a pyramid. This takes a huge amount of back-breaking labor from ordinary human workers (or slaves). Clearly some investment in worker enhancement would be desirable. But there are two ways of going about it. You could either invest in human enhancement technologies, looking into drugs or other supplements to increase the strength, stamina, and endurance of workers, maybe even creating robotic limbs that graft onto their current limbs. Or you could invest in other "enhancing" technologies, such as machines to sculpt and haul the stone blocks needed for construction. Which investment strategy do you choose?

Agar thinks the answer is obvious. You should clearly favor the external, automating solutions. They are cheaper, carry less risk, and are more likely to get the job done.

The point is that the practical impediments to technical cyborgization are significant. They might encourage us to favor more automation and external dependency in the short term, and thus prevent us from realizing the full potential of the Cyborg Utopia. It might be up to a handful of daring cyborg pioneers to show us the way, and they may suffer great losses and ridicule in the interim.

Conclusion: Not the Utopia We Are Looking For

This chapter has evaluated the potential for a post-work Cyborg Utopia. The Cyborg Utopia is a possible future world (or, rather, a set of possible future worlds) in which humans try to retain their dominance of the cognitive niche through technological augmentation. This vision has a number of attractions and, on an initial pass, scores highly on the utopian scorecard. It promises to stave off the five threats of automation by using technology to retain human agency, autonomy, and understanding; it facilitates pluralism by allowing people to experiment with different modes of being; it maintains a nice balance between stability and dynamism, giving humanity a number of horizons toward which to aim; and it gives us hope for the future, both for ourselves and for our offspring.

But on a second pass, we see that there are a number of problems with this vision. By trying to conserve our current evaluative equilibrium, it may go too far and also conserve the world of work. It may not allow for a radically different future in which we escape the depredations of paid employment. It may lead us to greater dependency on (and possibly enslavement to) machines, rather than freedom from their clutches. It may not be rationally intelligible to creatures like us: in certain forms it could lead to the inversion or destruction of too many of the values we now care about (humanism, individualism, and clear boundaries between what is permissible and what is not). Finally, and perhaps most importantly from our current perspective, it may not be practicable any time soon. Cyborg pioneers like Harbisson, Warwick, and others can tinker with current technology all they like and not get very far. While we are waiting for the technology to improve, we are likely to favor external automating technologies over cyborg ones, thus exacerbating the potential threats of automation that were outlined in Chapter 4.

Still, I would not wish for the reader to go away with the impression that I am completely down on the idea of a Cyborg Utopia. It has its allure, and, as a long-term project, it may be worth keeping on the back burner. But despite its allure, it is not as utopian as it first seems. In the next chapter, I want to consider an alternative utopian proposal: the Virtual Utopia. This proposal, in many ways, suffers from the inverse fate of the Cyborg Utopia: it seems neither utopian nor practical at a first pass, but on closer inspection proves to be very attractive.

CHAPTER 7

The Virtual Utopia

ON SEPTEMBER 23, 2016, Ana Swanson wrote an article for the *Washington Post* with the title "Why Amazing Video Games Could Be Causing a Problem for America."[1] The article reported on research that had just been done by a group of economists about young men and their attraction to video games. According to this research, in the United States as of 2015 there were fewer young men (as a percentage of the population) at work or looking for work than ever before. The researchers argued that this was partly due to young men's overwhelming attraction to video games.

Shortly after Swanson's article appeared, one of the researchers, Erik Hurst, expounded on the results in a speech given to the Booth School at the University of Chicago, reporting that[2]

> on average, lower-skilled men in their 20s increased "leisure time" by about four hours per week between the early 2000s and 2015 . . . Of that four-hours-per-week increase in leisure, three of those hours were spent playing video games! The average young, lower-skilled, non-employed man in 2014 spent about two hours per day on video games. That is the average. Twenty-five

> percent reported playing at least three hours per day. About
> 10 percent reported playing for six hours per day. The life of
> these nonworking, lower-skilled young men looks like what my
> son wishes his life was like now: not in school, not at work, and
> lots of video games.

Hurst seems relatively sanguine about this state of affairs, more interested in understanding the trends than lamenting them. And some, including perhaps most notably the entrepreneur and (at the time of this writing) 2020 Democratic presidential primary candidate Andrew Yang, have argued that a life filled with video games may not be all that bad or all that different from a life of work, at least for young men.[3]

Others have been less sanguine. Nicholas Eberstadt's book *Men without Work*,[4] though not ostensibly about video games, laments the general withdrawal of men from the American workforce (approximately seven million men are missing in action, according to his findings) and worries deeply about the effects this is having on traditional family values and personal vices. He believes that the men who have withdrawn from the world of work are living lives of less flourishing and meaning, and are consequently drawn to vices such as laziness, drugs, and video games. Philip Zimbardo and Nikita Coulombe, in an even more alarmist tract, are deeply critical of the world of video games, and argue that the male withdrawal into virtual and online worlds is having a dramatic and deleterious impact on cognitive development and social orientation.[5]

The focus on men is interesting, particularly in light of the fact that research suggests that women spend as much (if not more) time playing video games.[6] But I won't dwell on the gender issue here. I want to focus on the deeper question prompted by these alarmist tracts: is the retreat from the world of work, and into virtual worlds such as those provided by video games, something to fear? The authors mentioned in the previous paragraph clearly see it as a dystopian move, as a shift away from what is natural and desirable. And you can see where they are coming from. The retreat to the virtual seems to be a retreat from the conditions of meaning and flourishing outlined in Chapter 4, from the very things we need to survive and thrive. If we spend all our time in virtual worlds, then surely we cut ourselves off from projects of objective significance (the Good, the True, and the Beautiful)? There is nothing in this retreat to the virtual that stirs us to heroic heights.

This dystopian take on the retreat to the virtual has its appeal. But in the remainder of this chapter I will argue that it is wrong. Far from being a dystopian move, the retreat to the virtual is, in fact, exactly what we need to realize a genuinely post-work utopia. In other words, in the remainder of this chapter, I will be defending the fourth, and final, proposition that I outlined in Chapter 1:

> **Proposition 4:** Another way to manage our relationship with technology would be to build a Virtual Utopia, and this is both more practical and utopian than is commonly assumed: instead of integrating ourselves with machines in an effort to maintain our relevance in the "real" world, we could retreat to "virtual" worlds that are created and sustained by the technological infrastructure that we have built. At first glance, this seems tantamount to giving up, but there are compelling philosophical and practical reasons for favoring this approach.

I will develop the case for the Virtual Utopia in four stages. First, I will spend a little time explaining what the Virtual Utopia would look like, focusing in particular on what distinguishes the virtual from the real. Second, I will use this understanding of the distinction between the virtual and the real to develop an argument in favor of the Virtual Utopia, one that is based on the work of Bernard Suits and his so-called utopia of games. Third, I will develop another argument for the Virtual Utopia, this time based on the work of Robert Nozick and his concept of a meta-utopia.[7] Fourth, and finally, I will respond to some criticisms of the Virtual Utopia and offer an overall assessment of its utopian merits.

In doing all this, I will be taking the reader on a journey, from what I suspect will be initial shock and distaste at the idea that we should "give up" and retreat to the virtual to an embrace of that idea. I may not succeed in taking all readers on this journey, but if I can make the majority less resistant and more open to the possibility, I will take that as a success.

The Troubled Boundary between the Real and the Virtual

What is real and what is virtual? The question sounds like the basis for a major metaphysical bullshitting session but it is a serious and important one. It's also one that defies an easy answer. Jaron Lanier, one of the early pioneers in the creation of virtual reality (or VR) technology, knows this only too well. In his part-memoir / part-manifesto, *Dawn of the New Everything*, Lanier offers readers fifty-one separate definitions of virtual reality technologies. Some of these are ironic and satirical (for example, definition 32: "The technology that is often misrepresented as being able to make so-called holograms float impossibly in the air"); some are insightful in an unusual way (for example, definition 24: "A cybernetic construction that measures the probing aspect of perception so that it is canceled out"); and some track closely with what we might call the stereotypical view of VR technology (for example, definition 4: "The substitution of the interface between a person and the physical environment with an interface to a simulated environment").[8]

The stereotypical view is a trope, something that has been depicted in countless science fiction novels, films, and TV series, and is now the basis of mainstream consumer products. According to this trope, a virtual reality is a computer-generated world, one that might be fantastical or a simulation of the real world. We immerse ourselves in this world either by entering a room in which the computer-generated world is broadcast to us from strategically located screens, or, more commonly, by donning a helmet or a set of goggles that broadcasts the simulation directly into our skulls. We might also wear some special clothing, or carry some special tool or object, that tracks our physical movement so that this can be projected into the computer simulation. If done well, the experience can be quite remarkable. You can lose your sense of belonging in the physical world and become absorbed in the simulated one.

A classic science fiction depiction of the stereotypical view can be found in Neal Stephenson's novel *Snow Crash*. Early on in the novel, Stephenson explains how the technology works by describing how one of the lead characters—Hiro Protagonist (get it?)—immerses himself in the exciting simulated world of the Metaverse. Hiro wears noise-canceling earphones and puts on a pair of goggles that "throw a light, smoky haze across his eyes and reflect a distorted wide-angle view of a brilliantly lit boulevard that stretches off into an infinite blackness. This boulevard does not really exist; it is a computer-rendered view of an imaginary place."[9] What's more, the book is not just a useful illustration of the stereotypical view. It is an inspiration for it. Many of the designers of actual VR tech cite Stephenson as a major influence on their work.[10] They want to bring his imagined world out of the pages of science fiction into our living rooms.

The stereotypical view thus sees virtual reality as a technological phenomenon, something that is only possible in a world of sophisticated computer-generated imagery, immersive headsets, and motion-capture body suits. This technologized understanding of virtual reality is intuitive. The computer-simulated world is obviously not real. It's ethereal and immaterial. It doesn't have the heft and weight of the real world of matter and molecules. But this judgment requires some qualification. After all, many of the things that happen to you in a computer-simulated environment can be just as real as if they happened to you in the physical world. You can have real conversations with people and form alliances and friendships with them. You can spend and lose real money. You can also experience things that have spillover effects into the real world. Some of these experiences might be traumatic, maybe even criminal.

Consider Jordan Belamire's (a pseudonym) experiences while playing the virtual reality game QuiVR. QuiVR is an archery game where players fight off marauding zombies. It can be played online with multiple users. Players appear to other users in a disembodied form as a floating helmet and a pair of hands. The only indication of gender comes through choice of name and voice used to communicate with other players. Jordan was playing the game in her home, with her husband and family nearby. While playing, another user—with the onscreen name of "BigBro442"—started to rub the area near where her breasts would be (if they were depicted in the environment). She screamed at him to stop, but he proceeded to chase her around the virtual environment and then to rub her virtual crotch. At first, she tried to laugh it off, but given the immersive nature of the game, she really didn't find it funny. The assault felt real to her and she says that she found it "scary as hell."[11] So, even with the highly technologized stereotypical view, we see that there is a fluid boundary between virtual and real. What we think of as being purely virtual—a game environment simulated inside a computer—can be studded with elements of reality.

The stereotypical view should be contrasted with something I shall call the "counterintuitive view." According to the counterintuitive view, virtual reality is not just a technological phenomenon; it's part of our everyday lives. Indeed, on the counterintuitive view, many of the things we think of as being real turn out to be virtual (and vice versa). There are some extreme proponents of this view. The psychedelic philosopher Terence McKenna once opined that "what we call reality is, in fact, nothing more than a culturally sanctioned and linguistically reinforced hallucination."[12] And there are some respectable and widely venerated philosophical traditions that endorse a broadly similar view. One of the key ideas in Kantian philosophy is that our perception of the world is not the perception of the world as it is in itself, but is rather a mental projection over that reality. In other words, the world as we perceive it is a simulation, not the real thing.

Of course, if you embrace such an extreme view, the distinction between the virtual and real breaks down entirely, and you have to start asking yourself questions like "what do I really mean when I say the chair in front of me is 'real' but the chair in the photograph is not?" There is obviously some distinction between the two things, and it is useful to be able to talk about that distinction. You need some vocabulary for doing this. So it may be that, if you embrace the Kantian view and accept that everything is virtual in some sense, you have to redefine the words "virtual" and "real" so that something of the old distinction remains.

Fortunately, you don't have to go as far as McKenna or Kant to think that much of what we call "real" is, in fact, virtual. Imagined realities are after all the lubricant of social life. One of the big promoters of this view in recent times is the historian / futurist Yuval Noah Harari. In his best-selling books *Sapiens* and *Home Deus,* Harari repeatedly emphasizes the idea that much of what we take for granted in our everyday lives is not inherent in the physical reality that we perceive.[13] It is, rather, a personal, cultural, or social construction that is layered over that reality. He argues that the cognitive ability to perform this virtual layering is one of the distinctive traits of humanity.

Examples of such constructions include imagined relationships of hierarchy and dominance, beliefs about what is natural and unnatural, money, jobs, laws, and other social institutions.

Harari runs quite far with this idea, delving into speculations about how this virtualized understanding of social life might help us to find meaning in a post-work world. Like me, he too is interested in the impact of automation on work and what it means for human flourishing. He is particularly interested in fears about the retreat to the virtual. But his response to these fears is simple and deflationary. In an op-ed written for *The Guardian*—entitled "The Meaning of Life in a World without Work"—he argues that there is nothing to worry about because much of our social and cultural life is already virtual.[14]

It's worth considering Harari's argument about this in some detail because it highlights both the attractions and the limitations of the counterintuitive view. Harari makes his case by drawing an analogy between his experiences playing the game Pokemon Go and the religious beliefs of Jews and Muslims living in Jerusalem. Pokemon Go is an "augmented reality" game that is played on a smartphone. The goal of the game is to collect "pokemon" (fantastical pocket monsters) from different locations in the physical world. The monsters are, of course, entirely computer simulated. They don't exist in the real physical world. But if you hold up the screen of your smartphone over the physical world, it will show you a picture of the monster displayed against the real physical landscape. The monsters are thus a computer projection onto the real world. While this digital augmentation is a neat technological trick, Harari points out that we don't need any technological assistance to project fantastical properties onto the real world. Religious believers do this all the time. This is where he draws an analogy with Jews and Muslims in Jerusalem: "When you look at the objective reality of Jerusalem, all you see are stones and buildings. There is no holiness anywhere. But when you look through the medium of smartbooks (such as the Bible and the Qu'ran) you see holy places and angels everywhere."[15] What's more, the religious believers take these mental projections very seriously because they imbue their world with meaning and value. And, in fact, it is not just religious believers who do this. Everyone does it all the time. As Harari puts it, "the meaning we ascribe to what we see is generated by our own minds."[16] It is never part of the fabric of reality.

We can distil this down into something I will call Harari's General Principle:

> *Harari's General Principle:* Much of the reality we experience (particularly the value and meaning we ascribe to it) is virtual in nature.

Harari uses this principle to provide existential reassurance when it comes to the idea of a future spent living inside virtual reality. His claim is that there is nothing bizarre or tragic about the retreat to the virtual world of video games because we already live inside big virtual reality games, ones from which we seem to derive great meaning, irrespective of their virtuality. He singles out religion and consumerism as two illustrations of the virtual reality games we already play.

> *Religion:* "What is religion if not a big virtual reality game played by millions of people together. Religions such as Islam and Christianity invent imaginary laws . . . Muslims and Christians go through life trying to gain points in their favorite virtual reality game . . . If by the end of your life you gain enough points, then after you die you go to the next level of the game (aka heaven)."[17]
>
> *Consumerism:* "Consumerism too is a virtual reality game. You gain points by acquiring new cars, buying expensive brands and taking vacations abroad, and if you have more points than everybody else, you tell yourself you won the game."[18]

There is a certain flippancy to Harari's claims, and he may push the game-like idea a bit too far in these descriptions, but we should give him his due. To those of us who are religious skeptics and reluctant capitalists, there is something plausible in what he is saying. I, for one, don't believe in angels or demons or gods. I really do think that religion is a virtual reality game: that all the rules and regulations are fake and illusory. I feel similarly about much of the economic activity that is incentivized by capitalism. I think it is unnecessary, competition for competition's sake, and not driven by any deep necessity. It is, consequently, very tempting for me to embrace Harari's logic.

But, in the end, I don't think Harari's argument works. In his desire to deflate the fears we might have about the retreat to the virtual, Harari pushes the counterintuitive view too far. The big problem is that his argument isn't true to the lived experiences of devoted religious believers and avid consumerists. They don't think that the reality in which they live is a virtual reality game. For example, I doubt that religious believers experience their daily practice in the gamified form that Harari ascribes to them. It's not about gaining points or leveling up; it's about being true to the commitments and requirements of authentic religious practice. His perspective is that of the outsider—someone who has seen through the sham—not that of the insider. The same, presumably, goes for consumerism, though there is more reason to question the plausibility of that example for the simple reason that I doubt many people take consumerism very seriously. They may get caught up in the practice of buying consumer goods, but they will do this for what they take to be serious and sometimes worthy ends, for example, because the products are necessary for their flourishing and well-being, or because they give genuine pleasure, or because they help them gain status and reputation over others, and so on.

This means that it is very difficult to draw any solace from Harari's deflationary argument. The cultural practices and beliefs from which we currently derive great meaning and value may be purely arbitrary mental projections, but they are not experienced or understood in that way. It requires a certain mentality and awareness to see them like that, and there is no guarantee that once you do you will continue to flourish and find meaning in your life. Harari has to argue for the plausibility of that; he can't simply assume it to be the case. Furthermore, even if Harari was right about religion and consumerism, there would still be some features of our day-to-day lives that would not be virtual or unreal even in his sense. The struggle for daily bread; the warmth of the sun; the tender embrace of our loved ones. These things will still carry the heft and weight of reality, no matter what Harari might say.

To summarize to this point, although the stereotypical view and the counterintuitive view differ on how they conceive of the distinction between the virtual and the real, on both views the boundary between the real and the virtual is fluid and poorly understood. Can we build a more nuanced under-standing of virtual reality that allows for some ambiguity and overlap between the virtual and the real, but that still allows for some genuine dif-ferences between them (and thus doesn't commit Harari's mistake?). We are going to need this if the Virtual Utopia is to be rationally intelligible. Fortunately, I think we can develop a rationally intelligible and appropri-ately nuanced understanding of virtual reality. It just takes a bit of time.

Philip Brey's ontology of the virtual helps to point the way to this more nuanced understanding.[19] I will be adopting a modified version of this on-tology as the foundation for the argument for the Virtual Utopia. So I will try to explain how it works over the next couple of pages. I warn you in ad-vance, however, that we will have to get into some serious metaphysical and philosophical weeds concerning different kinds of reality and how best to differentiate between them in order to understand this ontology. The dis-tinctions are straightforward, but there are a lot of them, and it's possible to get lost in the conceptual tangle. I can only reassure you that I will summa-rize the trickier parts as I go along, and that they do feed into what I think is a compelling understanding of what a Virtual Utopia would be. So it is worth it in the end.

Let's get started. Brey develops his ontology with the stereotypical view of virtual reality initially in mind. He supposes that when people talk about virtual reality they are talking about computer-simulated worlds and com-munities. He uses this supposition to force us to see that "reality" is multi-valent. There are different kinds of things out there in the world, and they have different conditions of reality associated with their existence. Some of them have to exist in the physical world to count as real; some of them can exist in mentally simulated, or computer-generated worlds, and still be per-fectly real. We have to appreciate these different forms of reality if we are to make sense of the distinction between the virtual and the real.

To see what Brey is talking about, let's use one of his examples. Imagine you are staring at a computer screen and on the computer screen there is a computer-generated image of an apple. As Brey points out, this "apple" clearly exists in some form. It is not a mirage or hallucination. It *really* ex-ists within the virtual environment. But its existence has a distinctive meta-physical quality to it. It does not exist as a real apple. You cannot bite into it or taste its flesh. But it does exist as a representation or simulation of an apple. In this sense it is somewhat like a fictional character in a novel. Sherlock Holmes is not real: there was no one by that name living at 221b Baker Street in London in the late 1800s. But Sherlock Holmes clearly does exist as a fictional character. There are agreed upon facts about his appearance, habits, and intellect, as well as what he did and did not do as a fictional character.

Sherlock Holmes and the apple have a simulative reality, but nothing more. They do not and cannot exist as a real apple or real person. But why not? The answer seems to lie in the essentially *physical* nature of apples and human detectives. An apple does not exist as a real apple unless it has certain physical properties and attributes. It has to have mass, occupy space, consist in a certain mix of proteins, sugars, and fats, and so on. A virtual apple cannot have those properties and hence cannot be the same thing as a real apple. The same goes for detectives like Sherlock Holmes. Although there are some complexities there. *Human* detectives have to have mass, occupy space, and consist in a certain mix of proteins and metabolic processes. But do all detectives have to have these properties? It seems to be at least conceivable that there could be a virtual detective that could solve real-world crimes in roughly the same manner as Sherlock Holmes. Imagine a really advanced artificial intelligence that is constantly fed data about crimes and criminal behavior. It spots patterns and learns how to solve crimes based on this data. You could feed information about new crimes into the AI and it could spit out a solution. This AI program would then be a "real" detective, not a mere simulation or representation of a detective. In fact, you don't really have to imagine this possibility. As discussed in Chapter 1, there are already companies trying to create such virtual detectives.

We can draw some lessons from these examples. First, we can see that there are entities—like apples and *human* detectives—that are essentially physical in nature. We can call them *essentially physical kinds.* These are objects, events, and states of affairs that must have some specific physical properties in order to qualify as a real instance of the relevant kind. Computer-generated versions of these kinds can never be fully real; they can only be simulations. But then there are other kinds that are not essentially physical in nature. A "detective" would be an example. A detective is a *non-physical functional kind:* an entity qualifies for membership of the class of detectives in virtue of the function it performs—attempting to investigate and solve crimes—not in virtue of any physical properties it might have. Virtual versions of these kinds can be every bit as real as their physical-world equivalents.

To be clear, not all functional kinds are non-physical. Some functional kinds are essentially physical in nature. A lever is an essentially physical functional kind. A wooden stick can be counted as a "real" instance of a lever in virtue of the function it performs, but it can only perform that function because it has certain physical characteristics. Just try lifting a heavy object with a computer image of a lever. You won't be able to do it. On the other hand, a spirit level does not require any particular physical shape or constitution to perform its function. You can quite happily assess the levelness of your bookshelf with a spirit level that has been simulated on the screen of your smartphone. Furthermore, the term "non-physical functional kind" is something of a misnomer. Objects and entities that belong to that class typically do have some physical instantiation: our mental projections and imaginings are instantiated in our brains; and computer-generated objects are physically instantiated, in some symbolic form, in computer hardware. It's just that they don't require any *particular* or *specific* physical characteristics in order to perform the relevant function. They are multiply realizable.

So there are some essentially physical kinds: virtual instances of these kinds can only be simulacra. There also some non-physical functional kinds: virtual instances of these kinds can be as real as their physical-world equivalents. The next question is whether there are any other kinds whose virtual instances can be every bit as real as their physical-world equivalents. Yes, there are: social kinds. These are a sub-category of non-physical functional kinds, which are particularly interesting because of their practical importance and their ontological origins. They are critical to the argument that follows.

In terms of their importance, it goes without saying that large chunks of the reality with which we engage on a daily basis is social in nature. Our relationships, jobs, financial assets, property, legal obligations, credentials, status, and so on are all socially constructed and socially sustained. These are the things that Harari focuses on in his analysis of human history and that support his belief that much of our lives are virtual. Brey's ontology essentially agrees with Harari on this point, albeit with one important qualification. Brey says that the mere fact that these things are socially constructed doesn't make them virtual or unreal. It's just that their reality doesn't require any particular physical instantiation. This means that social reality can be recreated in many forms—it is multiply realizable. Furthermore, Brey argues that we can use John Searle's theory of social reality as a guide to when and whether social kinds can be "ontologically reproduced" (as he puts it) in a computerized or simulated forum.

Searle's theory of social reality distinguishes physical kinds and social kinds along two dimensions: their ontology (what they are) and their epistemology (how we come to know of their existence).[20] He argues that physical kinds are distinctive in virtue of the fact that they are *ontologically objective* and *epistemically objective*. An apple does not depend on the presence of a human mind for its existence—it is thus ontologically objective. Furthermore, we can come to know of its existence through intersubjectively agreed-upon methods of inquiry—it is thus epistemically objective. Social kinds are distinctive because they are *ontologically subjective* and *epistemically objective*. Money depends on human minds for its existence. Gold, silver, paper, and other physical tokens do not count as money in virtue of their physical properties or characteristics. They count as money because human minds have conferred the functional status of money on them through an exercise of collective imagination. In theory, we can confer the functional status of money on any token, be it an exquisitely sculpted metal coin or a digital register of bank balances. In practice, certain tokens are better suited to the functional task than others. This is due to their durability and incorruptibility. Nevertheless, this hasn't stopped us from conferring the functional status of money on many different kinds of tokens over the years. Most money that is in existence today is non-physical in nature: it only exists in digital bank balances. This virtual money is still epistemically objective in nature. I cannot unilaterally imagine more money into my bank account. My current financial status is a matter of intersubjectively agreed-upon facts.

Searle argues that many social kinds share these twin properties of ontological subjectivity and epistemic objectivity. Examples include marriages, property rights, legal rights and duties generally, corporations, political offices, and so on. He calls these "institutional facts." They are social kinds that come into existence through collective agreement upon a *constitutive rule.* The constitutive rule takes the form "X counts as Y in context C." In the case of money, the constitutive rule might read something like "precious metal coins with features a, b, c, count as money for the purposes of purchasing goods and services." Searle doesn't think that we explicitly formulate constitutive rules for all social objects and events. Some constitutive rules are implicit in how we behave and act; others are more explicit.

Searle's theory clearly implies that much of our everyday social reality is, in a certain sense, virtual in nature. Money, marriages, property, rights, duties, political offices, and the like do not exist "out there" in the physical world; they exist inside our (collective) minds. They are, as Harari has argued, fictional projections of our minds over the physical reality we inhabit. In principle, we can project the same social reality over any physical token, including the representations and simulations that exist within a computer-simulated reality. All it takes is some collective imagination and will.

Let's now summarize the important points from this discussion. Brey's ontology argues that in order to distinguish the real from the virtual we need to be sensitive to the different kinds of things that can exist and the different conditions of reality that attach to them. Three distinctions are particularly important:

Essentially physical kinds: these are entities that must have some specific physical properties or characteristics in order to count as "real" (apples, chairs, cars. etc.).

Non-physical functional kinds: these are entities that perform functions that do not depend on any particular physical properties or characteristics; they can be "real" in a number of different forms, including computer simulations.

Social kinds: these are a subset of non-physical functional kinds whose existence depends on collective coordination and agreement upon a constitutive rule (of the form "X counts as Y in C"); they can be "real" wherever there is collective mental agreement.

Note that this ontology only covers *objects, events,* and *states of affairs.* It does not include *actions.* As Brey points out in his paper, actions have to be treated differently for the simple reason that their "reality" depends partly on their effects. For example, actions performed in a computer-generated environment can have "extravirtual" origins and effects, and this means that they have an even more fluid relationship with reality than do simulated objects and events. This is clear from Jordan Belamire's experiences in QuiVR.

For what it is worth, I think Brey's theory is pretty much spot on and provides the nuance we need to make the Virtual Utopia rationally intelligible. Although Brey limits himself to casting light on the many layers of reality that exist in a computer simulation, his ontology also sheds light on one of the key insights from Harari: that there is, or can be, something obviously fake or illusory about many of our cultural beliefs and practices that involve creating mental projections over the physical world. Harari pushes it too far by including systems of belief and practice that people think to be real in his theory of the virtual, but if he limited himself to other examples, he would be on firmer ground. For example, what Harari says about virtual reality games would appear to be clearly true of many of the sports and other games that we do, in fact, play in the real physical world. There is nothing in the physical reality of a chessboard that dictates that the pieces be moved in a particular way to achieve a particular end. Those restrictions depend on the mental projection of constitutive rules onto our experience of the chessboard. But, unlike in the case of religious rules and practices, when we play chess we are cognizant of the mentally arbitrary nature of the rules. We realize that we are imposing a structure on reality that is not really out there, and that what we are doing (in playing the game) does not have some deeper cosmic significance. It is important that we capture these kinds of virtual reality—ones that take place in the real physical world but lack real stakes or consequences—within our model of the Virtual Utopia. Indeed, I would go so far as to suggest that the absence of real stakes or consequences, and the awareness of the arbitrary nature of the rules and constraints we impose on our actions, are among the more distinctive features of the "virtual" (in everyday parlance).

Rather than belaboring the point any further, let me just spell out what my preferred understanding of "virtual reality" is and how it relates to the

Virtual Utopia. It starts with the recognition that the distinction between the virtual and the real is fluid and that there is nothing that is wholly virtual or wholly real. Even in a purely fantastical computer-generated world, with no other human characters or avatars, we ourselves are going to be "real," and our experiences of that world will have some reality. Furthermore, even in the physical world of matter and molecules, we are always adding details to our perception of reality that are not actually there. Granting this, I think we should abandon the idea that there is some hard and fast distinction between the virtual and the real. Instead, I believe it makes most sense to think of the virtual and the real as phenomena that can be arranged along a spectrum, probably a multidimensional one that acknowledges the different "kinds" of things that can exist and the different conditions of reality that attach to them. This means that some things can be classified as being more virtual and some as more real, but there are many things that are neither wholly one nor the other. If we do this, I think the challenge for the remainder of this chapter becomes clearer: we have to figure out where, along this spectrum (or in this multidimensional space), does the preferred vision of the Virtual Utopia lie.

My answer to this question, taking into consideration the fears about the retreat to the virtual that opened this chapter, and the discussion in previous chapters about the options facing humanity in an automated future, is that the most credible and distinctive vision of the Virtual Utopia will have three main qualities:

(a) It will focus on activities that are undertaken or pursued for *trivial or relatively inconsequential stakes.* In other words, it will focus on those activities that do not determine our continued survival, and do not contribute anything of great value to the world in terms of the Good, the True, and the Beautiful (although I will offer some caveats about this below).

(b) It will concern itself with activities that are *known* by the participants in the world to be relatively trivial or inconsequential. In other words, the participants will know that they are operating within an arbitrarily structured or simulated environment and hence not playing for big or important stakes. This condition is important as it rules out a Harari-like understanding of virtual reality, and avoids the "Matrix problem,"[21] namely, the possibility that people within the Virtual Utopia are tricked into believing that what they do is real. Allowing for both of those things would make it too easy to address the fears of those who worry about the retreat to the virtual, and make the Virtual Utopia a less compelling and less distinctive vision of the ideal society.

(c) It will be *technologically agnostic.* In other words, it will not depend on any particular technology for its instantiation. Computer-generated simulations, that we immersively participate in, are an obvious means of creating a Virtual Utopia. These could be realized in a variety of different ways, for example, through VR headsets, *Star Trek*-like holodecks, or augmented reality projections over the physical world. Furthermore, as will be pointed out below, these technologies may enable more elaborate and exciting versions of the Virtual Utopia. Nevertheless, they are not, strictly speaking, necessary for it. Game-like environments in the physical world—devoid of all technological frills—can also count as part of the Virtual Utopia.

In short, the Virtual Utopia is a set of possible worlds each of which is characterized by a *triviality* condition, a *knowledge* condition, and a *technological agnosticism* condition. It should be clear from this description that a Virtual Utopia, so understood, will still contain many "real" things. We will be able to have real emotional reactions to the experiences we have in that world; we will be able to build real moral virtues through our actions in that world; we will be able to develop real skills and abilities (proficiency in activities) in that world; and many of our current social institutions can exist in a perfectly real form in a virtual world. It should also be clear from this description that the Virtual Utopia does not have any single settled final form: many possible worlds could fit the bill.

Is there any reason to think that this vision of the Virtual Utopia provides us with the post-work utopia we are looking for? I will now present two arguments in support of this view.

The Virtual Utopia as a Utopia of Games

The first argument in favor of the Virtual Utopia is inspired by Bernard Suits's book *The Grasshopper.*[22] This book is a dialogue in which the lead characters spend the majority of their time debating the definition of the word "game." In doing this, they try to respond to a famous argument from Ludwig Wittgenstein that claimed that it was impossible to come up with a single satisfactory definition of "game." What could possibly link together Tiddliwinks, poker, football, hockey, Mario Kart, and Grand Theft Auto? Wittgenstein argued that nothing could. These games shared some properties but not others. There was no essential property (or set of properties) shared by all, though there may be family resemblances across the class of games.

The characters in *The Grasshopper* dispute this. They argue that there is a common core to all games: all games are voluntary attempts to overcome unnecessary obstacles. More precisely, they argue that games are anything with the following three features:

Prelusory Goals: These are outcomes or changes in the world that are intelligible apart from the game itself. For example, in a game like golf, the prelusory goal would be something like "putting a small, dimpled ball into a hole marked by a flag." In a game like tic-tac-toe (or noughts-and-crosses) it would be something like "being the first to mark three X's or O's in row, and / or preventing someone else from doing the same." The prelusory goals are the states of affairs that help us keep track of what is going on in the game, and to determine who wins or loses the game.

Constitutive Rules: These are the rules that determine how the prelusory goal is to be attained. We encountered them previously when discussing Searle's theory of social reality. The constitutive rules in the game set up artificial obstacles that prevent the players from achieving the prelusory goal in the most straightforward and efficient manner. For example, the most efficient and straightforward way to get a dimpled ball in a hole would probably be to pick up the ball and drop it directly in the hole. But the constitutive rules of golf do not allow the player to do this. Instead, they have to manipulate the ball through the air and along the ground using a set of clubs, in a very constrained environment. These artificial constraints are what make the game interesting.

Lusory Attitude: This is the psychological orientation of the game players to the game itself. In order for a game to work, the players have to accept the constraints imposed by the constitutive rules. This is an obvious point. Golf could not survive as a game if the players refused to use their clubs to get the ball into the hole.

In broad outline, this approach to defining games is quite illuminating. We could quibble about some of the details, of course. For example, some games are probably more nebulous and incomplete than this theory lets on. In some cases, keeping score may not be particularly important to a game; the game might be more open-ended or allow the player to determine their own goals. Many online, multiplayer game-worlds have this feature. Furthermore, even when there is a score, it might be determined by many different prelusory goals that are revised over time. Similarly, it is unlikely that every game we play comes with a predetermined set of constitutive rules. These are more likely to be open to specification, qualification, and revision as we learn more about the landscape of the game, and as players innovate within that landscape. For example, should golfers be allowed to putt the ball using a claw grip or an elongated putter that they can anchor in their chests? The constitutive rules of golf have changed the answer to those questions over time. These quibbles are something to be aware of and to keep in mind when we think about games. We shouldn't, however, let them distract us from the overarching value of this theory of games.

You may have noticed that this theory of games overlaps with my proposed model of the Virtual Utopia. That is no accident. I deliberately crafted my model to make room for games so defined. And although the Virtual Utopia as I have defined it is not limited to games, they are an important element of it. Why is this? The answer can be found toward the end of Suits's dialogue. In the latter stages of the dialogue, after the definitional debate has ended, Suits's characters discuss the utopian nature of games. They invite the reader to imagine a world in which automated technologies have been perfected, and in which super smart machines can cater to every human whim. In this world, if you want a house, all you have to do is press a button or, since the machines can read your mind, just wish for one. It will appear.

This automated utopia has some of the features of a utopian world as classically conceived. As discussed in Chapter 5, the medieval land of Cockaygne was the land of plenty. So too was the Garden of Eden. Utopias are often imagined to be the places where the struggles, deprivations, and demands of "real" life come to an end. Taking this idea onboard, Suits asks us what it is that humans will do when they attain this level of technologically facilitated abundance. What will they do when there is nothing that they have to do? The answer, according to him, is that they will play games. Game playing consequently represents the apotheosis of human existence: it is the thing that we have been striving for through our technological and cultural development. The arc of human history bends toward a utopia of games.

One of Suits's reasons for arguing this is that any human activity in a future of perfected technologically facilitated abundance would be a game. Remember, in this imaginary world, you can get everything you want or need by simply flicking a switch or wishing that it be so. You never need lift a finger again. It follows, by necessity, that *any action* you do perform involves the voluntary assumption of unnecessary obstacles. Houses are available, in all shapes and sizes, to cater to every whim and preference, at the flick of a switch. No effort, no blood, no sweat. But suppose you don't want to flick the switch. Suppose you want to build the house with your own bare hands. You want to draw up the blueprints, source the materials, lay the foundations, pour the concrete, cement the bricks, tile the floors, and so on. You have turned house building into a game in which the prelusory goal (the construction of the house) is achieved by overcoming voluntarily imposed obstacles.

There is more to Suits's game-playing ideal than this. He's not arguing for the utopian potential of games simply by default. That would be a pretty hollow victory for the Virtual Utopia. His claim is that in the absence of need or want, we can spend our time inventing and playing games that are more deeply engaging and absorbing than any game we have ever played before. These games will allow us to achieve idealized forms of human flourishing. They will, in short, be "Utopian Games."

Defending the Utopia of Games

That's Suits's vision. Why do I think we should embrace it? In addition to agreeing with Suits that this represents an obvious ideal endpoint to human technological development, and that removing want and need from our lives is an obvious utopian goal, I think there are four major reasons to think that a world in which we play games is a world in which we can flourish and find meaning.

The first is that creating such a world can help to stave off many of the threats of automation that were discussed in Chapter 4. It cannot stave them all off, of course. That is very obvious. For example, if we are to arrive at the utopia of games, we need to make our peace with the severance problem. This problem, as you will recall, stems from the fact that automating technologies threaten to sever the link between human activity and objectively valuable outcomes, such as the pursuit of knowledge, the satisfaction of human needs, and the resolution of distributive moral problems. We're going to have to resign ourselves to this fate in the utopia of games. But we can do this safe in the knowledge that the other problems of automation (the threats to autonomy and agency) can be ameliorated through game playing. Games will be arenas in which human autonomy and agency can be nurtured and developed. They will provide opportunities for humans to think, plan, and decide; to cultivate moral virtues such as courage, generosity, and fair play; and to display ingenuity and creativity. This is not an unusual or alien idea. People have long argued that the value of sports, for example, lies in their capacity to develop such attributes and provide outlets for human agency to flourish. The philosopher Mike McNamee, for example, argues that sports should be understood as "morality plays" that provide an idealized forum in which players can develop their own moral virtues, and model them to the rest of us.[23] Graham McFee, in a similar vein, argues that sports can function as moral laboratories in which people hone their moral agency.[24] McFee's assumption is that this will then be carried over from the laboratory into real life. What I am arguing here is for vision of a world in which there is no "real" life to carry it over into. The game laboratory itself will have to suffice. The utopia of games could thus be seen as a compromise, something that allows us to retain some, but not all, of our humanistic attributes, but since we are forced to compromise on so many of them in the present-day world (and may be forced to do so even more in the future), that is hardly a demerit for the utopia of games. On the contrary, the fact that the utopia of games provides idealized and protected fora for honing our agency and autonomy seems like a net advantage.

The second reason for embracing the utopia of games is that it satisfies several of the other criteria set out on our utopian scorecard. As you'll recall, one of the aims of utopianism is to provide a balance between stability and dynamism in future social development. We must not try to impose a rigid blueprint on future societies (rigid blueprints are what lead to dissatisfaction and violence), but rather provide them with horizonal projects to which they can aspire. Though it may not look like it at first glance, the utopia of games can provide this. This is because the actual games that we play in this future world are open-ended. We will not end up like the denizens of Herman Hesse's *The Glass Bead Game,* where one particular game becomes the societal focus. There is an infinite landscape of games to be explored. Each of these games can push us and develop us in unexpected ways. The horizons on this landscape of games are another new frontier against which we can expand. Furthermore, and for similar reasons, the utopia of games can also help to ensure that the utopian project is pluralistic and doesn't impose a single set of values or goals on any one individual. There will be many games to be played, and these will appeal to many different tastes and predilections.

The third reason for embracing the utopia of games is that games, rightly done, provide a way in which to realize two important conditions of meaning and flourishing in their most purified and idealized form. This is an argument that was originally developed by the philosopher Thomas Hurka and it requires some unpacking.[25] Hurka asks us to think in more detail about both the structure of means-end reasoning (or practical reasoning, if you prefer) and the nature of achievement. Means-end reasoning is all about working out the most appropriate course of action for realizing some particular goal. Once you figure out the correct means to an end, and implement that means, you can *achieve* the goal. The more difficult this process is, the greater the achievement. A well-designed game allows for complexity in the relationship between means and ends. When one finally attains the game's ends, there is a great sense of *achievement* involved (you have overcome the obstacles established by the rules of the game). This sense of achievement, according to Hurka, is an important source of value. This should be a familiar thought. I discussed the importance of achievement in Chapter 4 when I described Gwen Bradford's theory of achievement and argued that it was integral to the good life. I used the theory to argue for the severance problem and to make the case for technological pessimism. What is interesting about Hurka's argument is that it helps to turns my earlier pessimism on its head. The rise of the machines may cause us to retreat to the world of games, but if Hurka is right, this might actually be a good thing because games provide a pure platform for realizing ever higher degrees of achievement.

Hurka uses an analogy to make the argument. Compare theoretical reasoning with practical reasoning. In theoretical reasoning, you are trying to attain true insights about the structure of the world around you. This enables you to realize a distinct value: knowledge / understanding (again something discussed in Chapter 4). This requires something more that the mere description of facts. To truly understand something, you need to identify general laws or principles that help to explain those facts. When you succeed in identifying those general laws or principles, you will have attained a deep level of insight. This has far more value than mere description. For example, when Newton identified his laws of gravity, he provided overarching principles that could explain many distinct facts. This was valuable in a way that simply describing facts about objects in motion was not. There is extra value to knowledge that is explanatorily integrated. Indeed, the more facts that are integrated into your explanatory framework, the better (see figure 7.1 for an illustration of this idea). Hurka argues that the parallel to knowledge in the practical domain is achievement and that it too can be improved or enhanced if the achievement integrates or draws together a number of different activities. In other words, he argues that there is some good to achievement of all kinds, but there is greater good in achievement that involves greater means-end complexity (see figure 7.2 for an illustration of this idea). Hurka points out that games, if they are well designed, can allow for almost any degree of depth and complexity in means-ends reasoning you desire. You can consequently have arbitrarily high levels of achievement through games.

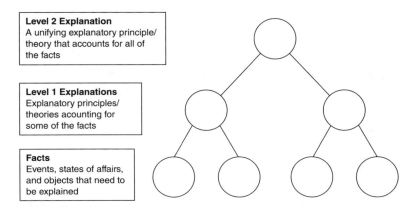

Level 2 Explanation
A unifying explanatory principle/
theory that accounts for all of
the facts

Level 1 Explanations
Explanatory principles/
theories acounting for
some of the facts

Facts
Events, states of affairs,
and objects that need to
be explained

Figure 7.1 Hurka's Levels of Explanatory Depth

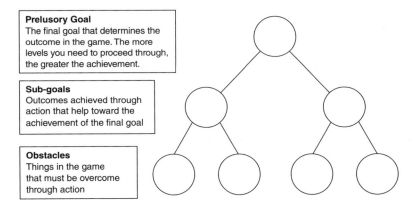

Prelusory Goal
The final goal that determines the
outcome in the game. The more
levels you need to proceed through,
the greater the achievement.

Sub-goals
Outcomes achieved through
action that help toward the
achievement of the final goal

Obstacles
Things in the game
that must be overcome
through action

Figure 7.2 Hurka's Levels of Achievement

This is not true in the real world, where the depth and complexity of means-end reasoning has limits imposed on it by the structure of reality

Hurka has a second argument that is possibly even more interesting. He claims that there is another, significant, source of value in game-playing. To understand this second source of value we need to understand a distinction that Aristotle once drew between two types of activity: *energeia* and *kineseis*. *Energeiai* are activities that are all about process, not about outcome. Aristotle thought that philosophy and self-examination were like this: they were constant processes of questioning and gaining insight; they never bottomed out in some goal or end state. *Kineseis* are the opposite. They are all about goals or end states. Aristotle thought that process-related activities were ultimately better than goal-related activities. The reason for this is that he thought the value of a kinesis was always trumped by or subordinate to its goal. It wasn't good in itself but good because of its outcome. This is why Aristotle advocated the life of contemplation and philosophizing. Such a life would be one in which the activity would be an end in itself: an endlessly rewarding and renewable source of value. Not something of which we could tire or get bored.

At first glance, it might seem like games don't fit neatly within this Aristotelian framework. They are goal-directed activities (the prelusory goal is part of their structure). And so this makes them look like *kineseis.* But remember, these goals are essentially inconsequential. They have no deeper meaning or significance. As a result, the game is really all about process. It is about finding ways to overcome the artificial obstacles established by the constitutive rules. As Hurka sees it, games are consequently excellent platforms for attaining the process-oriented goods that Aristotle extolled. They are activities directed at some external end, but the internal process is the sole source of value. Indeed, there is a sense in which they are an even purer way of achieving Aristotle's ideal than the way suggested by Aristotle himself. The problem with Aristotle's suggestion that the best life is the life of intellectual virtue is that intellectual activity often does have goals lurking in the background (for example, attaining a true insight). The people engaging in those activities don't think of them as having no end goal. There is always the risk that these goals trump the inherent value of the intellectual process. With games, you never have that risk. The goals are valueless from the get-go: all you have to care about is the process. Purely procedural goods can really flourish in the world of games.

Hurka himself expresses some doubts about all this. While he accepts that the game-playing life allows for some flourishing, he still thinks it is of a weaker or inferior sort to an activity that serves some objectively valuable end. As he puts it, "excellence in games, though admirable, is less so than success in equally challenging activities that produce a great good or prevent a great evil."[26] Hurka may be correct in this. It may be better, all things considered, if our activities have both intrinsic and instrumental value. But in the context of this book and this chapter, his caution is less compelling. I argued in Chapter 4 that we may need to resile ourselves to a fate in which automating technologies, not human beings, achieve the important and consequential outcomes. In other words, we may need to make do with less. This may look like a dispiriting compromise, but it is actually not. The reality is that the higher forms of achievement to which Hurka alludes—the achievements of the political reformers and medical researchers—have never been widely available. They have always been the preserve of an elite few. Most people have to make do with lesser kinds of achievement anyway, including achievements in sports and games. If the utopia of games provides an idealized forum for those kinds of achievement, there is reason to welcome it, rather than rebuff it.

The final reason for embracing the utopia of games is closely allied to Hurka's argument. It is that it could provide an ideal society for pursuing the value of *craft*. This is an argument that requires some unpacking. Dedicating one's life to honing a set of skills, using those skills to produce certain kinds of outcomes, and being totally absorbed by this process, are the hallmarks of crafting. The skilled blacksmith or furniture maker, for example, will have spent many years attuning themselves to the demands of their crafts. They will know how to make precise, skilled movements that accommodate and work with the materials they use. They will be absorbed by the process of working the metal, or honing the wood, knowing that in doing so they are guided by forces (the standards of beauty / elegance / skill) beyond themselves. This may not always involve working with physical materials, as in the case of the blacksmith and carpenter; it may also involve a purely physical or intellectual skillset, as in the case of the musician or fiction writer. Ideally, the craftsperson will do this work for its own sake, not because it pays them or serves some hunger for glory. As Richard Sennett puts it in his paean to craftsmanship, the craftsman is "dedicated to good work for its own sake. Theirs is practical activity but not simply a means to another end . . . [they] represent the special human condition of being engaged."[27]

Sennett goes on to lament the perverse and distorting effects that economic and governmental incentives have on the pursuit of craftsmanship. The competitive standards of capitalism can sacrifice quality to mass production; the conformist standards of communism can sacrifice quality to mediocrity and incompetence. These instrumental ends take people out of the skilled absorption that makes craft such a valuable art. For Sennett, this value has deep biological and historical roots. We are embodied beings who make our way in the world through physical and cognitive engagement with our surroundings. We anticipate, predict, adapt, and respond. The craftsperson, in his/her mature form, has mastered that physical engagement, at least in a certain domain. This is something that human civilization has long valued and recognized. In the West, Sennett traces it back to the Homeric hymn to Hephaestus, the god of craftsmen, which holds crafting out as the harbinger of peace and the catalyst of civilization.[28]

Sennett is not alone in his defense of craft. Hubert Dreyfus and Sean Dorrance Kelly, in their critique of modern nihilism—which they see as the product of secularization and mechanization—believe that the ideal of craftsmanship offers hope for meaning and flourishing in our jaded times. Indeed, they go so far as to argue that craftwork, broadly understood to include the mastery of physical and intellectual skills, provides us with a secular equivalent of the sacred. They use the example of Roger Federer, whose grace and skill on the tennis court is widely renowned, to make this point, suggesting that the way he uses his body to perform his craft (playing tennis) helps us to explore the horizons of what is possible within an embodied human form.[29]

This might push the value of craft too far. I'm not sure that we should be interested in recovering some secularized sense of the sacred. Nevertheless, there is something to what Dreyfus, Kelly, and Sennett have to say. In trying to master a skillset, you have to attune yourself to standards and qualities that are not purely self-determined; you have to focus on something that is larger than yourself. The pursuit of such mastery was identified in Chapter 3 as one of the potential goods of work (other than money) that we would need to think about preserving in a post-work utopia. The pursuit of such mastery is not, as Dreyfus and Kelly point out, merely about achieving technical proficiency in a physical skill; it is about seeing the world in a different way. It is about recognizing variables and attributes in activities that were previously hidden. As they put it: "Learning a skill is learning to see the world differently . . . [it] allows [the craftsperson] to see meaningful distinctions that others without their skill cannot."[30]

Furthermore, developing the skill of the craftsperson is not something that is subject to limits or quickly engenders boredom. Repetition and practice often reveal greater depths in the skillset that were previously unappreciated. As Sennett points out, "as skill expands, the capacity to sustain repetition increases. In music this is the so-called Isaac Stern rule, the great violinist declaring that the better your technique, the longer you can rehearse without becoming bored."[31]

In short, the life of craft is one that can sustain human flourishing and meaning. It is also an ideal that has a long and venerable history. The argument I make here, similar to that of Hurka's, is that the utopia of games provides an ideal forum for pursuing this lifestyle. A life of games can be the ultimate life of craftsmanship. People can dedicate themselves to honing and refining their skillsets in various games. They can approach these games with a craftsman-like mindset. What's more, they can do this without the distorting or contaminating incentives that typically pollute the pursuit of craft for its own sake in our current world. The craft does not need to be pursued for economic gain or necessity. It does not have to be subject to the crushing demands of a hypercompetitive market, or the motivation-sapping tedium of governmental standards and compliance.

Again, this is not an unusual or alien idea. In many cases, those who currently pursue ancient crafts—like blacksmithing, or furniture making, or artisanal beer-brewing—are already engaging in games (in the Suitsian sense). Machines can do all of these things with greater speed, precision, and efficiency than humans can. People are deliberately imposing unnecessary obstacles on themselves in the pursuit of these crafts. The only difference between the present reality and the reality imagined by Suits (and me) is that sometimes these things are still done for economic gain or within work structures that have all the negative features that I discussed in Chapter 3. I am arguing that we set that to the side and let the crafting ethos shine.

Critiquing the Utopia of Games

But surely this cannot be a serious argument? Surely, I am not saying that we should give up on making a difference to the world and retreat to the world of games? There are several misconceptions of the argument that need to be dealt with, as well as several objections that need to be rebuffed, before the idea can be taken seriously.

I'll deal with the misconceptions first. People who balk at the idea of the utopia of games usually do so on the assumption that the future that is being imagined is one in which we do nothing other than play games, and that we will do so alone, in isolated, self-obsessed bubbles. This is not the case. Games can be social activities, and outside the games there will still be time for relationships, families, food, music, and many of the other activities that sustain us and make our lives more meaningful in the present world. The big change is that we will replace our current obsession with work—and its associated work ethic—with games and their associated game ethic. Instead of work providing a privileged forum for attaining goods such as mastery and a sense of community, games are going to provide that forum.[32]

People may also balk at the idea because they imagine that there is nothing real or worthwhile going on in games. But this is not the case. As should be clear from the extended discussion of reality vs. virtuality earlier in this chapter, there will be many "real" things in the "virtual" world of games. Real experiences, real emotions, real virtues, and real relationships will all be present. These will all provide the basis for objective goods, not merely trivial or secondary goods. People can grow and develop their agency in the game-world. They can acquire understanding and competence in the game-world. They can have fun, find satisfaction, and make friends. Something will be missing—some connection with larger, consequentially significant goods like knowledge—but these could never provide the basis for mass flourishing anyway. They were always the preserve of an elite.

Finally, people may not take the utopia of games seriously because they assume it requires the perfected technologies that Suits imagines in his dialogue. In other words, it is not until machines can read our minds and print into existence anything we desire that we will have reached the utopia of games. Until that day, any discussion about it will be necessarily speculative and distracting. But this is not true. Suits may himself have imagined a world of perfected technologies, but there is no reason why we have to achieve such perfection (if that is even a coherent notion) before we start to take the utopia of games seriously. As noted in earlier chapters, machines may not render everyone unemployed in the future. There may still be an elite few workers who are needed to keep the engines of productivity turning. But there will be a growing surplus population who need to find outlets for their yearning for meaning and flourishing. You may find yourself among them. Indeed, you may already be among them. We, as a society, will need to start thinking about developing outlets for these affected individuals long before we arrive at Suits's imagined techno-utopia.

That said, it is true that one aspect of Suits's argument will not work until we arrive at his imagined world. This is the part of the argument that claims that every human activity is by default a game because, in a world of perfected technologies, all human activity is unnecessary. But as suggested above, it's not clear what role that idea really plays in Suits's case for the utopia of games. Suits doesn't make explicit arguments—he expresses himself through the more obscure medium of dialogue. This makes it difficult to know what he really thinks. Christopher Yorke suggests Suits equivocates between arguing that the utopia of games is desirable and arguing that it is inevitable.[33] This might suggest that he is a little unsure about the desirability of his imagined utopia. I don't think there is any need to be so equivocal. Suits's world of perfected technologies may, ultimately, be inevitable. But I suspect that we are a long way from reaching it. In the meantime, there will be many human activities that will become unnecessary due to advances in automation, and some that will not. This doesn't undermine the reasons given above for thinking that the utopia of games is desirable, nor does it obviate the case for pursuing it as an ideal.

So much for the misconceptions about the utopia of games. What about the objections to it? Is there any reason to think that it just isn't a very good or plausible utopian vision? There are several that are worth entertaining. M. Andrew Holowchak, for instance, argues that the Suitsian vision is incoherent/undesirable on the grounds that Suits ignores a key part of what makes games fun.[34] Holowchak presents two versions of this objection. One version claims Suits overlooks the need for failure in games. It is no fun playing a game if you can win, with ease, every time. But in Suits's imagined utopia failure is never possible: if anything goes wrong, you can simply wish for the desired outcome and a machine will do it for you. The other version, which Holowchak himself prefers, argues that Suits's analysis ignores the need for contention or competition in successful games. In other words, there needs to be some psychological desire to beat yourself or beat your opponent in order for there to be a game. But, again, in Suits's imagined utopia there is no real contention or competition. He supposes that any psychological desire for contention or competition can be cured through our perfected technology.

Neither of these versions of the objection is persuasive, even when engaged on their own terms. If failure, contention, and competition were essential requirements for games, then games themselves would be impossible. Both versions of the objection claim that we cannot fake the possibility of failure or the desire for competition / contention. But clearly we can do this. Think about it. There is no possibility of failure and no real contention / competition in most of the games we currently play. Not really anyway. It is all facade and artifice. It is only by accepting the constitutive rules of the game that failure and contention enter the fray. When I play golf, I can, if I like, pick my ball up and just drop it in the hole. I need never fail to achieve the prelusory goal in an efficient manner. But of course I don't do that because I accept the constitutive rules. I go along with the facade of needing to use clubs to manipulate the ball through the air and over the ground. Accepting these constraints doesn't make my eventual triumph in getting the ball into the hole any less authentic or real, but it does add the potential for failure and contention to the proceedings. Furthermore, even if I am wrong about this, neither of the objections has any weight until we arrive at Suits's hypothetical world of perfected technology, which I have just argued is not needed in order to embrace the utopia of games.

A more substantive set of objections has been developed by Christopher Yorke.[35] He argues that Suits's utopia of games is problematic because it is rationally unintelligible: there's too much distance between the world as it is currently constituted and the world as Suits would like it to be. Rational intelligibility was, as you recall, a key criterion on our utopian scorecard. But I hope that I have already provided several reasons for thinking that the utopia of games is more intelligible than might first be supposed. I have pointed out that it builds on models (the value of sports, the value of craft) that are already familiar to us, and I have argued that many "real" things that are widely recognized to be of value will still be accessible in the utopia of games (achievement, virtue, the development of agency). Nevertheless, it is worth considering Yorke's objections in more detail in order to see whether they give any additional reason to doubt my earlier enthusiasm for games. I don't think they do, but seeing why I think this will help further clarify exactly what I understand the utopia of games to be.

Yorke's first objection focuses on the nature of the games we will be playing in Suits's imagined techno-utopia. Yorke claims that in order for Suits's utopia to be rationally intelligible, we need to have some clear sense of the games we will be playing in it. But Suits doesn't provide us with this. And, when we think about it in the required detail, we see that games in Suits's world of advanced automated technologies would be very strange indeed. Part of the problem is that Suits provides two different conceptions of a utopian game in his work. As we have already seen, given how he defines games (as the achievement of arbitrary goals through the voluntary triumph over artificial obstacles) and how he imagines our technological future, there is a sense in which any activity undertaken in a world of perfect automation counts as a game. Such "games by default" should be contrasted with what we might call "games by design," which are deliberately designed to function as games, and are always and everywhere game-like, irrespective of the technological backdrop. As noted, Suits seems to think that we will need games by design, not just games by default, in a future of perfected automation. In other words, he doesn't think that games by default will be enough to sustain the utopia. For what it is worth, I don't quite agree with this. I think games by default could be enough to sustain meaning and flourishing, and to stave off boredom, because they would essentially consist of many of the activities that motivate us today, performed for fun (for their intrinsic merits) rather than economic or other necessity.

But Yorke resists this interpretation of the utopia of games because he thinks it doesn't account for what Suits actually says, and I'm willing to concede this point because I think it would be better, all things considered, if games by design were added to the mix. They would add something to the utopia of games that would otherwise be lacking: a novel horizon of possibility against which we can test human ingenuity and capacity. So this means that we need some account of the games by design that will be worth playing in a future of perfected automation. The problem is that Suits provides no guidance as to what these games will look like. You can, however, read between the lines of his book and find some guidance as to what they will *not look like.* And this is where Yorke thinks it all starts to unravel. For example, Suits stipulates that in his imagined utopia no one can be wronged or harmed. Yorke argues that this rules out immoral games: "games that necessarily, in the course of playing them, incur irreparable physical harm upon their participants—such as Russian Roulette and boxing—will be excluded from the utopian set. Similarly, games that require players to engage in immoral behaviors like bald-faced lying in order to play effectively—Werewolf and Diplomacy come to mind—will be off the menu."[36] Suits also argues that all interpersonal problems will be eliminated in his utopia, which suggests that all cheating or unsportsmanlike behavior will be banned from his utopian games: "in Suits's utopia, his utopian games will not be ruined by the bad behavior of their players. Cheating, trifling, spoilsporting, bullying, and grousing behaviors will all be preemptively (if somewhat rather mysteriously) eliminated."[37] Finally, Suits says that utopian games cannot be boring. This, according to Yorke, rules out quite a large number of games: "boring games would include soluble games (those with a dominant strategy that, once known, leave no opportunity for the exercise of meaningful player agency, like Tic Tac Toe), games of pure chance (those that leave no opportunity for the exercise of meaningful player agency because strategy and tactics cannot have an impact on their outcome, such as Snakes and Ladders), and games of pure skill (like Chess—since utopians will have endless hours to devote to its study, and potentially live in a time 'when everything knowable was in fact known')."[38]

The problem, according to Yorke, is that once you rule out all of these kinds of games—immoral ones, ones that involve unsportsmanlike behavior, and ones that are boring—you end up with a set of possible utopian games that is epistemically inaccessible to creatures like us. The utopian games are clearly going to be very different from the kinds of games we currently play: so different, in fact, that we have no concrete idea of what they will actually involve. This makes the utopia of games rationally unintelligible.

There are, however, several problems with this argument. For starters, many of the issues that Yorke identifies stem from the additional assumptions that Suits makes about his automated utopia, none of which are strictly necessary for us to get behind the utopia of games. There is nothing in the nature of an automated future (or, indeed, a utopian one) that requires the absence of all immorality and harm, or all forms of boredom; their minimization perhaps, but not their elimination. Furthermore, the problems to which Yorke alludes all seem to arise at a level of extreme technological advancement, which is not what I assume or argue for here. Still, even if you set those problems to the side, and you engage Yorke's objection on its own terms, I think it is easy to see that he sets far too high a standard on what counts as immoral and boring and so makes the utopia of games more unintelligible than it needs to be.

Consider the idea of immoral games first. I would argue that the immorality of conduct depends largely on the context in which the conduct is performed and the consequences of the conduct. Boxing might be immoral if it entails, as Yorke insists, irreparable harm (though you might even dispute this on the grounds that people can consent to such harm). But why assume that harm would be irreparable in Suits's utopia? If we have reached a state of technological perfection, would this not also include medical perfection that could quickly repair any apparent harm? Think again about the world of *Star Trek*. There are several episodes where crew members are injured playing games on the holodeck only to have their injuries quickly healed by the advanced medical technology. If that becomes possible for boxing-related injuries, then I don't see how boxing retains its immorality in a future of perfected technology. If all injuries are trivial and reversible, then there may be nothing harmful or immoral about the game. This is similar to the point made in the previous chapter about fungibility and replaceability of human body parts and their effects on our moral beliefs. Likewise, I would argue that within the context of a game, behavior that would ordinarily count as lying or deception can lose any hint of immorality, particularly if it is required for success in the game. For example, I would argue that it is not even possible to "lie" when playing a game like Diplomacy. The standard philosophical definition of lying is to utter deliberate falsehoods *in a context that ordinarily requires truth telling*. The context of the game Diplomacy is not one that ordinarily requires truth telling. Deception is built into the fabric of the game: it's part of what makes it fun. And since there are no serious long-term consequences of this deception, it is once again hard to see where the immorality is (the card game poker is also like this with the complication that it is sometimes played for real economic stakes). So the kinds of games that Yorke is so quick to rule out would not actually be ruled out in Suits's utopia.

Similar issues arise with Yorke's characterization of boring games. Soluble games and games of pure chance and pure skill might eventually become boring, but that doesn't mean that they couldn't be entertaining for a period of time (while people are figuring out the solution or developing the skill), and it doesn't mean that we couldn't create a never-ending series of such games to stave off the boredom. In other words, Suits's injunction against boredom need not be interpreted as an injunction against individual games that might eventually become boring, but as an injunction against the total set of games that all utopians might ever play. Unless we think that total set has very few members, or that we will exhaust it very quickly, there is nothing to worry about. In addition to this, just because a game might be soluble in principle does not mean that humans will be able to solve it using their cognitive capacities. Machines might be able to solve many games that humans currently cannot, but that does not mean that the machine solutions will be epistemically accessible to humans. A world of technological abundance is not necessarily one in which humans acquire superior cognitive abilities. In other words, the Virtual Utopia is not necessarily a Cyborg Utopia, and this means that there is more utopian potential in the world of games than Yorke presumes.

Yorke has another argument for unintelligibility that is worth considering. This one takes aim at the technologically perfected society that Suits imagines, not at the games that are played in that society. Yorke argues that Suits's imagined society seems to be a post-instrumentalist society: it is a world in which the need for all instrumental activities has been eliminated. Yorke then argues that there is a significant cultural gap between our society and this post-instrumentalist one. This post-instrumentalist society is consequently unintelligible to us from our current standpoint and hence the utopia of games is unintelligible.

One way you can test this unintelligibility is to look to Suits's descriptions of his imagined society. Are those descriptions consistently post-instrumentalist? Do they hang together coherently? Yorke argues that they do not. For example, Suits still talks about the need to eat to stave off hunger and the need to do things to stave off boredom. These are both instrumental goals that need to be solved by instrumental activities. This means that the imagined world is not consistently post-instrumental. Furthermore, Yorke argues that there is good reason for Suits's inability to imagine a truly post-instrumentalist society. The human species is uniquely instrumentalist in nature: we have evolved to fill the cognitive niche, to use our brains to solve problems and achieve goals. It's very difficult for us to escape this way of engaging with the world.[39]

Yorke's point is that a truly post-instrumentalist society would be one in which humans are radically different from what they currently are, namely, one in which they have achieved some "posthuman" state of existence. But since we have not currently achieved this state of existence, the idea is clearly unintelligible to creatures like us. In other words, Yorke argues that we would need to achieve the Cyborg Utopia (and its posthuman state of existence) before we could really appreciate Suits's utopia. Consequently, the cultural gap problems that plague the Cyborg Utopia also plague the utopia of games.

Again, I don't think that this objection is persuasive. As Yorke himself points out, since the idea of a truly post-instrumentalist society is so difficult to imagine, it's probably not what Suits was trying to describe or defend, nor is it something that we need to defend to embrace the utopia of games. We can think of the instrumentalist nature of a society as something that exists by degrees. We currently live in a strongly instrumentalist society—one in which instrumentalist activity is common and central to our existence. That said, some of our needs are routinely satisfied with technological assistance: we are not living on an existential knife-edge where everything we do is subservient to our basic survival needs. In other words, we do not live in a hyper-instrumentalist society in which all activities are valued for their instrumental properties. A hyper-instrumentalist society would represent one extreme end of the spectrum of possible societies. At the other end is the completely post-instrumentalist society—the one in which the need for instrumentalist activity has been completely eliminated. Between these two extremes, there are many other possible societies, including what we might call a hypo-instrumentalist society—the one in which many, but not all, instrumentalist activities have been eliminated.

It's likely that Suits's utopia of games is intended to exist in a hypo-instrumentalist society, not a truly post-instrumentalist society. In particular, it is likely that it is supposed to exist in a society in which the need for physical labor in order to secure the basic goods of life—food, shelter, material consumables, etc.—has been eliminated, but in which other instrumental needs—for example, the need for status, friendship, entertainment—remain. Moving Suits's utopia away from the extreme of post-instrumentalism can make his imagined world much more rationally intelligible, but it all depends on how far from the extreme of post-instrumentalism we can take it. Yorke seems to think that Suits's imagined world of plenitude is so irreducibly foreign to our world of scarcity that, even in a watered-down hypo-instrumentalist form, it is unintelligible to us.[40] But this is much too strong a claim. Although there is undoubtedly much poverty and immiseration in the world today, there are clearly some pockets of post-scarcity and hypo-instrumentalism. In developed economies there is an abundance of material goods, food, and energy.[41] It may well be a fragile state of affairs—and one that is revealed as such in emergency situations—but for all practical, day-to-day purposes it gets pretty close to a form of post-scarcity. Furthermore, there are certain groups of people within our societies—super-wealthy elites—who probably get very close to living a post-scarcity life when it comes to all material goods and services. And while they may live lives that are different to our own, they are not completely alien. We can understand what motivates them and gives them a sense of purpose. The cultural gap is not as wide as Yorke supposes.

There are also some deep philosophical problems with the ideas of hypo-instrumentalism and post-scarcity that motivate Yorke's argument. The main one is that the human capacity for finding new forms of instrumentalism, and for finding new forms of scarcity, may be infinite. What were once wants can quickly turn into needs and can be pursued with all the vigor and urgency that entails. So while we may eliminate certain instrumental needs from human life (for example, the need for food or shelter), it's likely that we will quickly reallocate our mental resources to other perceived needs (for example, the need for social status). These new needs could then be pursued in a strongly instrumentalist way, and thus become the major focal point in society. One could easily imagine this happening inside Suits's utopia of games in such a way that status and ranking within a game become a major form of scarcity for which people compete. So I'm not sure that we can ever achieve a pronounced form of hypo-instrumentalism. That said, I don't think this makes Suits's claim that games represent an ideal of existence unintelligible or undesirable. It might make particular readings or interpretations of that ideal unintelligible, but the basic idea that we would be better off playing games than dedicating our time to securing our basic material well-being would still be intelligible. Furthermore, reallocating mental resources from one form of scarcity to another could be highly desirable, for the reasons given above.

In summary, I think the utopia of games does offer a credible utopian project for humanity. Getting to a world in which we spend the majority of our time playing games would represent a significant societal achievement. It would mean that we have removed several forms of scarcity and want. And games themselves can provide us with a potentially infinite set of worlds in which we can flourish and find meaning. This may require some compromises, but those compromises would be worth it, and would build upon long-standing human ideals such as the ideals of craftsmanship, play, achievement, and virtue-building. It is a much more plausible and practical utopia than might initially seem to be the case.

A Virtual Meta-Utopia

The second argument for the Virtual Utopia is a little different. It does not claim that virtual reality provides a pathway to a particular vision of the good life (like mastery of games). It is agnostic on this matter. Instead, it claims that virtual reality is desirable because it offers us a world-building mechanism that allows us to realize (in virtual form) any vision of the good life that we may desire. Unlike the utopia of games, this argument does rely on a more technologized understanding of the Virtual Utopia because it works only to the extent that we can simulate and/or construct different possible worlds through technology.

The argument is based on the work of Robert Nozick. In his famous book *Anarchy, State and Utopia*, Nozick makes the case for a libertarian view of individual rights and the political desirability of a minimal state.[42] He covers these topics in the first two-thirds of the book. Then, in the last third, he offers an original analysis of what a utopian world would look like. For some reason, Nozick's vision of utopia has been much less widely discussed than his libertarianism and minimal statism. This is somewhat surprising since his analysis of utopianism is perhaps the most interesting and novel aspect of the book. Whatever the reasons may be for this neglect, I think it is time to resurrect Nozick's ideas and reconsider them in light of advances in the technology of virtual reality. I cannot claim originality for doing this. Others have highlighted the link between digital technologies and Nozick's ideas before.[43] What I do hope to offer is a more detailed appraisal and evaluation of a technologized version of Nozick's proposal, and to present it as part of a larger case for the Virtual Utopia. To do this, I will first discuss Nozick's proposal, explaining how it works and some of the problems to which it gives rise. I will then explain how the proposal could be implemented using virtual reality technology and argue that there are many advantages to this method of implementation.

(Note: Readers who are familiar with Nozick's work will know that he would probably object to this entire line of argument on the grounds that a virtual reality cannot provide the kinds of value that we are looking for in life. To those readers, I ask for some patience. I will deal with Nozick's criticisms of virtual reality in the penultimate section of this chapter.)

Understanding Nozick's Meta-Utopia

Nozick's utopian vision can be simply stated: there is (in all likelihood) no single utopian world; so we should not try to identify, describe, or build such a world. We should, instead, focus on the possibility of creating a meta-utopian world, that is, a world in which many different worlds can be constructed and joined, according to individual preference. Nozick presents a three-step argument for this view. The first step provides a conceptual analysis of what is meant by the word "utopia." The second step is to argue that there is no single utopian world. The third step is to argue that a meta-utopia is the only stable structure that can accommodate the fact that there is no single utopia.

Let's start with the conceptual analysis. For Nozick, a utopia is the best of all possible worlds. Now, I already discussed the concept of a utopia at length in Chapter 5, and although I argued in favor of a "possible worlds" rendering of utopianism, I rejected this particular understanding of what a utopia is: utopias are sets of possible worlds that represent some radical improvement over the current world. But since it is important to Nozick's argument, and since Nozick uses it to end up somewhere quite similar to where I ended up in Chapter 5, we can accept this definition for the time being and move on. The challenge, for Nozick, is in working out what the best of all possible worlds might look like. Nozick tries to make the task more manageable by asking us to imagine we have the power to create any possible world we like. If we had that power, which world would we construct and what would lead us to call it a utopia? He argues that the utopian world would be the one that is *stable*, that is, the world we most want to be in and that is judged by us to be the most desirable. This gives us Nozick's "stability analysis" of utopia:

> **Stability Condition**: A world W is stable if it is judged by its members to be the best possible world, that is, there is no world they would rather be in.
>
> **Utopia**: A world W is utopian only if it is stable.

This brings us to the second step of Nozick's argument. As you will have noted, his analysis places *internal* standards of judgment at the core of what it is to live in a utopia. A world is utopian if it is judged by its members to be the best of all possible worlds. The judgments of the people living in the world are paramount, not the judgments of some external authority or the application of some objective standard of betterness to rank possible worlds. Nozick thinks this reliance on internal standards is justified (we'll come back to this) but that it creates some obvious problems. If internal standards are what matters in the assessment of possible utopias, we run into the problem that there is probably no shared, intersubjective standard of what makes one world better than another. This makes it highly unlikely that there is a single world in which the stability condition is met for all inhabitants of that world. Some of the inhabitants might think there is no place they'd rather be than the world they happen to be in; but others are likely to imagine a better world that is just around the corner. You might think a stable happy family life is what matters for the good life, whereas others prioritize success in their careers, and so on. This is the problem of pluralism that was outlined in

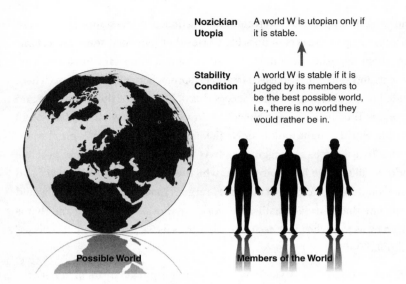

Nozickian Utopia — A world W is utopian only if it is stable.

Stability Condition — A world W is stable if it is judged by its members to be the best possible world, i.e., there is no world they would rather be in.

Possible World   Members of the World

Figure 7.3 Nozick's Analysis of Utopia

Chapter 5 (see figure 7.4). The challenge is to figure out how we can realize a utopian world when there is such pluralism.

Two caveats are worth bearing in mind about this second step in the argument. First, note how Nozick's claim is not that a single utopian world is impossible, merely that it is highly unlikely. It is possible that everyone's internal standards of betterness perfectly coincide, but it is not very likely and does not track with what we know about the world. Second, when we say that standards of betterness vary, this does not mean that there are no shared, objective values—that is, no grounds for agreement on what makes for a good life. There could be widespread agreement about that without there being shared standards of betterness. You and I could both agree that success in work and success in family life are important values, but we might disagree on their order of priority. So a devout Nozickian could agree that the conditions of meaning and flourishing that were laid out in Chapter 4 are central to the good life, but simply disagree on how those conditions are prioritized.

This brings us to the third step in Nozick's argument. Since there is probably no single utopian world—no single world that meets the stability con-

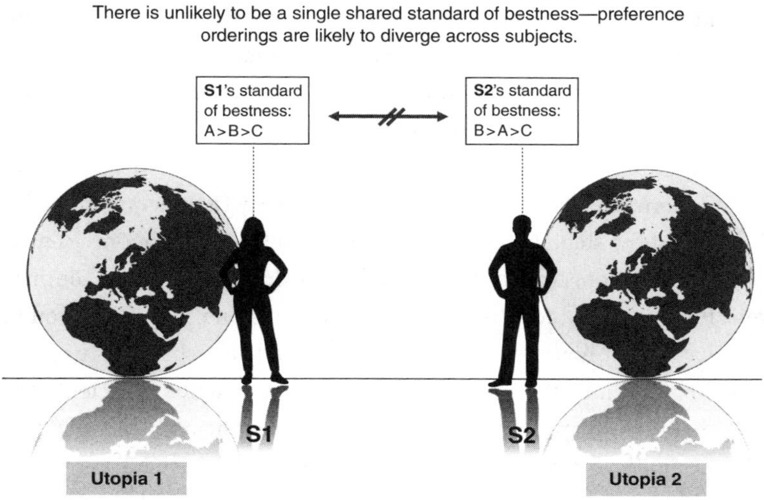

There is unlikely to be a single shared standard of bestness—preference orderings are likely to diverge across subjects.

| S1's standard of bestness: A > B > C | | S2's standard of bestness: B > A > C |

Figure 7.4 The Plurality Problem

dition for everyone—it follows that the closest thing to a utopian world will be a meta-utopian world, namely, one in which it is possible to create and join many different worlds. In other words, a world in which we are free to build and join the possible worlds that meet our own internal stability conditions. This world is the one that allows a thousand worlds to bloom. Nozick's claim is that no matter what your internal standards for betterness are, you are likely to agree that the meta-utopia is the best chance of realizing your own personal utopia. This world does not presuppose or dictate any particular vision of the good life. It simply provides an overarching structure in which multiple conceptions of the good life can be pursued.

There is something very attractive about Nozick's meta-utopian ideal. The idea that we shouldn't try to create a single, "best" world, but should instead give people the means to create and join different possible worlds that conform to their own understanding of what is best, is intuitively compelling. It is particularly compelling when you realize that it doesn't depend on a crude relativism about what makes for a good life, but rather emerges from the fact that there is reasonable disagreement about how to prioritize that which is objectively valuable. Nevertheless, there are some problems with Nozick's vision, and I want to discuss a few of them here. Each of these problems helps to explain why I think a version of Nozick's argument that makes use of virtual reality technologies would be a better approximation of the meta-utopia than his own preferred libertarian minimal state.

The first comes from Ralf Bader's critical appraisal of Nozick's meta-utopia.[44] It concerns the stability condition. It is easy to understand the intention behind the stability condition. It's a sop to liberal, autonomy-centric moral presuppositions, which state that the individual should be the ultimate arbiter of what is good for them. The ideal world is one that allows you to choose that which matches your preferences. But no self-respecting autonomy fanatic thinks that preference matching by itself is sufficient. The preferences you have must be arrived at through a sufficiently independent and autonomous process. Suppose you express a preference for a world in which you get to be a professional dancer. But suppose further that your preference for being a professional dancer was drilled into you from an early age by your overbearing mother. She always wanted to be a professional dancer herself but failed in her ambitions. She is living vicariously through you. Anytime you expressed an aptitude and desire to do something else, she berated you and convinced you that dancing was the way to go. Eventually you came around to her way of seeing things. You took her preferences on as your own. Would we really say that a world in which your preference for being a dancer is met is the best possible world for you? The problem with saying that is that it seems to assign too much normative weight to preferences that might not be authentically yours, that is, preferences that have been coerced, manipulated, and brainwashed, which suggests that we may need to modify Nozick's stability condition by adding an "authenticity" clause:

> **Stability Condition***: A world W is stable if it is judged by its members to be the best possible world. This means that there is no world they would rather be in, and their judgments are authentic, autonomously derived reflections of what they truly prefer.

The problem with the additional clause is that it makes the practical realization of Nozick's meta-utopia much more difficult. Suddenly it looks like you have to bring in external judges to determine whether a preference is authentic, and there is probably going to be disagreement among those judges, at least some of the time, about what this means. This might be tolerable. We might be able to reach agreement on some clear-cut cases of inauthenticity and make adjustments for this in the meta-utopia, for example, by encouraging people to experiment before settling on a particular world. But the modified version of the stability condition creates another problem, one that is likely going to be more serious in practice. If the meta-utopia needs to filter out worlds that are the result of manipulated or coerced judgments of betterness, then it seems like it entails a paradox—namely, it cannot accommodate those worlds where people's judgments of betterness require the freedom to impose their will on others. Nozick was aware of this. In his original discussion, he noted that there are three kinds of community that could exist in a meta-utopian world:

Existentialist Communities: These are communities that adopt a pluralistic view as to what makes for the best world, and have no desire to impose any particular conception of "bestness" on others. They are willing to tolerate the multiplicity of worlds that the meta-utopia entails.

Missionary Communities: These are communities that adopt a monistic view as to what makes for the best world and wish to convert everyone to their view of bestness, but they do so through rational debate and persuasion, not through manipulation and coercion.

Imperialist Communities: These are communities that adopt a monistic view as to what makes for the best world and wish to convert everyone to their view of bestness. They are willing to do so through manipulation, coercion, and force if needs be.

While a meta-utopian institutional framework could be created that accommodates existential and missionary communities, it could not accommodate an imperialist community. The existence of such a community would violate the modified stability condition. You might say this is okay because imperialist preferences shouldn't be allowed. But if you do so, you start to undercut some of the original appeal of the meta-utopian argument. The appeal of Nozick's analysis was that it didn't seem to take any particular stance on what made for the best possible world: it allowed people to determine this for themselves. But now it seems like we have to start putting our foot down and ruling out some particular conceptions of bestness. This makes the argument less philosophically pure and more difficult to implement, given that there are many imperialist communities already in existence.

One way in which you could resolve the imperialist problem would be to avoid the original sin of the stability condition, that is, not give so much weight to internal standards when judging which world is best; you could use objective standards instead, ones that could rule out the justifiability of imperialism. But, of course, this is itself replete with practical problems. What are these objective standards? Who determines what they are? And, most important, who determines the priority ranking of those standards? It is those very problems that make the appeal to internal standards quite attractive. Still, many will feel jittery about the use of internal standards because of the potential anarchy it could justify, and this prompts the question: can we say anything to assuage these jitters and remain committed to the use of internal standards in determining what a utopia is? Bader argues that we can, for three reasons.

The first is that there is still a strong case for the use of internal standards in determining what counts as a utopia. Bader thinks that the internalist approach makes for a substantive and theoretically interesting account of utopia—namely, a utopia is a world that is preferred to all other possible worlds by its members. This seems to be both a novel and interesting approach to utopian thinking. Appealing to external standards is less substantive and theoretically interesting. For the externalist, the account of utopia falls out of the particular theory of value to which they adhere. This means all the theoretical and argumentative heavy lifting is borne by that theory (be it utilitarian or otherwise). So the externalist approach to utopia just replicates centuries of debate about value. The internalist approach, in addition to paying heed to the practical reality of pluralism and diversity, holds out the promise of providing something different.

The second reason is that there are plausible grounds for thinking that internal and external standards should join up at some point. The thinking here is that a plausible theory of external value would have to incorporate an "endorsement condition," that is, it would have be something that can be endorsed and agreed upon by everyone who is subject to it. As Bader puts it: "What is objectively best should ideally not be completely disconnected from what the subjects take to be best."[45]

The third reason is a practical one. It suggests that epistemic humility is a must when it comes to utopian thinking. If we have learned anything from history, it is that utopian world builders often get things wrong and cause great hardship and suffering in the process. We should guard against repeating such mistakes. This means that we shouldn't be too bullish about any particular external theory of value. Even if we think it is on the right lines, we should factor in some element of risk and uncertainty. If you incorporate this epistemic humility into your externalist theory, you'll end up with something pretty similar to Nozick's internalist theory. This is because an epistemically humble approach would require some accommodation to the views of others and some degree of experimentation with world-building. This is essentially what Karl Popper argued in his famous critique of utopianism that we discussed back in Chapter 5.

I agree with nearly all of this: I agree that a predominantly internalist approach to determining what is best offers a viable and attractive take on utopianism, one that can score highly on the utopian scorecard in terms of its allowance for pluralism and dynamism. Furthermore, I think it is consistent with the approach to flourishing and meaning that I set out in Chapter 4: that approach made much of the need to marry together subjective and objective understandings of the good life.

But even if we can feel comfortable about the predominantly internalist approach to determining which of all the possible worlds would be best for us, we must still confront the practical problem of imperialism. As Nozick conceives it, the meta-utopia is a relatively minimalist and value-neutral phenomenon. It is just a mechanism that allows people to create and join different possible worlds. But now that we have run through some of the objections to Nozick's vision, we see that things are not so straightforward. It looks like the meta-utopian mechanism is going to have to play a larger and more interventionist role in policing the possible worlds that people might want to create and impose on others. This makes the meta-utopia more cumbersome and less practicable in the real world—how do you effectively police the boundaries between different communities so as to control the imperialists?—and brings it much further away from the libertarian minimalism preferred by Nozick.[46] In doing so, it highlights the attractions of a virtual form of the meta-utopia.

Could We Create a Virtual Meta-Utopia?

The argument I defend here is that virtual reality technologies, specifically those that allow for the creation of immersive, simulated worlds, provide a better infrastructure for implementing Nozick's meta-utopian ideal. Thus, to the extent that we think Nozick's meta-utopian ideal is compelling and genuinely utopian, we should wish to create a virtualized version of it. Why would anyone accept this?

The obvious reason is that there are, as we just saw, some serious problems with implementing the meta-utopian idea in the "real" world. These problems dissolve when you try to implement it in a virtual world. How do you allow people to create and join their own preferred possible world in physical reality? This would presumably entail setting up geographically isolated communities that adhere to particular individuals' preferred values. People in those communities would then have to find like-minded souls that are willing to join their community and maintain its integrity. They would have to locate the relevant material and physical resources to sustain the community. They would also have to police the boundaries of the community themselves, or fund and sustain a state that can do this job for them. There would be many physical limits on the possible worlds they could create. The physical world is disappointingly constraining in this respect. It would not be easy for them to create a completely isolated, hermit-like world, if that is what they desire. There would also be many legal and political constraints on the worlds they could create. One of the consequences of human expansion around the globe is that there are few, if any, parts of the world that are not owned by someone or some organization. Setting up a community on someone else's land would be financially costly and legally contentious. Many people simply wouldn't have the resources to do this. Consequently, the capacity to set up isolated utopian communities would be the preserve of the rich. Consider, for example, the techno-utopian dream of sea-steading communities. These are isolated, floating cities / communities that exist in one of the few places not owned or controlled by a single authority: the high seas. Sea-steading communities are not some science fictional dream. There are dedicated groups of individuals who are interested in creating them.[47] They are, however, incredibly expensive to create and maintain—something that might be a twinkle in the eye of a tech billionaire like Peter Thiel,[48] but out of reach for the vast majority of humanity. Nozick's meta-utopia is, consequently, not something that is easily achievable in physical reality.

But most of these practical problems dissolve, or at least ameliorate, if we switch to virtual reality. Computer-simulated worlds are not subject to the same physical and legal limitations. You do not need to access someone else's land to create and join your own preferred virtual world. You can do all this in a simulated environment. This is, consequently, a version of the meta-utopian ideal that can be more widely distributed and not simply the preserve of a wealthy elite. What's more, there can be much greater diversity in the types of possible worlds that can be created in virtual reality. If you want to live a completely isolated, hermit-like existence, you can; if you want to join a community with thousands or millions of others, you can. Some of these others need not be human; they could themselves be simulated characters. We already have prototypes for this kind of virtual existence. Online worlds like Second Life and World of Warcraft provide two, very different, examples of what is possible in virtual reality. They are not totally immersive, and cannot completely replace physical reality, but they showcase the diversity that is possible in a simulated environment and give us a sense of where the technology might lead.

It will also be relatively easier to maintain the boundaries between possible worlds in a virtual meta-utopian architecture. You can keep the would-be imperialists from encroaching on other possible worlds by isolating their simulated world from the others. To keep them happy, you could allow them to play "imperialist games" inside their virtual realms, that is, give them the sense that they are forcefully converting others to their worldview, when in reality they are converting computer-simulated characters. If their lust for imperialism is truly insatiable, you could even trick them into thinking this is real. This is not something I recommend lightly. I previously insisted that there be a knowledge condition embedded into our definition of virtuality, which would seem to rule out this kind of deception. But deception could be justifiably worked into the system as a kind of punishment: individuals and communities that repeatedly attempt to invade other virtual worlds and forcibly convert others could be punished by being locked inside a simulated world that allows them to play these imperialist games without their knowledge. Obviously, the success of this would depend on how immersive the simulation would be, or on our capacity to alter someone's perception of that world so that they think it is real. But, outside of this special case, the virtual instantiation of the meta-utopia does not depend on the virtual world being a completely immersive simulation. As long as it is good enough to keep people engaged—as many of our currently crude simulated realities already seem to be able to do—this is acceptable.

This is not to say that the virtual instantiation of the meta-utopia is without its problems. Obvious questions arise as to who owns and controls the world-building architecture itself. Is this something that will be owned by large technology corporations? Will there be a free market in different world-building mechanisms? Could machines themselves take control (*Matrix*-style)? Could the acceptance of a virtual meta-utopia amount to a kind of technological enslavement, similar to that discussed in the previous chapter? These are important questions. The ideal solution would, presumably, be that the world-building architecture is something that is owned in common and is managed and maintained in such a way that preserves the meta-utopian aim of the system. Creating a constitutional order that does this and protects the system from being taken over by a nefarious actor will be a delicate process, but one that is not radically different from the kinds of constitutional problems humanity has always faced. As for the worry about technological enslavement, this is worth taking seriously, but it should be understood in light of the argument made in the previous chapter: there are many dimensions to freedom. Embracing the virtual meta-utopia might allow us to maximize freedom along some dimensions while limiting it along others. The compromise might be worth it if it brings us closer to a utopian mode of existence.

Another concern is that a virtual meta-utopia won't have the same subjective appeal as Nozick's real-world meta-utopia because it will lack "real stakes." This is a particular problem for me since it is crucial to my definition of the Virtual Utopia that people *know* they are living in a virtual world. Surely no died-in-the-wool imperialist or missionary will be happy playing games in a virtual world? Surely no wannabe scientist will be happy faking experiments in a virtual lab? I hope I have said enough already to convince you that the "real stakes" objection has less force than might first be supposed. Even within simulated virtual worlds, there is a lot of real stuff going on. Furthermore, even in our physical world as currently constituted, many people live lives that are relatively devoid of real stakes—they are not radically reforming our knowledge of the world, building great art, or solving significant moral problems. For them, the virtual meta-utopia would actually be a significant improvement over the status quo. This is not to deny that something will be missing from the virtual meta-utopia for some people. It's just that accepting the absence of *some* real stakes may be a good compromise.

One final point that is worth emphasizing is the relationship between the virtual meta-utopia and the utopia of games. As I see it, these are not mutually exclusive variations on the Virtual Utopia. It is possible for them to co-exist. It's possible to spend some of our time in virtual worlds that are simulated and that correspond with our own preferred conception of what is best; it's also possible to spend some of our time playing games in the physical world. We could also simulate games within a simulated environment. Combining the two visions in this way allows for a strengthened, and more appealing, conception of the Virtual Utopia.

Two General Objections to the Virtual Utopia

I will now address two general objections to the idea of the Virtual Utopia. These objections come at the idea from different angles. They do not target either of the two specific versions of the Virtual Utopia that I discussed above. They stem from general concerns about the kinds of lives we might live in a virtual world.

The first of these objections comes from Robert Nozick. Although I co-opted his work in defense of the virtual meta-utopia, I noted at the outset that Nozick himself would no doubt disapprove. This is because Nozick is famous for having developed another argument that speaks decisively against the idea of a virtual life. I have, in a way, anticipated and responded to parts of this argument in the preceding discussion, but it's worth discussing it on its own, partly because readers with some philosophical background will expect it to be discussed, and partly because in doing so we can further underscore the claim that I have been defending throughout this chapter, namely, that a Virtual Utopia is not something that is completely alien, unintelligible, or undesirable to creatures like us.

Nozick's argument arises out of the following thought experiment:

> Imagine a machine that could give you any experience (or sequence of experiences) you might desire. When connected to this experience machine, you can have the experience of writing a great poem or bringing about world peace or loving someone and being loved in return. You can experience the felt pleasures of these things, how they feel "from the inside." You can program your experiences for . . . the rest of your life. If your imagination is impoverished, you can use the library of suggestions extracted from biographies and enhanced by novelists and psychologists. You can live your fondest dreams "from the inside." Would you choose to do this for the rest of your life? . . . Upon entering the machine you will not remember having done this; so no pleasures will get ruined by realizing they are machine-produced.[49]

This has become known as the "experience machine" thought experiment.[50] Nozick's intuition, and the intuition of many people who have been presented with the thought experiment in classrooms and experimental tests over the years, is that you wouldn't plug into the machine.[51] Nozick uses this result to make the case against hedonism, which is the view that subjective experience is the sole source of value. If you plug into the machine, you are being offered subjective experiences that are as good as, if not far better than, those you would be offered in the "real" world. The fact that most people know this and still resist the idea of being plugged into the experience machine suggests that there is more to value than the hedonist appreciates. Some connection to reality is also important. A truly flourishing human life requires this; we won't (and shouldn't) be satisfied without it.

I have no particular interest in defending hedonism against Nozick's attack. All I am interested in here is whether the experience machine thought experiment also gives some reason to call in question the desirability of the Virtual Utopia. I think it does not, for two important reasons.

The first reason is that the Virtual Utopia is sufficiently different from the experience machine to cast doubt on whether the same intuitive dissatisfaction would hold. As I have repeatedly emphasized throughout this chapter, the Virtual Utopia is not a surrealist dreamworld in which nothing is "real." There is plenty of real stuff going on in it. If we follow the "utopia of games" model, many of our experiences could take place in the real physical world and involve interactions with real physical people. When we are not playing games, we can have relationships and experiences with our family and friends. Even if we follow the "virtual meta-utopia" model, we do not have to live isolated lives inside a computer-simulated environment. We can still interact with other real people, through virtual representations, and have real conversations and real shared experiences with them. In signing up to the Virtual Utopia, you are not being asked to plug into a machine, have your memory wiped clean, and discard everything you have known up until that point. You may lose contact with some aspects of reality as currently conceived, but these will be compensated by other gains. These differences should be sufficient to undermine any attempt to use Nozick's argument to challenge the Virtual Utopia.

The second reason to doubt the relevance of the experience machine argument is that a series of experimental tests of Nozick's thought experiment have revealed that the anti-virtuality intuition that underscores it may not be as robust as Nozick originally supposed. The problem is that Nozick's original formulation of the thought experiment is replete with biases that prompt a negative intuitive reaction. You are being asked to plug into a wholly fake world from your current position in the real world. You are being told that you will not know that you have been plugged into that world. It's not clear that people can really imagine themselves lacking this knowledge, or overcome their attachment to the world as they know it. Backing this up, Felipe De Brigard has performed experimental tests that show how the common intuitive reaction to Nozick's thought experiment may be the result of status quo bias. If you change the formulation so that people are asked to plug out of an experience machine that they have just learned they have been living in, you get a different reaction. Suddenly people are not so keen on the real world.[52] Similarly, Dan Weijers has worked to create a bias-free version of the experience machine thought experiment and to test people's reactions to it. He finds that when you de-bias the thought experiment as much as possible, the experimental results neither support nor deny Nozick's view. In other words, the experimental evidence is neutral on the desirability of the experience machine.[53] This gives further reason to doubt the relevance of the experience machine thought experiment to the assessment of the Virtual Utopia.

There is, however, another general objection to the Virtual Utopia that is worth considering. Unlike Nozick's objection—which criticizes the Virtual Utopia for not being real enough—this one takes the opposite tack and criticizes it for being too real. This objection holds that the Virtual Utopia is not desirable because it offers us a "playground for immorality." Virtual reality is often portrayed to us in popular media and science fiction in these terms. Computer games often allow gamers to perform acts of great cruelty and violence in a simulated form. We seem to tolerate some forms of this, but feel queasier and more uncertain about others, for example, gratuitous sadism or acts of sexual violence are still frowned upon in computer simulated environments.[54] Fantastical projections of what future virtual reality technologies might be like take this a step further. The novel, movie, and now TV series *Westworld* provides possibly the clearest illustration. It suggests that people will use immersive, virtual reality worlds to act out rape and murder fantasies. Donning a virtual reality helmet will, according to this view, be like donning the Ring of Gyges:[55] it will free us from the usual moral constraints of the physical and give us a license for cruelty, depravity, and violence.

The ethics of actions in virtual worlds, particularly actions performed against or toward simulated persons or creatures, are complex and subject to much debate.[56] I myself have many views about them that I have set out in previous work.[57] I am not going to summarize those views here. Two observations do seem appropriate though. First, and in keeping with the general theme of this chapter, I do not think that the mere fact that our actions are performed in a "virtual" world means that they are suddenly free from all moral constraints. Contrary to the popular myth, I think moral standards can and will apply to much of what happens in virtual reality. The moral virtues that we cultivate through our actions in virtual worlds will be every bit as real as those we cultivate in the physical world. This means that people can be rightly criticized and reprimanded for failing to live up to those standards in virtual reality. Furthermore, some of the people with whom we interact in the Virtual Utopia will be real, not simulations or artificial agents. Most of the normal moral rules will apply to our interactions with them. That said, there is no denying that virtuality may require some revision to our moral norms. Actions that we would deem immoral in the real physical world may no longer be immoral in a virtual world. I made this point earlier when discussing immorality in the context of Suits's utopia of games. There, I noted that whether an act of deception or violence counted as being immoral was, to some extent, contingent on both the rules of the game and the consequences of the action. The fact that virtual actions might be easily reversible or repairable, for example, might denude them of their immorality. There is a potential lightness of being in a virtual world that is akin to the lightness of being a cyborg.

That said, the impact of repairability and reversibility on our approach to virtual morality depends, critically, on how much of a role consequences play in our understanding of immorality. If an action is deemed immoral primarily because of its intrinsic qualities, then the fact that its consequences might be reversible or repairable might mean nothing when it comes to its moral assessment. Contrariwise, if its consequences are what matter most, the reversibility and repairability of those consequences might count for a lot. Consider an act of sexual violence (in which there is some kind of nonconsensual sexual touching / penetration) versus an act of physical violence (in which there is touching that occasions some kind of bodily harm). I tend to think that sexual violence is wrong primarily because of its intrinsic qualities (its nonconsensual sexual nature), not because of its consequences. Just because a rape victim is resilient and unperturbed by her assault does not mean that her rape was any less serious. On the other hand, the immorality of physical violence does seem to depend heavily on its consequences. A physical assault that results in serious bodily harm (or psychological trauma) is judged to be morally worse than an assault that results in fleeting discomfort. You could apply this logic to the assessment of acts in a virtual world and hold that, say, acts of sexual violence—performed via virtual representations—should be judged more harshly than acts of physical violence—performed via virtual representations. You could also apply the reasoning more generally in order to determine how many of our moral standards need to be revised when it comes to virtual actions.

The bottom line then is that the Virtual Utopia does not give us the playground for immorality that many people suppose. Many moral rules and standards will apply equally well to virtual actions because they will have a real impact on our character / virtue and on the lives of others. That said, some revision to our moral standards may be required, but will be justified by reference to the criteria of immorality that apply in the physical world. These revisions won't turn the Virtual Utopia into a playground for immorality any more than playing a game of Diplomacy turns deception into a vice. They will simply change what counts as moral / immoral. Furthermore, there will, presumably, be new moral rules that apply specifically to the virtual world, for example, rules of fair play and gamesmanship, or rules that ban the use of viruses to infect a computer-simulated avatar. Far from experiencing a moral drought, inhabitants of the Virtual Utopia will have to develop and adapt their moral systems to get accustomed to their new ways of life. This could represent an exciting new project in exploring the bounds of moral possibility.

This is, of course, to focus solely on whether the virtual nature of our actions gives us some license for immorality. It does not focus on the related question of whether the Virtual Utopia will motivate or entice people to engage in acts of morality—acts that they and everyone else judge to be wrong in spite of their virtual nature. This is to be expected for the obvious reason that lots of people are enticed to immorality in the physical world. Unless we combine the pursuit of the Virtual Utopia with some radical program of cyborg moral enhancement, we cannot expect to change fundamental facts of human nature. So there will still be some need for law and order in the Virtual Utopia. That said, some of the obvious excuses / rationalizations for immorality in the physical world may dissipate in the Virtual World (for example, if we achieve a post-scarcity, abundant society, one of the common motivators of violence and theft would be eliminated), and the automated technologies that sustain and enable the Virtual Utopia could be leveraged to keep the peace.

Conclusion

I want to close this chapter by going back to where it started: Ana Swanson's article about the retreat of young men from the world of work into the world of video games. One of the men profiled in Swanson's article was Danny Izquierdo. At the time of article's publication, Danny was a young man, in his early twenties, who lived in Maryland in the United States. He had a college degree and he had worked at a few odd jobs, but found them all frustrating because he felt his rewards were not matched to his efforts. He preferred to play video games. He said he was attracted to the sense of community and meritocracy that he found within them. The real world, for Danny, was too difficult and too competitive, with no obvious sense of meaning or reward for what he did. Now, I don't want to dwell too much on Danny. He is just one person chosen, probably unfairly, to be emblematic of the more general trend: the retreat from reality. But I do want to see if, after the various twists and turns of this chapter, I can give a clear answer to the question that his attitude prompts: would we be better off by following his lead?

In a famous speech delivered in San Francisco in 1967, the acid-dropping psychologist Timothy Leary counseled his generation to "turn on, tune in, and drop out." He argued that psychedelics were the key to doing this. They were a gateway to a new kind of spiritual enlightenment. Once you had a good trip, you could see the world in a different way. The traditional categories, institutions, and norms no longer made sense. Why slave away for decades to climb the corporate ladder when you could experience a profound sense of oneness with the whole of humanity? Psychedelics haven't gone away since 1967—indeed, they may be experiencing something of a resurgence in popularity[58]—but for this generation the retreat to the virtual holds similar promise.[59] It offers us a mode of existence that is detached from, and free from, many (but not all) of the institutions and concerns of everyday life. Why not embrace it and "drop out" from the competitive demands of the cognitive niche?

To some people this attitude is the knell that rings in the death of human civilization. But I hope to have demonstrated that this is not the case. Embracing the Virtual Utopia does not mean that we must embrace the death of all that is good and pure in human life. On the contrary, it can allow for the highest expressions of human agency, virtue, and talent (in the form of the utopia of games), and the most stable and pluralistic understanding of the ideal society (in the form of the virtual meta-utopia). It offers up a vast horizon of possible worlds into which we can grow and mature. What's more, the idea that this entails giving up on reality rests on a mistaken and naive understanding of what is virtual and what is real. You can never completely remove reality from any form of life. Our experiences, our relationships, our institutions, and many of our actions in a Virtual Utopia will be just as "real" as they ever were. We may have to give up on some things—some severance from objectively valuable ends must be tolerated—but this looks to be the best compromise between obtaining the benefits of advanced automation and ensuring that humans can live a flourishing and meaningful life. In short, the Virtual Utopia could be the utopia we are looking for.

Epilogue
The Unending Quest

I WANT TO END THIS BOOK with some final reflections on human obsolescence and the quest for meaning. I will do so by a reference to Jorge Luis Borges's short story "The Library of Babel." The story is an epistle, written by a librarian, living in a fictional universe that consists of a single, never-ending library. The library is made up of a series of hexagonal galleries, connected by staircases and hallways, repeating indefinitely, in the exact same form, in every direction. The library contains an unimaginably vast number of books, all of the exact same form: 410 pages, 40 lines per page, and 80 characters per line.[1] There are twenty-five possible orthographic symbols that occupy these lines, and each book varies randomly in the symbols it contains. Consequently, in the vastness of the library, all possible books exist.

This story has been subject to many interpretations over the years. Borges was obsessed with the mathematics of the infinite, and some people see it as an attempt to explore and explain the concept of infinity. There is certainly evidence for this interpretation. But I want to offer an alternative interpretation. I see the story more as a meditation on the meaning of life in a universe of infinite possibilities. As Borges notes in the story, because the library contains all possible books, it must contain, somewhere within its recesses, books that explain the secrets of the universe, that set out all possible truths, and that vindicate the life of the reader. Borges's librarian tells us this and also tells us that when the citizens of the library realized this, there was much rejoicing: "When it was announced that the Library contained all books, the first reaction was unbounded joy. All men felt themselves the possessors of an intact and secret treasure. There was no personal problem, no world problem, whose eloquent solution did not exist—somewhere in some hexagon."[2]

But this joy soon turned to despair. Because the vast majority of books in any given hexagon were meaningless gibberish (just symbols arranged in random order), the chances of finding the books that unlocked the riddles of existence were infinitesimal. What's more, even if you did find the books that conveyed the truth, how would you recognize them? The library would also contain a vast number of contradictory books that would refute or deny the truth of any such book, or would offer subtle variations on it that gave you some, but not all, of the truth: "That unbridled hopefulness was succeeded, naturally enough, by a similarly disproportionate depression. The certainty that some bookshelf in some hexagon contained precious books, yet that those precious books were forever out of reach, was almost unbearable."[3]

And yet, despite this realization, the vast majority of people living in the library continue in the unending quest, stumbling through the darkness in the hopes of finding the books that will unlock the mysteries of existence. In fact, this quest seems to be all-consuming. There is no time for anything else in Borges's imaginary world. There is no mention of home or family life; no mention of recreation and leisure; everyone in this imaginary universe is either contributing to, or actively contesting, the quest to make sense of it all.

Although this may be trite and contrived, I think you can view our current predicament—as evolved apes living on the upward arc of an ongoing technological revolution—as being analogous to that of the citizens of Borges's imagined library. Through centuries of technological progress we have been trying to unlock the mysteries of the universe and to achieve mastery over our environment. In the past couple of centuries, we have witnessed accelerating progress in this enterprise. This should be a cause for much rejoicing. But, as we have seen, it can also be a cause for much despair. For there is a paradox at the heart of our technological progress. It has been undertaken to serve human interests and human needs, but at the same time it renders humans themselves obsolescent and threatens to cut them off from traditional sources of value and meaning. This has many people worried, as they scramble desperately to figure out how humans will find a place in this bold new future.

This book has offered several responses to this paradox. It has argued that we should embrace our obsolescence from the world of work, but worry about the impact of automation beyond work. It has argued that the crisis of automation may represent an opportunity for budding utopianists. From the ashes of human life as currently conceived, it has suggested that we can forge a radically better future. It has argued that we can, if we wish, seek to transcend our human limitations and become more like the machines that provoke our obsolescence through a process of cyborgization. This would be an ambitious project with many potential advantages, but also one that carries several risks and may not be practicable in the short- to medium-term future. Alternatively, it has argued that we can embrace our growing obsolescence and retreat to virtual worlds. In doing so, we may have to let go of some long-standing aspirations and hopes, but the costs of this should not be overestimated. We do not have to forgo everything in the retreat to the virtual; and we can pursue some sources of meaning with greater vigor and fewer encumbrances than ever before.

This, then, is the primary message of this book. We shouldn't make the same mistake as Borges's librarians. We shouldn't keep searching through the infinite darkness for something we ourselves can never obtain; we shouldn't sacrifice everything else that is good in life for an unending, and unrealizable, goal.

Notes

1. The Autumn of Humanity

Epigraph: Used with permission from https://kajsotala.fi/.

1. From G. MacCready, "An Ambivalent Luddite at a Technological Feast," *Designfax* (August 1999). Quoted in D. Dennett, *From Bacteria to Bach and Back: The Evolution of Minds* (New York: W. W. Norton, 2017), 8–9.

2. For example Nick Bostrom, "Existential Risk Prevention as a Global Priority," *Global Policy* no. 4 (2013): 15–31; Nick Bostrom, *Superintelligence: Paths, Dangers, Strategies* (Oxford: Oxford University Press, 2014); Olle Haggstrom, *Here Be Dragons: Science, Technology and the Future of Humanity* (Oxford: Oxford University Press, 2016); and Phil Torres, *Morality, Foresight and Human Flourishing: An Introduction to Existential Risks* (Durham, NC: Pitchstone Publishing, 2017).

3. Nicholas Carr, *The Glass Cage: Where Automation Is Taking Us* (London: Bodley Head, 2015).

4. Those with overly optimistic views might include Peter Diamandis and Steven Kotler, *Abundance: The future Is Better than You Think* (New York: Free Press, 2012); and R. Kurzweil, *The Singularity Is Near: When Humans Transcend Biology* (New York: Viking, 2005). Those with overly pessimistic views might include Carr, *The Glass Cage*; Matthew Crawford, *The World Beyond Your Head: How to Flourish in an Age of Distraction* (London: Penguin,

2015); and Brett Frischmann and Evan Selinger, *Re-engineering Humanity* (Cambridge: Cambridge University Press, 2018).

5. Catherine Panter-Brick et al., eds., *Hunter-Gatherers: An Interdisciplinary Perspective* (Cambridge: Cambridge University Press, 2001).

6. Ian Morris, *Foragers, Farmers and Fossil Fuels* (Princeton NJ: Princeton University Press, 2015), 52 and 55.

7. Ibid., 71–92.

8. Charles Mann, *The Wizard and the Prophet: Science and the Future of Our Planet* (London: Picador, 2018).

9. The data comes from Max Roser, "Agricultural Employment," *OurWorldInData.org,* 2017. https://ourworldindata.org/agricultural-employment/.

10. Tom Simonite, "Apple Picking Robot Prepares to Compete for Farm Jobs," *MIT Technology Review,* May 3, 2017, https://www.technologyreview.com/s /604303/apple-picking-robot-prepares-to-compete-for-farm-jobs/; and Nicholas Geranios, "Robotic Fruit Pickers May Help Orchards with Worker Shortage," *Associated Press,* April 28, 2017, https://www.usnews.com/news /best-states/washington/articles/2017-04-28/a-robot-that-picks-apples -replacing-humans-worries-some.

11. Joel Mokyr, *A Culture of Growth: The Origins of the Modern Economy* (Princeton, NJ: Princeton University Press, 2016); and Roger Osborne, *Iron, Steam & Money: The Making of the Industrial Revolution* (London: Pimlico, 2014).

12. Causation is often disputed here. Some think the values drove the material revolution; some think the material revolution drove the values. The wording suggests I favor the latter explanation, but I take no particular stance on the dispute since it does not affect the point being made about the march toward obsolescence. On the link, see Ian Morris, *Foragers,* and Deirdre McCloskey, *Bourgeois Dignity: Why Economics Can't Explain the Modern World* (Chicago: University of Chicago Press, 2010).

13. Eric Brynjolfsson and Andrew McAfee, *The Second Machine Age* (New York: W. W. Norton, 2014).

14. Steven McNamara, "The Law and Ethics of High Frequency Trading," *Minnesota Journal of Law Science and Technology,* no. 17 (2016): 71–152.

15. Michael Wellman and Uday Rajan, "Ethical Issues for Autonomous Trading Agents," *Minds and Machines* 27, no. 4 (2017): 609–624.

16. Ibid., 610.

17. The "flash crash" is the name that is usually applied to an event that took place on May 6, 2010, when the Dow Jones Industrial Average dropped 998.5 points. Trading algorithms (specifically high-frequency trading algorithms)

were initially blamed, though the official report into the incident suggested they played a secondary role. Although the term "flash crash" has become closely associated with that particular event, it can be applied more broadly to any sudden drop in the market. See "Commodities Futures Trading Commission and the Securities Exchange Commission," *Findings Regarding the Market Events of May 6th, 2010*, 2010, https://www.sec.gov/news/studies/2010/marketevents-report.pdf.

18. Jonathan Cohn, "The Robot Will See You Now," *The Atlantic*, March 2013, https://www.theatlantic.com/magazine/archive/2013/03/the-robot-will-see-you-now/309216/; Siddhartha Mukherjee, "AI versus MD: What Happens When Diagnosis Is Automated?" *New Yorker*, April 3, 2017; and Richard Susskind and Daniel Susskind, *The Future of the Professions* (Oxford: Oxford University Press, 2015), chapter 5.

19. The comparison comes from Mukherjee, "AI vs MD."

20. Ibid.

21. Susskind and Susskind, *Future of the Profession*, 48.

22. Eliza Strickland, "Autonomous Robot Surgeon Bests Humans in World First," *IEEE Spectrum*, May 6, 2016, http://spectrum.ieee.org/the-human-os/robotics/medical-robots/autonomous-robot-surgeon-bests-human-surgeons-in-world-first.

23. Robert Sparrow and Linda Sparrow, "In the Hands of the Machines? The Future of Aged Care," *Minds and Machines*, no. 16 (2006): 141–161; Amanda Sharkey and Noel Sharkey, "Granny and the Robots: Ethical Issues in Robot Care for the Elderly," *Ethics and Information Technology*, no. 14 (2010): 27–40; and Mark Coeckelbergh, "Artificial Agents, Good Care, and Modernity," *Theoretical Medical Bioethics*, no. 36 (2015): 265–277.

24. I have argued that it is possible to have a friendly and loving relationship with a robot. I see no reason why it isn't also possible to have a caring relationship with one. See John Danaher, "The Philosophical Case for Robot Friendship," *Journal of Posthuman Studies* 3, no. 1 (2019), https://philpapers.org/rec/DANTPC-3; and John Danaher, "Programmed to Love: Is a Human-Robot Relationship Wrong?" *Aeon Magazine*, March 19, 2018, https://aeon.co/essays/programmed-to-love-is-a-human-robot-relationship-wrong.

25. See, for example, the MARIO project: http://www.mario-project.eu/portal/. On Japanese attitudes to robots, see Jennifer Robertson, *Robo Sapiens Japanicus: Robots, Gender, Family and the Japanese Nation* (Oakland: University of California Press, 2017).

26. For barristers (courtroom specialists in the UK, Ireland, and some other common law jurisdictions) it is still essential to be a member of an Inn of

Court, where one of the qualification requirements is to attend a certain number of dinners.

27. Richard Susskind, *Tomorrow's Lawyers* (Oxford: Oxford University Press, 2013).

28. For details, see the Ross Intelligence website: http://www.rossintelligence.com. See also Jason Koebler, "The Rise of the Robolawyer," *The Atlantic*, April 2017.

29. See https://lexmachina.com for details.

30. F. J. Buera and J. P. Kaboski, "The Rise of the Service Economy," *American Economic Review*, no. 102 (2012): 2540–2569.

31. David Autor, "Why Are There Still So Many Jobs? The History and Future of Workplace Automation," *Journal of Economic Perspectives*, no. 29 (2015): 3–30; and Hans Moravec, *Mind Children* (Cambridge, MA: Harvard University Press, 1988), 15–16.

32. N. Garun, "Amazon Just Launched a Cashier-Free Convenience Store," *The Verge*, December 5, 2016, https://www.theverge.com/2016/12/5/13842592 /amazon-go-new-cashier-less-convenience-store.

33. C. Welch, "Google Just Gave a Stunning Demo of Assistant Making an Actual Phone Call," *The Verge*, May 8, 2018, https://www.theverge.com/2018 /5/8/17332070/google-assistant-makes-phone-call-demo-duplex-io-2018.

34. Oracle, *Can Virtual Experiences Replace Reality? The Future Role for Humans in Delivering Customer Experience*, https://www.oracle.com/webfolder/s /delivery_production/docs/FY16h1/doc35/CXResearchVirtualExperiences .pdf; and A. Zhou, "How Artificial Intelligence Is Transforming Enterprise Customer Service," *Forbes*, February 27, 2017, https://www.forbes.com/sites /adelynzhou/2017/02/27/how-artificial-intelligence-is-transforming -enterprise-customer-service/#7b415c131483.

35. Martin Ford, *The Rise of the Robots: Technology and the Threat of Mass Unemployment* (New York: Basic Books, 2016), 14.

36. M. Robinson, "This Robot-Powered Restaurant Is One Step Closer to Putting Fast-Food Workers Out of a Job," *Business Insider* June 12, 2017, http://uk.businessinsider.com/momentum-machines-funding-robot-burger -restaurant-2017-6?r=US&IR=T.

37. Marco della Cava, "Robots Invade Foodie San Francisco, Promising Low Prices, Tasty Meals and Cheap Labor," *USA Today*, April 8, 2019, https://eu .usatoday.com/story/news/2019/04/06/robots-invade-foodie-san-francisco -promising-low-prices-cheap-labor/3334069002/.

38. The term "automation wave" is taken from Ford, *Rise of the Robots*.

39. Andrew Yang, *The War on Normal People* (New York: Hachette, 2018). Chapter 5 has an extended discussion of the automation of trucking and its possibly negative social consequences.

40. André Gorz, *Critique of Economic Reason* (London: Verso, 1989), 14.

41. Frederick Taylor, *The Principles of Scientific Management* (New York: Harper and Brothers, 1911).

42. Max Weber, *The Theory of Social and Economic Organization* (New York: Free Press, 1947); and R. M. Kanter, "The Future of Bureaucracy and Hierarchy in Organizational Theory," in *Social Theory for a Changing Society*, ed. P. Bourdieu and J. Coleman (Boulder, CO: Westview, 1991).

43. Ian Hacking, *The Emergence of Probability*, 2nd ed. (Cambridge: Cambridge University Press, 2006); E Medina, *Cybernetic Revolutionaries: Technology and Politics in Allende's Chile* (Cambridge, MA: MIT Press, 2011); and E. Morozov, "The Planning Machine: Project Cybersyn and the Origins of the Big Data Nation," October 13, 2014, *New Yorker*, https://www.newyorker.com/magazine/2014/10/13/planning-machine.

44. John Danaher, "The Threat of Algocracy: Reality, Resistance and Accommodation," *Philosophy and Technology*, no. 29 (2016): 245–268; and John Danaher et al., "Algorithmic Governance: Developing a Research Agenda through the Power of Collective Intelligence," *Big Data and Society*, September 19, 2017, https://doi.org/10.1177/2053951717726554.

45. Andrew G. Ferguson, "Policing Predictive Policing," *Washington University Law Review*, no. 94 (2017): 1–78; and Andrew G. Ferguson, *The Rise of Big Data Policing* (New York: NYU Press, 2017).

46. W. Hartzog, G. Conti, J. Nelson, and L. A. Shay, "Inefficiently Automated Law Enforcement," *Michigan State Law Review* (2015): 1763–1795.

47. Luke Dormehl, *The Formula: How Algorithms Solve All Our Problems . . . And Create More* (London: W. H. Allen, 2014), 157–158.

48. For information, see http://www.knightscope.com.

49. H. Shaban, "Automated Police Cars to Start Patrolling the Streets of Dubai before the End of the Year," July 1, 2017, *The Independent*, https://www.independent.co.uk/news/world/middle-east/dubai-automated-police-cars-end-year-a7818661.html.

50. Jamie Susskind, *Future Politics* (Oxford: Oxford University Press, 2018).

51. Richard Dawkins, *The Blind Watchmaker* (London: Longman, 1986), 2.

52. Yuval Noah Harari, *Sapiens: A Brief History of Humankind* (London: Harvill Secker, 2014), chapter 14.

53. For a good illustration of this, see Laura Snyder, *The Philosophical Breakfast Cub* (New York: Broadway, 2011).

54. D. MacKenzie, "The Automation of Proof: A Historical and Sociological Exploration," *IEEE Annals of the History of Computing*, no. 17 (1995): 7–29.

55. G. Conthier, "Formal Proof—The Four-Color Theorem," *Notices of the American Mathematical Society*, no. 55 (2008): 1382–1393.

56. C. Edwards, "Automating Proofs," *Communications of the ACM*, no. 59 (2016): 13–15.

57. M. Harris, "Mathematicians of the Future," *Slate Magazine*, March 15, 2015, https://slate.com/technology/2015/03/computers-proving-mathematical -theorems-how-artificial-intelligence-could-change-math.html.

58. A. Sparkes, W. Aubrey, E. Byrne, A. Clare, M. N. Khan, M. Liakata, M. Markham, J. Rowland, L. N. Soldatova, K. E. Whelan, M. Young, and R. D. King, "Towards Robot Scientists for Autonomous Scientific Discovery," *Automated Experimentation Journal*, no. 2 (2010): 1; and E. Yong, "Enter Adam, the Robot Scientist," April 2, 2009, *National Geographic News*, https://www.nationalgeographic.com/science/phenomena/2009/04/02/enter -adam-the-robot-scientist/.

59. K. Williams, E. Bilsland, A. Sparkes, W. Aubrey, M. Young, L. N. Soldatova, K. de Grave, J. Ramon, M. de Clare, W. Sirawaraporn, S. G. Oliver, and R. D. King, "Cheaper Faster Drug Development Validated by the Repositioning of Drugs against Neglected Tropical Diseases," *Journal of the Royal Society: Interface*, no. 12 (2015); and A. Extance, "Robot Scientist Discovers Potential Anti-Malaria Drug," *Scientific American*, February 5, 2015, https://www.scientificamerican.com /article/robot-scientist-discovers-potential-malaria-drug/.

2. The Case for Technological Unemployment

1. A small sample would include Andrew Yang, *The War on Normal People* (New York: Hachette, 2018); Ryan Avent, *The Wealth of Humans: Work, Power and Status in the 21st Century* (New York: St Martin's Press, 2016); Erik Brynjolfsson and Andrew McAfee, *The Second Machine Age* (New York: W. W. Norton, 2014); Martin Ford, *The Rise of the Robots: Technology and the Threat of Mass Unemployment* (New York: Basic Books, 2015); Richard Susskind and Daniel Susskind, *The Future of the Professions* (Oxford: Oxford University Press, 2015); Mark Reiff, *On Unemployment*, vols. 1 and 2 (London: Palgrave MacMillan, 2015); Calum Chace, *The Economic Singularity: Artificial Intelligence and the Death of Capitalism*, 2nd ed. (San Manteo, CA: Three Cs, 2016); C. B. Frey and M. A. Osborne, "The Future of Employment: How Susceptible

Are Jobs to Automation?" *Technological Forecasting and Social Change*, no. 114 (2017): 254–280; J. Manyika, M. Chui, M. Miremadi, J. Bughin, K. George, P. Willmott, and M. Dewhurst, *A Future That Works: Automation, Employment and Productivity*, McKinsey Global Institute Report, 2017; David Autor, "Why Are There Still So Many Jobs? The History and Future of Workplace Automation," *Journal of Economic Perspectives*, no. 29 (2015): 3–30; and John Danaher, "Will Life Be Worth Living in a World without Work? Technological Unemployment and the Meaning of Life," *Science and Engineering Ethics*, no. 23 (2017): 41–64.

2. Bertrand Russell, *In Praise of Idleness* (London: Routledge, 2004; originally published 1935), 3.

3. John Danaher, "Will Life Be Worth Living in a World Without Work?," 42–43.

4. Peter Fleming, *The Mythology of Work: How Capitalism Persists Despite Itself* (London: Pluto Press, 2017), 1.

5. David Graeber, *Bullshit Jobs: A Theory* (New York: Simon and Schuster, 2018).

6. André Gorz, *Critique of Economic Reason* (London: Verso, 1989).

7. This is a modification and updating of a definition I previously offered in "Will Life Be Worth Living in a World Without Work?"

8. My colleague Sven Nyholm suggests that philosophers might have a nitpicky objection to my definition. They might argue that since my definition focuses on economically rewarded activity, and since, presumably, machines will not be economically rewarded for their activity, machines cannot really eliminate work (because once the activity is performed by a machine, it is no longer economically rewarded and it no longer counts as work). But, of course, this truly is nit-picking. The point is that machines can replace activities that *previously counted* as work. Indeed, it is the slow erosion of such activities that is the heart of the case for technological unemployment.

9. Danaher, "Will Life Be Worth Living?"

10. Frey and Osborne, "The Future of Employment."

11. Manyika et al., *A Future That Works*, and J. Manyika, M. Chui, M. Miremadi, J. Bughin, K. George, P. Willmott, and M. Dewhurst, *Harnessing Automation for a Future That Works*, McKinsey Global Institute, January 2017.

12. PriceWaterhouseCooper, *Will Robots Really Steal Our Jobs? An International Analysis of the Long Term Potential of Automation*, https://www.pwc.com/hu/hu/kiadvanyok/assets/pdf/impact_of_automation_on_jobs.pdf.

13. Larry Elliott, "Robots to Replace 1 in 3 UK Jobs over Next 20 Years, Warns IPPR," *The Guardian*, April 15, 2017, https://www.theguardian.com/technology/2017/apr/15/uk-government-urged-help-low-skilled-workers-replaced-robots.

14. For example, R. D. Atkinson, and J. Wu, *False Alarmism: Technological Disruption and the U.S. Labor Market, 1850–2015*, ITIF @Work Series (Washington, D.C.: Information Technology and Innovation Foundation, 2017).

15. Frey and Osborne, "The Future of Employment," 263.

16. Manyika et al, *A Future That Works*, 4–5.

17. Ibid., 5–6.

18. The phrase is taken from Brynjolfsson and McAfee, *The Second Machine Age*.

19. Estimates for the rate of new jobs can be found in Darren Acemoglu and Pascual Restrepo, "The Race between Man and Machine: Implications of Technology for Growth, Factor Shares, and Employment," *American Economic Review*, no. 108 (2018): 1488–1542.

20. This is, effectively, the argument in Atkinson and Wu, "False Alarmism."

21. These effects are discussed in Brynjolfsson and McAfee, *The Second Machine Age*, and Autor "Why Are There Still So Many Jobs."

22. The focus on comparative advantage is central to the model for understanding technology and automation that is developed in Acemoglu and Restrepo, "The Race between Man and Machine."

23. Set out in full in Autor, "Why Are There Still So Many Jobs?"

24. World Economic Forum, Centre for the New Economy and Society, *The Future of Jobs Report 2018*, http://www3.weforum.org/docs/WEF_Future_of _Jobs_2018.pdf. For a similar argument, see also R. Jesuthasan and J. Boudreau, *Reinventing Jobs: A 4-Step Approach to for Applying Automation to Work* (Cambridge, MA: Harvard Business Press, 2018).

25. Darren Acemoglu and Pascual Restrepo, "Robots and Jobs: Evidence from US Labor Markets," NBER Working Paper no. 23285, March 2017.

26. Ibid., 4.

27. Ibid., 4–5.

28. Ibid., figure 1.

29. Acemoglu and Restrepo, "The Race between Man and Machine."

30. Brynjolfsson and McAfee, *The Second Machine Age;* and Ray Kurzweil, *The Singularity Is Near: When Humans Transcend Biology* (New York: Viking, 2005).

31. These figures come from the American Trucking Association: https://www .trucking.org/News_and_Information_Reports_Industry_Data.aspx. They are consistent with the results from the US Bureau of Labor Statistics for 2016: https://www.bls.gov/emp/tables/employment-by-major-industry-sector.htm.

32. This might be confusing. A positive feedback loop is one in which an effect is continuously amplified, not equilibrated, over time; a negative feedback loop

is one in which an effect is equilibrated. The use of the terms "positive" or "negative" has nothing to do with whether the effect is a good or bad thing.

33. E. Pol and J. Reveley, "Robot Induced Technological Change: Toward a Youth-Focused Coping Strategy," *Psychosociological Issues in Human Resource Management,* no. 5 (2017): 169–186.

34. Bryan Caplan, *The Case against Education* (Princeton, NJ: Princeton University Press, 2018).

35. On this idea, see Nicholas Rescher, *Scientific Progress: A Philosophical Essay on the Economics of Research in Natural Science* (Pittsburgh: University of Pittsburgh Press, 1978); and Joseph Tainter, *The Collapse of Complex Civilisations* (Cambridge: Cambridge University Press, 1988), chapter 4.

36. Nicholas Bloom, Charles Jones, John Van Reenen, and Michael Webb, "Are Ideas Getting Harder to Find?" NBER Working Paper, version 2.0, March 5, 2018, https://web.stanford.edu/~chadj/IdeaPF.pdf.

37. Erik Brynjolfsson, Daniel Rock, and Chad Syverson, "Artificial Intelligence and the Modern Productivity Paradox: A Clash of Expectations and Statistics," NBER Working Paper no. 24001, November 2017.

38. Ibid., 18.

39. Michael Polanyi, *The Tacit Dimension* (Chicago: University of Chicago Press, 1966).

40. Hans Moravec, *Mind Children* (Cambridge, MA: Harvard University Press, 1988).

41. Autor "Why Are There Still So Many Jobs?" 26.

42. Daniel Susskind presents a more formal economic model that captures this idea in a working paper: "A Model of Technological Unemployment," Oxford University Discussion Paper no. 819, July 2017.

43. Jerry Kaplan, *Humans Need Not Apply* (New Haven, CT: Yale University Press, 2015).

44. Sherwin Rosen, "The Economics of Superstars," *American Economic Review,* no. 71 (1981): 845–858, 845.

45. Tyler Cowen, *Average Is Over* (London: Dutton, 2013); and Robert Frank, *Success and Luck* (Princeton, NJ: Princeton University Press, 2016).

46. Jeremy Rifkin, *The Zero Marginal Cost Society* (London: Palgrave Mac-Millan, 2014).

47. It is trotted out in Frey and Osborne, "The Future of Employment."

48. Darren Acemoglu and Jason Robinson, *Why Nations Fail* (New York: Random House, 2012), 182.

49. Martin Upchurch and Phoebe Moore, "Deep Automation and the World of Work," in *Humans and Machines at Work,* ed. P. Moore, M. Upchurch, and X. Whitakker, 45–71 (London: Palgrave MacMillan, 2017); and a similar point about policy / regulation and automation is made in Anthony Atkinson, *Inequality: What Is to Be Done?* (Cambridge, MA: Harvard University Press, 2015).

50. Philippe Van Parijs and Yannick Vanderborght, *Basic Income: A Radical Proposal for a Free Society and a Sane Economy* (Cambridge, MA: Harvard University Press, 2017); Rutger Bregman, *Utopia for Realists: And How We Can Get There* (London: Bloomsbury, 2017); and Ford, *Rise of the Robots.*

3. Why You Should Hate Your Job

1. John Danaher, "Will Life Be Worth Living in a World without Work? Technological Unemployment and the Meaning of Life," *Science and Engineering Ethics,* no. 23 (2017): 41–64.

2. I offered a preview of this argument in a short article published in 2018. See John Danaher, "The Case against Work," *Philosopher's Magazine,* no. 81 (2018): 90–94.

3. Elizabeth Anderson, *Private Government: How Employers Rule Our Lives (And Why We Don't Talk about It)* (Princeton, NJ: Princeton University Press, 2017).

4. Gerald Gaus, *The Order of Reason* (Cambridge: Cambridge University Press, 2010); and Gerald Gaus, *Contemporary Theories of Liberalism* (London: Sage, 2003).

5. For overviews of the debate, see Quentin Skinner, "The Genealogy of Liberty," public lecture, University of California–Berkley, September 15, 2008; Philip Pettit, *Just Freedom* (New York: W. W. Norton, 2014); and Philip Pettit, *Republicanism* (Oxford: Oxford University Press, 1997).

6. There may also be a third school of thought—"positive freedom"—which holds that freedom is the authentic expression of the self. See Skinner, "The Genealogy of Liberty," for more on this third conception. It is often associated with thinkers like Arendt and Hegel.

7. Alan Ryan, *The Making of Modern Liberalism* (Princeton, NJ: Princeton University Press, 2012).

8. Pettit, *Just Freedom,* xiv.

9. Ibid., xv.

10. Tyler Cowen, "Work Isn't So Bad after All," a response essay to Elizabeth Anderson that appears in Anderson, *Private Government,* 108–116.

11. Anderson, *Private Government,* 134–135.

12. Ibid., 136–137.

13. Phoebe Moore, *The Quantified Self in Precarity* (London: Routledge, 2017); and Gordon Hull and Frank Pasquale, "Toward a Critical Theory of Corporate Wellness," *BioSocieties*, no. 13 (2018): 190–212.

14. D. Silverberg, "The Company That Pays Its Staff to Sleep," *BBC News,* June 20, 2016. As a further illustration of this, in September 2018, the insurance company John Hancock announced that it will give incentives to anyone willing to submit to health and fitness tracking on its life insurance policies. See C. Wischover, "A Life Insurance Company Wants to Track Your Fitness Data," *Vox.com*, September, 20, 2018, https://www.vox.com/the-goods/2018/9 /20/17883720/fitbit-john-hancock-interactive-life-insurance.

15. Moore, *The Quantified Self in Precarity,* has a nice case study on this with a Dutch company.

16. Anderson, *Private Government,* 66–69.

17. David Frayne, *The Refusal of Work* (London: ZED Books, 2015).

18. I take the term "functionally agentless" from J. M. Hoye and J. Monaghan, "Surveillance, Freedom and the Republic," *European Journal of Political Theory*, no.17 (2018): 343–363.

19. Andrew Weil, *The Fissured Workplace: How Work Became So Bad for So Many and What Can Be Done about It* (Cambridge, MA: Harvard University Press, 2014); Guy Standing, *The Corruption of Capitalism: Why Rentiers Thrive and Work Does Not Pay* (London: Biteback Publishing, 2016); and Guy Standing, *The Precariat: The New Dangerous Class* (London: Bloomsbury, 2011).

20. Weil, *The Fissured Workplace,* chapter 2 discusses this at length.

21. Ibid., 7–8.

22. Ibid., 270–271,

23. Standing, *The Corruption of Capitalism;* and Erik Brynjolfsson and Andrew McAfee, *Machine, Platform, Crowd* (New York: W. W. Norton, 2017).

24. Standing, *The Corruption of Capitalism,* 210.

25. For an excellent description of how this plays out, see Alex Rosenblat, *Uberland: How Algorithms Are Rewriting the Rules of Work* (Oakland: University of California Press, 2018).

26. J. Manyika, S. Lund, J. Bughin, K. Robinson, J. Mischke, and D. Mahajan, *Independent Work: Choice, Necessity, and the Gig Economy,* McKinsey Global Institute Report, 2016.

27. Ronald Coase, "The Nature of the Firm," *Economica,* no. 4 (1937): 386–405.

28. Weil, *The Fissured Workplace,* 60.

29. Ibid., 62.

30. Ibid., chapter 8.

31. Weil, *The Fissured Workplace,* 88–91. There is some complexity here. As Standing points out in *The Corruption of Capitalism* (216–217), some digital platform providers are backed by a significant amount of venture capital and can operate at a loss while they are growing their customer base. This means they can sometimes afford to pay workers premium rates as they try to defeat any competitors. This has happened with Uber as it has expanded around the world. Thus, workers can experience a short-term gain as firms try to gain dominance in a market. The longer-term prospects, however, are grim, as once dominance has been achieved, the platform providers can set prices at a level that is less good for workers. This has also happened in American cities in which Uber now dominates: Uber drivers earn noticeably less than taxi drivers once did.

32. Standing, *The Corruption of Capitalism,* 217–232.

33. *Uber B.V. and Others vs. Mr. Y. Aslam and Others,* UKEAT/0056/17/DA, judgment delivered on November 10, 2017.

34. *Uber B.V. and Others vs. Aslam and Others* [2018], EWCA Civ 2748,

35. M. Taylor, G. Marsh, D. Nicol, and P. Broadbent, *Good Work: The Taylor Review of Modern Working Practices,* July 2017, https://assets.publishing .service.gov.uk/government/uploads/system/uploads/attachment_data/file /627671/good-work-taylor-review-modern-working-practices-rg.pdf.

36. S. Butler, "Deliveroo Wins the Right Not to Give Riders Minimum Wage or Holiday Pay," *The Guardian,* November 14, 2017, https://www.theguardian .com/business/2017/nov/14/deliveroo-couriers-minimum-wage-holiday-pay; and also "Deliveroo Wins Latest Battle Over Riders Rights", *BBC News* 5 December 2018, https://www.bbc.com/news/business-46455190.

37. I focus on pay here, though non-pay benefits are probably not equally shared either. I discuss this in more detail later in this chapter. See Christian Timmerman, "Contributive Justice: An Exploration of the Wider Provision of Meaningful Work," *Social Justice Research,* no. 31 (2018): 85–111, for more on this important topic.

38. Two caveats: (i) the justifiability of differences due to skill and effort depends, in part, on whether you think individuals are personally responsible for that effort and skill—this may not always be the case; (ii) in a world of machine-mediated innovation, the need to incentivize human-led innovation may not arise.

39. These figures come from a report prepared by Oxfam entitled "An Economy for the 99%" for the World Economic Forum: https://policy-practice .oxfam.org.uk/publications/an-economy-for-the-99-its-time-to-build-a -human-economy-that-benefits-everyone-620170.

40. Thomas Piketty, *Capital in the Twenty-First Century* (Cambridge, MA: Harvard University Press, 2014), and Anthony Atkinson, *Inequality: What Is to Be Done?* (Cambridge, MA: Harvard University Press, 2015).

41. Piketty, *Capital,* 303–304.

42. Note that Piketty and his colleagues have a particular methodology for estimating total income that can be challenged. Some of the figures they use—particularly those relating to labor income—are fairly robust as they are based on national income tax return statements. Others—particularly those relating to capital income—require more guesswork and estimation.

43. All the figures come from Piketty, *Capital,* 311.

44. David Autor, "Why Are There Still So Many Jobs? The History And Future of Workplace Automation," *Journal of Economic Perspectives,* no. 29 (2015): 3–30.

45. Ibid., 9–14.

46. Ibid., 18.

47. Piketty, *Capital,* 396–397.

48. Ibid., 397ff.

49. Ibid., 403.

50. Ibid., 404.

51. C. D. Goldin, and L. Katz, *The Race between Education and Technology: The Evolution of US Educational Wage Differentials, 1890–2005* (Cambridge, MA: Harvard University Press, 2010).

52. For this argument, see Piketty, *Capital;* Bryan Caplan, *The Case against Education* (Princeton, NJ: Princeton University Press, 2018); and Ryan Avent, *The Wealth of Humans* (New York: St Martin's Press, 2016).

53. Piketty, *Capital,* 395–396.

54. Ibid., 387–388.

55. Though note that recent French labor market reforms will have some impact on this.

56. As Walter Scheidel notes in *The Great Leveler* (Princeton, NJ: Princeton University Press, 2017), there is a general historical trend toward increased inequality in any society that produces a social surplus. It is very difficult to

redress this trend without a major calamity such as climate change, mass warfare, or disease.

57. Frayne, *The Refusal of Work*, 70.

58. Some people argue that "leisure" is itself a work-saturated concept, meaning that it only makes sense in a society that is organized around work. The true oasis of unmediated life is idleness, which is genuinely undirected activity. On this point, see Brian O'Connor's wonderful philosophical essay *On Idleness* (Princeton, NJ: Princeton University Press, 2018).

59. Steven Pinker, *Enlightenment Now: The Case for Reason, Science, Humanism, and Progress* (London: Penguin, 2018).

60. Marshall Sahlins, *Stone Age Economics* (Chicago: Aldine-Atherton, 1972).

61. Jonathan Crary, *24/7: Late Capitalism and the End of Sleep* (London: Verso, 2014).

62. Frayne, *The Refusal of Work*, 73ff.

63. Ibid., 75.

64. Heather Boushey, *Finding Time: The Economics of Work-Life Conflict* (Cambridge, MA: Harvard University Press, 2016).

65. Ibid., 54–57 and 60–61.

66. Ibid., 63.

67. Ibid., 68. Ironically, Pinker in his optimistic and upbeat book *Enlightenment Now* cites similar figures as evidence of a positive change in family life, suggesting that we now have more time for such family-related activities. Boushey argues that it is evidence of increased stress and expectations around "helicopter" parenting.

68. Boushey, *Finding Time*, 74.

69. Ibid., 79–80.

70. Ibid., 77.

71. Arlie Hochschild, *The Outsourced Self* (New York: Picador, 2012).

72. Scott Peppet, "Unraveling Privacy: The Personal Prospectus and the Threat of a Full Disclosure Future," *Northwestern University Law Review*, no. 105 (2011): 1153.

73. Gallup, "State of the Global Workplace Report 2013," http://www.gallup .com/services/178517/state-global-workplace.aspx; and also S. Crabtree, "Worldwide 13% of Employees Are Engaged at Work," *Gallup News*, October 8, 2013, http://news.gallup.com/poll/165269/worldwide-employees-engaged -work.aspx.

74. Gallup, "State of the Global Workplace Report 2017: Executive Summary," http://news.gallup.com/reports/220313/state-global-workplace-2017 .aspx#formheader.

75. Ibid., 8.

76. Ibid., 4, 9, and 14.

77. Daniel Kahneman and Angus Deaton, "High Income Improves Evaluation of Life But Not Emotional Well-being," *Proceedings of the National Academy of Sciences*, no. 107 (2010): 16489–16493.

78. E. Ortiz-Ospina and M. Roser, "Happiness and Life Satisfaction," Our World in Data, https://ourworldindata.org/happiness-and-life-satisfaction; and B. Stevenson and J. Wolfers, "Economic Growth and Subjective Wellbeing: Reassessing the Easterlin Paradox," *Brookings Papers on Economic Activity* (Spring 2008), 1–87.

79. Anca Gheaus and Lisa Herzog, "The Goods of Work (Other Than Money)," *Journal of Social Philosophy*, no. 47 (2016): 70–89. They don't call it the structural goodness thesis and they don't make it explicitly in response to anti-work arguments. Consequently, it is difficult to say whether they are pro-work or not. Norman Bowie also defends a similar view in his paper "Dignity and Meaningful Work," in *The Oxford Handbook of Meaningful Work*, ed. R. Yeoman, C. Bailey, A. Madden, and M. Thompson, 36–50 (Oxford: Oxford University Press, 2018).

80. In brief: social status in the sense of social recognition and validation is important; social status in the sense of achieving some sense of superiority over another is much less so.

81. Timmerman "Contributive Justice"; and Michele Loi, "Technological Unemployment and Human Disenhancement," *Ethics and Information Technology*, no. 17 (2015): 201–210.

82. Derek Parfit, *On What Matters*, vol. 1 (Oxford: Oxford University Press, 2011); K. Lazari-Radek and P. Singer, *The Point of View of the Universe: Sidgwick and Contemporary Ethics* (Oxford: Oxford University Press, 2014).

4. Giving Techno-Pessimism Its Due

1. There are several examples of this. Bob Black has written an extremely popular and influential argument against work, detailing various ways in which it impedes our flourishing, but when it comes time to describe his preferred post-work reality he resorts to general and vague descriptors. He talks about the possibility of a "ludic" (game-playing) life without adequately defending or explaining why this vision should appeal to us. See Bob Black,

The Abolition of Work and Other Essays (Port Townshend, WA: Loompanics Unlimited, 1986). Similarly, Nick Srnicek and Alex Williams in their book *Inventing the Future* (London: Verso, 2015) present an excoriating, Marxist critique of work that is disappointingly vague when it comes time to articulate the post-work reality. Instead, they favor a view in which the post-work world is a project that needs to be pursued in the right way. There is some wisdom to this. As we will see in later chapters, utopian projects that are too precise in their visions often mutate into dystopias and fail to be fully persuasive. Still, some reassurance that the project is proceeding along the right lines is required, and that's what I hope to provide in the remainder of this book.

2. Ben Bramble, *The Passing of Temporal Well-Being* (London: Routledge, 2018).

3. G. Fletcher, *The Philosophy of Well-Being: An Introduction* (London: Routledge, 2016); B. Bradley, *Wellbeing* (London: Polity Press, 2015); and D. Haybron, *The Pursuit of Unhappiness: The Elusive Psychology of Wellbeing* (Oxford: Oxford University Press, 2010).

4. Ben Bramble, "A New Defense of Hedonism about Well-Being," *Ergo,* no. 3 (2016): 4, https://quod.lib.umich.edu/e/ergo/12405314.0003.004?view =text;rgn=main; and C. Heathwood, "Desire Satisfactionism and Hedonism," *Philosophical Studies,* no. 128 (2006), 539–563.

5. I use the awkward phrase "objectively determined states of being" because the states in question are still ones that occur to individuals and are experienced by them, subjectively. It's just that the assessment of whether or not they are satisfied is something that is objectively decided.

6. G. Fletcher, "Objective List Theories," in *The Routledge Handbook of Philosophy of Well-Being,* ed. G. Fletcher, 148–160 (London: Routledge, 2016).

7. Martha Nussbaum, *Creating Capabilities: The Human Development Approach* (Cambridge, MA: Harvard University Press, 2011); and Amartya, Sen *Development as Freedom* (Oxford: Oxford University Press, 1999).

8. Thaddeus Metz, *Meaning in Life: An Analytic Study* (Oxford: Oxford University Press, 2013); Iddo Landau, *Finding Meaning in an Imperfect World* (Oxford: Oxford University Press, 2017); and Aaron Smuts, "The Good Cause Account of Meaning in Life," *Southern Journal of Philosophy,* no. 51(2013): 536–562.

9. I take this, in modified form, from S. Campbell and S. Nyholm, "Anti-Meaning and Why It Matters," *Journal of the American Philosophical Association,* no. 1 (2015): 694–711, who argue that there are four schools of thought. I have blended together two of their schools of thought.

10. Richard Taylor, "The Meaning of Life," in *The Meaning of Life,* ed. E. D. Klemke and Steven M. Cahn, chapter 12 (New York: Oxford University Press,

2008); and Gwen Bradford, *Achievement* (Oxford: Oxford University Press, 2016).

11. Thaddeus Metz, "The Good, the True, and the Beautiful: Toward a Unified Account of Great Meaning in Life," *Religious Studies*, no. 47 (2011): 389–409.

12. Susan Wolf, *Meaning in Life and Why It Matters* (Princeton, NJ: Princeton University Press, 2010).

13. William L. Craig, *Reasonable Faith*, 3rd ed. (Downers Grove, IL: Intervarsity Press, 2007); and John Cottingham, *The Spiritual Dimension* (Cambridge: Cambridge University Press, 2005).

14. Landau, *Finding Meaning*, chapter 5.

15. Thaddeus Metz, "The Immortality Requirement for Life's Meaning," *Ratio*, no. 16 (2003): 161–177; and Daniel Weijers, "Optimistic Naturalism: Scientific Advancement and the Meaning of Life," *Sophia*, no. 53 (2013): 1–18.

16. Gianluca Di Muzio, "Theism and the Meaning of Life," *Ars Disputandi* 6 (2006): 128–139.

17. John Danaher, "Why We Should Create Artificial Offspring: Meaning and the Collective Afterlife," *Science and Engineering Ethics*, no. 24 (2018): 1097–1118.

18. In personal correspondence, Sven Nyholm points out that apart from considerations of intellectual humility and convenience, there are good reasons to favor the ecumenical approach. As he puts it "the sorts of things people tend to take pleasure in or desire to have in their lives tend to match up with the sorts of things that objective list theorists put on their lists of objective goods. For example, people get pleasure from and desire things like love, friendship, art, mastery / skills, knowledge, and so on." I discuss this important point again in Chapter 7 when I discuss Nozick's meta-utopian theory.

19. For example, Catholic natural law theory, influenced as it is by Aristotle's account of the good life, would effectively agree with the objective list approach to flourishing outlined in the text. On this see John Finnis, *Natural Law and Natural Rights* (Oxford: Oxford University Press, 1979).

20. Jean Baudrillard, *La Guerre du Golfe n'a pas eu lieu* (Paris: Galilée, 1991).

21. The term was invented by the psychologist James Gibson. He used it to refer to the things afforded to an animal or human by their environment. He argued that it arose from a complementarity between the animal and the material environment. For example, the handle on a cup, when complemented by the existence of a hand that could grasp the handle, creates an affordance.

22. Plato, *The Phaedrus*, 274d.

23. Richard Heersmink, "A Taxonomy of Cognitive Artifacts: Function, Information and Categories," *Review of Philosophical Psychology,* no. 4 (2013): 465–481; Richard Heersmink, "Extended Mind and Cognitive Enhancement: Moral Aspects of Extended Cognition," *Phenomenal Cognitive Science,* no. 16 (2017): 17–32; D. Kirsh "Thinking with External Representations," *AI and Society,* no. 25 (2010): 441–454; D. Kirsh, "The Intelligent Use of Space," *Artificial Intelligence* no. 73 (1995): 31–68; D. Norman "Cognitive Artifacts," in *Designing Interaction: Psychology at the Human-Computer Interface,* ed. J. M. Carroll, 17–38 (Cambridge: Cambridge University Press, 1991); and Matthew Crawford, *The World beyond Your Head: How to Flourish in an Age of Distraction* (London: Penguin, 2015).

24. Norman "Cognitive Artifacts," and Heersmink "A Taxonomy of Cognitive Artifacts."

25. Heersmink, "A Taxonomy of Cognitive Artifacts," 465–466.

26. Ibid., and Kirsch "Thinking with External Representations."

27. David Krakauer, "Will AI Harm Us? Better to Ask How We'll Reckon with Our Hybrid Nature," *Nautilus,* September 6, 2016, http://nautil.us/blog/will-ai -harm-us-better-to-ask-how-well-reckon-with-our-hybrid-nature.

28. Norman, "Cognitive Artifacts."

29. Philippe Van Parijs and Yannick Vanderborght, *Basic Income: A Radical Proposal for a Free Society and a Sane Economy* (Cambridge, MA: Harvard University Press, 2017); K. Widerquist, J. Noguera, Y. Vanderbroght, and J. de Wispelaere, *Basic Income: An Anthology of Contemporary Research* (Sussex: Wiley-Blackwell, 2013); Jeremy Rifkin, *The Zero Marginal Cost Society* (London: Palgrave MacMillan, 2014); Martin Ford, *The Rise of the Robots: Technology and the Threat of Mass Unemployment* (New York: Basic Books, 2015); and Erik Brynjolfsson and Andrew McAfee, *The Second Machine Age* (New York: W. W. Norton, 2014).

30. Unless, of course, the technologies push us toward life in a virtual world. I discuss this in more detail in later chapters.

31. Gwen Bradford, *Achievement;* and Gwen Bradford "The Value of Achievements," *Pacific Philosophical Quarterly,* no. 94 (2012): 202–224.

32. Nyholm argues that humans could be seen to form collaborative partnerships with automating technologies, which might allow us to attribute responsibility to them for the actions performed on their behalf by the automating technologies. This is only going to be true, however, if humans can set the goals and targets for the machines and maintain some supervisory control over what they do. Furthermore, even if Nyholm is correct that this

will enable us to attribute legal or moral responsibility to the humans that control the machines, it does not follow that this will allow us to attribute achievements to them. Achievement is a different thing. See Sven Nyholm, "Attributing Agency to Automated Systems: Reflections on Human–Robot Collaborations and Responsibility-Loci," *Science and Engineering Ethics*, no. 24 (2018): 1201–1219.

33. Excluding problems of interpersonal morality and duty. The focus in the text is really on problems of axiological deprivation.

34. See, for example, Cathy O'Neil, *Weapons of Math Destruction* (London: Penguin, 2016); Virginia Eubanks, *Automating Inequality: How High-Tech Tools Profile, Police and Punish the Poor* (New York: St. Martin's Press, 2018); and Safiya Noble, *Algorithms of Oppression* (New York: NYU Press, 2018).

35. For examples of robot art, I recommend checking out the robot art competition at https://robotart.org. For examples of robot musicians, I recommend M. Bretan and G. Weinberg "A Survey of Robotic Musicianship," *Communications of the ACM* 59, no. 5 (2016): 100–109. Other useful sources include David Cope's algorithmic composer EMI, which is described in the book *Virtual Music* (Cambridge, MA: MIT Press, 2001); Simon Colton, "The Painting Fool: Stories from Building an Automated Painter," in *Computers and Creativity*, ed. J. McCormack and M. d'Inverno, 3–38 (Berlin: Springer Verlag, 2012); and the papers contained in the special section—"Rethinking Art and Aesthetics in the Age of Creative Machines"—of the journal *Philosophy and Technology* 30, no. 3 (2017). I would like to thank an anonymous reviewer for directing me to these sources.

36. Indeed, Einstein was famously racing against David Hilbert to formulate the general theory.

37. Crawford, *The World beyond Your Head*; Mark Bartholomew, *Adcreep: The Case against Modern Marketing* (Stanford, CA: Stanford University Press, 2017); Tim Wu, *The Attention* Merchants (London: Atlantic Books, 2017); and Adam Alter, *Irresistible* (London: Bodley Head, 2017).

38. One caveat here: on a purely objectivist theory of meaning, my individual experiences may not matter to how meaningful my life actually is. The philosopher Aaron Smuts in "The Good Cause Account of Meaning in Life" illustrates this point by using the example of George Bailey in *It's a Wonderful Life*. Bailey tries to commit suicide on Christmas Eve because he so depressed with his life. An angel visits him to show him what an important contribution he makes to the lives of others living in his town and to talk him down from the ledge. Smuts argues that Bailey's life has been meaningful all along, he just didn't realize it. I ignore the purely objectivist theories here because (a) they

apply to meaning only, not to well-being, and (b) I think theories of meaning that fuse the objective and subjective are more plausible.

39. W. Gallagher, *Rapt: Attention and the Focused Life* (New York: Penguin Random House, 2009).

40. Robert Wright, *Why Buddhism Is True* (New York: Simon and Schuster, 2017).

41. Mihaly Cskikszentmihalyi, *Flow: The Psychology of Optimal Experience* (New York: Harper & Row, 1990); Mihaly Cskikszentmihalyi, *Finding Flow: The Psychology of Engagement with Everyday Life* (New York: Basic Books, 1997); and Mihaly Cskikszentmihalyi, *Experience Sampling Method: Measuring the Quality of Everyday Life* (Thousand Oaks, CA: Sage Publications, 2007).

42. On these points, see Alter, *Irresistible*, Bartholomew, *Adcreep*, and Wu, *The Attention Merchants*.

43. The one major exception would be absorbing video games that do enable you to develop certain skills and allow you to enter into flow states. I discuss games, in general, as a utopian project in Chapter 7.

44. Shoshana Zuboff, "Big Other: Surveillance Capitalism and the Prospects of an Information Civilization," *Journal of Information Technology* 30, no. 1 (2015): 75–91; and Shoshana. Zuboff, *The Age of Surveillance Capitalism* (London: Profile Books, 2019)

45. Wu discusses the attention-sapping power of the state and religion in *The Attention Merchants*.

46. Nick Bostrom and Toby Ord, "The Reversal Test: Eliminating Status Quo Bias in Applied Ethics," *Ethics*, no. 116 (2006): 656–679.

47. On this, see Hubert Dreyfus and Sean Dorrance Kelly, *All Things Shining* (New York: Free Press, 2011), chapter 3; and Walter Burkert, *Greek Religion*. (Cambridge, MA: Harvard University Press, 1987).

48. B. F. Skinner, "'Superstition' in the Pigeon," *Journal of Experimental Psychology*, no. 38 (1948): 168–172.

49. Sean Carroll, "Why Is There Something Rather Than Nothing?," 2018, http://arxiv.org/abs/1802.02231v1.

50. Charles Mann, *The Wizard and the Prophet* (London: Picador, 2018); and L. Hesser, *The Man Who Fed the World* (Dallas, TX: Durban House, 2006).

51. S. Grimm, "The Value of Understanding," *Philosophy Compass*, no. 7 (2012): 103–117.

52. Linda Zagzebski, *Virtues of the Mind* (Cambridge: Cambridge University Press, 1996); and Linda Zagzebski, "Recovering Understanding," in *Knowl-*

edge, Truth, and Duty: Essays on Epistemic Justification, Responsibility, and Virtue, ed. M. Steup, 235–252 (Oxford: Oxford University Press, 2001).

53. Duncan Pritchard, "Knowing the Answer, Understanding and Epistemic Value," *Grazer Philosophische Studien,* no. 77 (2008): 325–339.

54. John Danaher, "The Threat of Algocracy: Reality, Resistance and Accommodation," *Philosophy and Technology,* no. 29 (2016): 245–268; Jenna Burrell, "How the Machine Thinks: Understanding Opacity in Machine Learning Systems," *Big Data and Society,* DOI: 10.1177/2053951715622512; and Frank Pasquale, *The Black Box Society* (Cambridge, MA: Harvard University Press, 2015).

55. Andrew Ferguson, *The Rise of Big Data Policing* (New York: NYU Press, 2017).

56. V. Mayer-Schonberger and K. Cukier *Big Data: A Revolution That Will Transform How We Live, Work and Think* (London: John Murray, 2013); and Sabina Leonelli, *Data-Centric Biology: A Philosophical Study* (Chicago: Chicago University Press, 2016).

57. Burrell, "How the Machine Thinks."

58. It may even be that most technical experts do not understand them.

59. For some good case studies on this, see Eubanks, *Automating Inequality,* and Noble, *Algorithms of Oppression.*

60. S. Sloman and P. Fernbach, *The Knowledge Illusion* (New York: Riverhead Books, 2017).

61. Nicholas Carr, *The Glass Cage: Where Automation Is Taking Us* (London: Bodley Head, 2015).

62. Rob Kitchin, "Thinking Critically about and Researching Algorithms," *Information, Communication and Society,* no. 20 (2017): 14–29.

63. Sandra Wachter, Brent Mittelstadt, and Luciano Floridi, "Why a Right to Explanation of Automated Decision-Making Does Not Exist in the General Data Protection Regulation," *International Data Privacy Law Journal,* no. 7 (2017): 76–99; and Andrew Selbst and Julia Powles, "Meaningful Information and the Right to Explanation," *International Data Privacy Law Journal,* no. 7 (2017): 233–242.

64. Danaher, "The Threat of Algocracy."

65. C. Edwards, "Automating Proofs," *Communications of the ACM,* no. 59 (2016): 13–15.

66. I use these terms somewhat interchangeably. I follow Gerald Dworkin, "The Concept of Autonomy," *Grazer Philosophische Studien* 12 (1981):

203–213 in believing that "freedom" is a property of particular decisions made by an agent, whereas "autonomy" is a property of the agent themselves, across several decisions.

67. Gerald Gaus, *The Order of Public Reason* (Cambridge: Cambridge University Press, 2010).

68. Michael Hauskeller, "The 'Little Alex' Problem," *Philosophers' Magazine,* no. 62 (2013): 74–78; Michael Hauskeller, "Is It Desirable to Be Able to Do the Undesirable? Moral Bioenhancement and the Little Alex Problem," *Cambridge Quarterly of Healthcare Ethics,* no. 26 (2017): 365–376.

69. For an illustration of this, see Brian Leiter, "The Case Against Free Speech," *Sydney Law Review,* no. 38 (2016): 407–439. I have, myself, defended an alternative to both of these views and claimed that autonomy is an *axiological catalyst,* that is, something that makes good things better and bad things worse. John Danaher, "Moral Enhancement and Moral Freedom: A Critique of the Little Alex Problem," in *Moral Enhancement: Critical Perspectives,* ed. M. Hauskeller and L. Coyne, 233–250, Philosophy Supplement (Cambridge: Cambridge University Press, 2018).

70. For critical perspectives on this, see Derk Pereboom, *Free Will, Agency and Meaning in Life* (Oxford: Oxford University Press, 2014); and Drew Chastain "Can Life Be Meaningful without Free Will?," *Philosophia* (2019), https://doi .org/10.1007/s11406-019-00054-y.

71. Joseph Raz, *The Morality of Freedom* (Oxford: Oxford University Press, 1986), 373.

72. Carr, *The Glass Cage.*

73. Krakauer, "Will AI Harm Us?"

74. Richard Thaler and Cass Sunstein, *Nudge: Improving Decisions about Health, Wealth and Happiness* (London: Penguin, 2009).

75. Barry Schwartz, *The Paradox of Choice: Why Less Is More* (New York: Harper Collins, 2004); and B. Scheibehenne, R. Greifeneder, and P. M. Todd, "Can There Ever Be Too Many Options? A Meta-analytic Review of Choice Overload," *Journal of Consumer Research,* no. 37 (2010): 409–425.

76. This is not hyperbolic. As noted in Chapter 3, insurance companies already provide such schemes, and automated systems are widely used to control access to government benefits. See Hull and Pasquale, "Towards a Critical Theory of Corporate Wellness," and Eubanks, *Automating Inequality,* on both.

77. Karen Yeung, "'Hypernudge': Big Data as a Mode of Regulation by Design," *Information, Communication and Society,* no. 20 (2017): 118–136.

78. Thaler and Sunstein, *Nudge.*

79. For more on the idea, see Marjolein Lanzing, "'Strongly Recommended' Revisiting Decisional Privacy to Judge Hypernudging in Self-Tracking Technologies," *Philosophy and Technology* (2018), https://doi.org/10.1007/s13347-018-0316-4.

80. J. M. Hoye and J. Monaghan, "Surveillance, Freedom and the Republic," *European Journal of Political Theory,* no. 17 (2018): 343–363.

81. I originally defended this argument in John Danaher, "The Rise of the Robots and the Crisis of Moral Patiency," *AI and Society* (2017), DOI: 10.1007 / s00146-017-0773-9.

82. David Gunkel, *The Machine Question* (Cambridge: Cambridge University Press, 2011); and David Gunkel, *Robot Rights* (Cambridge: Cambridge University Press, 2018).

83. See Danaher, "The Rise of the Robots," and Danaher, "Moral Enhancement and Moral Freedom," for more on this conception of agency.

84. Gunkel, *The Machine Question,* 94.

85. There is now an active debate about whether robots / AIs can be moral agents / patients. I am sidestepping that debate for the time being. Gunkel's *Robot Rights* covers this in detail.

86. It may be very minimal. A sea slug may have the capacity to feel pain and so count as a moral patient, but we might not take this very seriously and seek to protect it at all costs.

87. Shannon Vallor, "Moral Deskilling and Upskilling in a New Machine Age: Reflections on the Ambiguous Future of Character," *Philosophy and Technology,* no. 28 (2014): 107–124; and Shannon Vallor, *Technology and the Virtues* (Oxford: Oxford University Press, 2016).

88. On these reasons, see Danaher, "The Rise of the Robots," and Gunkel, *The Machine Question,* 89.

89. Nick Bostrom, *Superintelligence: Paths, Dangers, Strategies* (Oxford: Oxford University Press, 2014); Roman Yampolskiy, *Artificial Superintelligence: A Futuristic Perspective* (Boca Raton, FL: Chapman and Hall / CRC Press, 2015); and Olle Haggström, *Here Be Dragons: Science, Technology and the Future of Humanity* (Oxford: Oxford University Press, 2016).

90. Steven Pinker, "The Cognitive Niche: Coevolution of Intelligence, Sociality, and Language," *Proceedings of the National Academy of Sciences,* no. 107 (2010, Supplement 2): 8993–8999.

91. Joseph Henrich, *The Secrets of Our Success* (Princeton, NJ: Princeton University Press, 2015).

5. In Search of Utopia

1. David Bramwell, *The No. 9 Bus to Utopia* (London: Unbound, 2014).

2. Ibid., 154.

3. Ibid., 157.

4. Ibid., 163.

5. Whether it deserves that label or not is a matter of some dispute. See Howard Segal, *Utopias: A Brief History from Ancient Writings to Virtual Communities* (Oxford: Wiley-Blackwell, 2012), 47–50, for an alternative view.

6. It is probably worth noting the etymology of the word "utopia." It comes from the combination of the Greek words "*ou*" and "*topos*" and translates, roughly, as "no place," suggesting that More was being ironic with his title.

7. Ruth Levitas, *The Concept of Utopia* (London: Phillip Allan, 1990).

8. J. C. Davis, *Utopia and the Ideal Society: A Study of English Utopian Writing 1516–1700* (Cambridge: Cambridge University Press, 1981).

9. Steven Pinker, in his book *Enlightenment Now* (London: Penguin, 2018) argues that, going by the medieval myth, we've already achieved the Cockaygne because we (in the West at least) live in a surreally bounteous world.

10. This is taken directly from an interview I did with Christopher Yorke for the podcast I run on my blog *Philosophical Disquisitions:* C. Yorke, and J. Danaher, *Episode 37—Yorke on the Philosophy of Utopianism* (I), http:// philosophicaldisquisitions.blogspot.com/2018/03/episode-37-york-on -philosophy-of.html.

11. Ibid.

12. David Lewis famously argued that all possible worlds exist in *On the Plurality of Worlds* (Oxford: Oxford University Press, 1986).

13. This makes no assumptions about whether or not metaphysical determinism is true or false. According to determinism, there is only one possible future, which means that there is only one way in which things can pan out. Even if this is true, we may not be able to perfectly predict what this is going to be. Consequently, from our epistemic perspective, there are still multiple possible futures.

14. This thought is not original to me. Many discussions of "ideal theory" in political philosophy make use of the possible worlds concept. For a lengthy discussion of this, see Gerald Gaus, *The Tyranny of the Ideal: Justice in Diverse Society* (Princeton, NJ: Princeton University Press, 2016).

15. Owen Flanagan, *The Geography of Morals: Varieties of Moral Possibility* (Oxford: Oxford University Press, 2018).

16. Ibid., chapters 8–10.

17. Ibid., 215.

18. Karl Popper, "Utopia and Violence," in *Conjectures and Refutations,* 2nd ed. (London: Routledge, 2002).

19. Ibid., 481.

20. Ibid., 483.

21. See "Letters of Note" for the text of the letter that Huxley sent to Orwell after the publication of *1984:* http://www.lettersofnote.com/2012/03/1984-v -brave-new-world.html.

22. David Harvey, *Seventeen Contradictions and the End of Capitalism* (London: Profile Books, 2014).

23. Thomas Hobbes, *Leviathan,* ed. C. B. MacPherson (London: Pelican Books, 1968; originally published 1651), part 1, chapter 13.

24. Immanuel Kant, *Perpetual Peace and Other Essays,* trans. Ted Humphrey (Indianapolis, IN: Hackett Publishing, 1983).

25. Francis Fukuyama, "The End of History," *National Interest,* no. 16 (1989): 3–18.

26. There is another argument worth considering here, which is that stability is, strictly speaking, impossible. Contrary to what Kant believes, there will always be the possibility of some new frontier of exploration opening up, and as long as there is that possibility, perpetual peace is impossible. Christopher Yorke makes this argument in his essay "Prospects for Utopia in Space," in *The Ethics of Space Exploration,* ed. James Schwartz and Tony Milligan, 61–71 (Dordrecht: Springer, 2016).

27. Ian Crawford, "Space, World Government, and the 'End of History,'" *Journal of the British Interplanetary Society,* no. 46 (1993): 415–420, 415.

28. Oscar Wilde, "The Soul of Man Under Socialism," *Fortnightly Review,* no. 292 (1891).

29. H. G. Wells, *A Modern Utopia* (Lincoln: University of Nebraska Press, 1967; originally published 1905), 5.

30. Yorke, "Prospects for Utopia in Space."

31. L. A. Paul, *Transformative Experience* (Oxford: Oxford University Press, 2014), 1.

32. Ibid., 2.

33. Paul evaluates many counterarguments to her skepticism in her book and does, in the end, argue that there is a kind of way to justify decision-making in the absence of experiential knowledge.

34. Christopher Yorke, "Endless Summer: What Kinds of Games Will Suits's Utopians Play?" *Journal of the Philosophy of Sport*, no. 44 (2017): 213–228.

6. The Cyborg Utopia

1. All the information about Harbisson is taken from his webpage: www
.neilharbisson.org, as well as from S. Jeffries, "Interview—Neil Harbisson: The World's First Cyborg Artist," *The Guardian*, May 6, 2014, https://www
.theguardian.com/artanddesign/2014/may/06/neil-harbisson-worlds-first-cyborg
-artist; and M. Donahue, "How a Color-Blind Artist Became the World's First Cyborg," *National Geographic*, April 3, 2017, https://news.nationalgeographic
.com/2017/04/worlds-first-cyborg-human-evolution-science/.

2. Or should that be Catalonia?

3. To be clear, Harbisson does not view his implant, even in its initial form, as a matter of compensation. He conceives of it as a way to create a new organ for seeing. See Donahue, "How a Color-Blind Artist Became the World's First Cyborg," on this point.

4. The quotes are taken from Jeffries, "Interview—Neil Harbisson."

5. Ibid.

6. Kevin Warwick, "Cyborgs—the Neuro-Tech Version," in *Implantable Bioelectronics—Devices, Materials and Applications*, ed. E. Katz, 115–132 (New York: Wiley, 2013); Kevin Warwick, "The Future of Artificial Intelligence and Cybernetics," in *There's a Future: Visions for a Better World*, ed. N. Al-Fodhan (Madrid: BBVA Open Mind, TF Editores, 2013); and Kevin Warwick, "The Cyborg Revolution," *Nanoethics*, no. 8 (2014): 263–273.

7. Mark O'Connell, *To Be a Machine* (London: Granta, 2017), 139. In saying this, Tim is allying himself with the broader transhumanist movement, though he may reject this label. Many transhumanists are proponents of cyborgification. They want to expand the possibility horizon for humanity by technologically aug-menting their bodies and escaping their evolved limitations. The transhumanist movement has strongly utopian leanings, so much so that some people have argued that it is intrinsically utopian, though this is rejected by others. On this, see Nick Bostrom, "A Letter from Utopia," 2010, https://nickbostrom.com/utopia
.pdf; Nick Bostrom, "Why I Want to Be Post-human When I Grow Up," in *Medical Enhancement and Posthumanity*, ed. B. Gordjin and R. Chadwick (Dordrecht: Springer, 2009); Michael Hauskeller, "Reinventing Cockaigne: Utopian Themes in Transhumanist Thought," *Hastings Center Report*, no. 42 (2012): 39–47; and Stefan Sorgner Lorenz, "Transhumanism in the Land of Cokaygne," *Trans-humanities*, no. 11 (2018): 161–184.

8. The idea that evolution is an optimizing process is rejected by biologists. It is generally viewed as a satisficing process.

9. Manfred E. Clynes and Nathan S, Kline, "Cyborgs and Space," *Astronautics,* September 1960, 26–27, 74–76.

10. Ibid., 27.

11. Ibid.

12. Amber Case, "We Are All Cyborgs Now," TED Talk, December 2010, https://www.ted.com/talks/amber_case_we_are_all_cyborgs_now; Donna Haraway, *Simians, Cyborgs and Women: The Reinvention of Nature* (New York: Routledge, 1991); Andy Clark *Natural-Born Cyborgs: Minds, Technologies and the Future of Human Intelligence* (Oxford: Oxford University Press, 2003).

13. David Gunkel, "Resistance Is Futile: Cyborgs, Humanism and the Borg," in *The Star Trek Universe: Franchising the Final Frontier,* ed. Douglas Brode and Shea T. Brose, 87–98 (New York: Rowman and Littlefield, 2015).

14. Gunkel identifies a third sense in his work: the ontological. This is based on the work of Donna Haraway and other scholars in the humanities. Haraway claims that we are ontological cyborgs because the classificatory boundaries between humans and other entities have become increasingly blurry in the recent past. Haraway argues that this is true in at least two respects. First, the boundary between humans and animals is much less distinct than it used to be. Capacities such as sentience, rationality, problem-solving, and morality have all traditionally been taken to be unique to humanity, but many now argue that (a) such capacities can be (and are) shared by animals, and (b) perhaps more importantly, are not obviously shared by all humans either. Thus the boundary between the human and animal has been deconstructed. Second, the same has happened with the boundary between human and machine. More and more machines are capable of doing things that were once thought to be uniquely human. I don't discuss the ontological sense of what it means to be a cyborg in the main text because to the extent that it provides the basis for a utopian vision I think it can be captured, adequately, by the conceptual sense of what it means to be a cyborg.

15. Clark, *Natural-Born Cyborgs.*

16. Andy Clark and David Chalmers, "The Extended Mind," *Analysis,* no. 58 (1998): 7–19.

17. Orestis Palermos, "Loops, Constitution and Cognitive Extension," *Cognitive Systems Research,* no. 27 (2014): 25–41; and Adam Carter and Orestis Palermos, "Is Having Your Computer Compromised a Personal Assault? The Ethics of Extended Cognition," *Journal of the American Philosophical Association,* no. 2 (2016): 542–560.

18. These examples are taken from Carter and Palermos, "Is Having Your Computer Compromised a Personal Assault?"

19. Richard Heersmink, "Distributed Cognition and Distributed Morality: Agency, Artifacts and Systems," *Science and Engineering Ethics*, no. 23 (2017): 431–448, 434.

20. The three pathways are set out in Warwick, "The Cyborg Revolution."

21. For a more detailed overview of the experiments on this technique, see Warwick, "Cyborgs—the Neuro-Tech Version"; Warwick, "The Future of Artificial Intelligence and Cybernetics"; and T. DeMarse, D. Wagenaar, A. Blau, and S. Potter, "The Neurally Controlled Animat: Biological Brain Acting with Simulated Bodies," *Autonomous Robotics*, no. 11(2001): 305–310.

22. Warwick, "The Cyborg Revolution," 267.

23. It's worth noting here that conservatism is, itself, a contested ideology. People who call themselves "conservatives" often have different moral outlooks and different understandings of what that means. For some it is a purely epistemological idea, relatively devoid of substantive content; for others it has some very specific substantive content. For an opinionated overview and introduction to conservatism, I recommend Ted Honderich, *Conservatism: Burke, Nozick, Bush, Blair?* (London: Pluto Press, 2005); and Kieron O'Hara, *Conservatism* (London: Reaktion Books, 2011).

24. O'Hara, *Conservatism*.

25. G. A. Cohen, "Rescuing Conservatism," in *Reasons and Recognition: Essays on the Philosophy of T. M. Scanlon*, ed. R. J. Wallace, R. Kumar, and S. Freeman, 203–230 (Oxford: Oxford University Press, 2011); and G. A. Cohen, "Rescuing Conservatism: A Defense of Existing Value," in *Finding Oneself in the Other*, ed. K. Otsuka, 143–174 (Princeton, NJ: Princeton University Press, 2012).

26. To be clear, I no longer think that *The Lord of the Rings* is as wonderful a book as I used to. I believe it was Terry Pratchett who once said that if you are twelve years old and you don't think *The Lord of the Rings* is the best book ever, there is probably something wrong with you. But if you are fifty-two years old and think the same thing, there is probably also something wrong with you. I'm not quite fifty-two yet, but Tolkien's spell has worn off.

27. Jonathan Pugh, Guy Kahane, and Julian Savulescu, "Cohen's Conservatism and Human Enhancement," *Journal of Ethics*, no. 17 (2013): 331–354.

28. This is an argument set out in Pugh, Kahane, and Savulescu "Cohen's Conservatism," and John Danaher "An Evaluative Conservative Case for Biomedical Enhancement," *Journal of Medical Ethics*, no. 42 (2016): 611–618.

29. Danaher, "An Evaluative Conservative Case," 612.

30. Examples would include Nicholas Agar, *Truly Human Enhancement* (Cambridge, MA: MIT Press, 2013); Matthew Crawford, *The World beyond Your Head: How to Flourish in an Age of Distraction* (London: Penguin, 2015); and Brett Frischmann and Evan Selinger, *Re-engineering Humanity* (Cambridge: Cambridge University Press, 2018).

31. This term comes from the work of Richard Dawkins *The Blind Watchmaker* (London: Penguin, 1986).

32. John Danaher, "Hyperagency and the Good Life—Does Extreme Enhancement Threaten Meaning?" *Neuroethics*, no. 7 (2014): 227–242; John Danaher, "Human Enhancement, Social Solidarity and the Distribution of Responsibility," *Ethical Theory and Moral Practice*, no. 19 (2016): 359–378; David Owens, "Disenchantment," in *Philosophers without Gods*, ed. L. Antony, 165–178 (Oxford: Oxford University Press, 2007).

33. Ted Chu, *Human Purpose and Transhuman Potential* (San Rafael, CA: Origin Press, 2014).

34. Pierre Teilhard de Chardin, *The Phenomenon of Man* (New York: Harper, 1965).

35. For a detailed exploration of the techno-utopian themes, see Manu Saadia, *Trekonomics: The Economics of Star Trek* (San Francisco, CA: Pipertext Publishing, 2016).

36. As with any sprawling fictional series, there are severe inconsistencies in the world of *Star Trek*. Money may not exist, but trade certainly does, and several of the species do use money. These points are addressed in Saadia, *Trekonomics.*

37. Christopher Yorke, "Prospects for Utopia in Space," in *The Ethics of Space Exploration*, ed. James Schwartz and Tony Milligan, 61–71(Dordrecht: Springer, 2016); and Christopher Yorke and John Danaher, "Episode 37—Yorke on the Philosophy of Utopianism," interview with the author, 2018, http://philosophicaldisquisitions.blogspot.com/2018/03/episode-37-york-on-philosophy-of.html.

38. Christopher Yorke, "Prospects for Utopia in Space," 67.

39. Ian Crawford, "Space, World Government, and the 'End of History,'" *Journal of the British Interplanetary Society*, no. 46 (1993): 415–420; and Ian Crawford, "Stapledon's Interplanetary Man: A Commonwealth of Worlds and the Ultimate Purpose of Space Colonisation," *Journal of the British Interplanetary Society*, no. 65 (2012): 13–19; Ian Crawford, "Avoiding Intellectual Stagnation: The Starship as an Expander of Minds," *Journal of the British Interplanetary Society*, no. 67 (2014): 253–257.

40. On this point, see Keith Abney, "Robots and Space Ethics," in *Robot Ethics 2.0: From Autonomous Cars to Artificial Intelligence,* ed. P. Lin, R. Jenkins and K. Abney, 354–368 (Oxford: Oxford University Press, 2017).

41. Karl Popper, "Three Worlds," in *Tanner Lectures on Human Values,* University of Michigan, April 7, 1978, https://tannerlectures.utah.edu/_documents/a-to-z/p/popper80.pdf.

42. Tony Milligan, *Nobody Owns the Moon: The Ethics of Space Exploitation* (Jefferson, NC: McFarland, 2015); and James Schwartz and Tony Milligan, eds., *The Ethics of Space Exploration* (Dordrecht: Springer, 2016).

43. Christopher Ketcham, "Towards an Ethic of Life," *Space Policy,* no. 38 (2016): 48–56.

44. There is one possible exception to this. According to a position known as anti-natalism, being alive is a very bad thing. Life is full of underappreciated suffering and harm. It would, consequently, be better if humanity went slowly extinct. To the extent that the elimination of suffering can be understood as a utopian project, this would seem to be an exception to the pro-survivalist position I advocate in the text. Anti-natalism is an unusual view but it has its dedicated and erudite advocates. I ignore it here both because I find it too counterintuitive and because I think the proponent of the Cyborg Utopia should be open to the possibility that the suffering that worries the anti-natalist can be eliminated through technological reform of our hardware. In other words, the problem with anti-natalism is that it is too fatalistic about the human condition. It assumes things are never going to get sufficiently better to make life worth living. For a sophisticated defense of anti-natalism, I recommend David Benatar, *Better Never to Have Been* (Oxford: Oxford University Press, 2006); and David Benatar, "Still Better Never to Have Been: A Reply to (More) of My Critics," *Journal of Ethics,* no. 17 (2012): 121–151.

45. James Schwartz, "Our Moral Obligation to Support Space Exploration," *Environmental Ethics,* no. 33 (2011): 67–88; Seth D. Baum, Stuart Armstrong, Timoteus Ekenstedt, Olle Häggström, Robin Hanson, Karin Kuhlemann, Matthijs M. Maas, James D. Miller, Markus Salmela, Anders Sandberg, Kaj Sotala, Phil Torres, Alexey Turchin, and Roman V. Yampolskiy, "Long Term Trajectories of Human Civilisation," *Foresight* (2018), DOI 10.1108/FS-04-2018-0037; and Abney, "Robots and Space Ethics."

46. Nick Bostrom, "Astronomical Waste: The Opportunity Cost of Delayed Technological Development," *Utilitas,* no. 15 (2003): 308.

47. Ketcham, "The Ethic of Life."

48. Phil Torres, "Space Colonization and Suffering Risks: Reassessing the 'Maxipok' Rule," *Futures,* no. 100 (2018): 74–85.

49. Christopher Davenport, *The Space Barons* (New York: Public Affairs, 2018).

50. John Danaher, "Why We Should Create Artificial Offspring: Meaning and the Collective Afterlife," *Science and Engineering Ethics*, no. 24 (2018): 1097–1118.

51. Samuel Scheffler, *Death and the Afterlife* (Oxford: Oxford University Press, 2013).

52. This is the plot of the book / film *The Children of Men*—Scheffler makes numerous references to this in his book.

53. Scheffler, *Death and the Afterlife*, 43.

54. This is a modified version of the argument originally presented in Danaher, "Why We Should Create."

55. Iddo Landau, *Finding Meaning in an Imperfect World* (Oxford: Oxford University Press, 2017), 66–67.

56. For an excellent, fair-minded analysis of these arguments, see James Warren, *Facing Death: Epicurus and His Critics* (Oxford: Clarendon Press, 2005).

57. Bernard Williams, "The Makropulus Case: Reflections on the Tedium of Immortality," *Problems of the Self* (Cambridge: Cambridge University Press, 1972).

58. Aaron Smuts, "Immortality and Significance," *Philosophy and Literature*, no. 35 (2011): 134–149.

59. Jorge Luis Borges, *The Aleph*, trans. Andrew Hurley (New York: Penguin, 1998), 14.

60. Tyler Cowen, *Average Is Over* (London: Dutton, 2013); Geoff Mulgan, *Big Mind: How Collective Intelligence Can Change the World* (Princeton, NJ: Princeton University Press, 2017); Thomas Malone, *Superminds: The Surprising Power of People and Computers Thinking Together* (London: Oneworld, 2018).

61. Arno Nickel, "Zor Winner in an Exciting Photo Finish," *Infinity Chess*, 2017, http://www.infinitychess.com/Page/Public/Article/DefaultArticle.aspx?id=322.

62. O'Connell, *To Be A Machine*, 6.

63. The claim I am making is not that unusual when it comes to important social values. There are all sorts of impossibility proofs in social choice theory and mathematics that show that it is impossible to satisfy certain seemingly desirable constraints at the same time. Kenneth Arrow's "impossibility theorem" is the classic example. It shows that it is impossible to create a perfectly democratic voting system. There are many other examples of this.

See, for example, John Roemer, *Equality of Opportunity* (Cambridge, MA: Harvard University Press, 1998).

64. Frederic Gilbert gives examples from a phenomenological study of patients with predictive brain implants—they don't feel the technology to be something "other" from them that undermines their autonomy. On the contrary, they see it as an autonomy-enhancing device. See Frederic Gilbert, "A Threat to Autonomy? The Intrusion of Predictive Brain Implants," *American Journal of Bioethics: Neuroscience*, no. 6 (2015): 4–11.

65. M. Ienca and P. Haselager, "Hacking the Brain: Brain-Computer Inter-facing Technology and the Ethics of Neurosecurity," *Ethics and Information Technology*, no. 18 (2016): 117–129.

66. Marc Goodman, *Future Crimes* (London: Bantam Press, 2015).

67. Frischmann and Selinger, *Re-engineering Humanity*.

68. Ibid., chapters 10 and 11.

69. For lengthier discussions of the risk of becoming borg-like, see Gunkel, "Resistance Is Futile," and R. Lipschulz and R. Hester, "We Are Borg: Assimila-tion into the Cellular Society," in *Uberveillance and the Social Implications of Microchip Implants: Emerging Technologies,* ed. M. G. Michael and Katina Michael, 366–384 (IGI Global, 2014).

70. *Star Trek* fans will know that I am simplifying. There are episodes in which some individuality emerges or is restored, and one major plotline in *Star Trek: The Next Generation* revolves around an attempt to introduce individuality into the Borg society. Furthermore, in the film *Star Trek: First Contact* it emerges that there is a single Queen that sits atop the Borg society, and she does have some sense of individuality.

71. Larry Siedentop, *Inventing the Individual* (London: Penguin, 2012).

72. Yes, the Latin is anachronistic.

73. Torres, "Space Colonization and Suffering Risks," 84.

74. As is much of the other reasoning in the existential risk debate, like Bostrom, "Astronomical Waste," and Brian Tomasik, "Risks of Astronomical Future Suffering," Foundational Research Institute, 2018, https://foundational-research.org/risks-of-astronomical-future-suffering/.

75. I hate to reference *Star Trek* again, but there is an interesting episode of *The Next Generation* that explores this idea. Following a thrilling intergalactic archaeology adventure, the crew of the Enterprise learns that all the major alien races in the galaxy (Vulcan, Klingon, Romulan, and Human) are evolved from a common ancestral species. But since they have taken different evolu-

tionary routes from that common ancestor, they have become violent and antagonistic toward one another.

76. Torres, "Space Colonization and Suffering Risks," 81.

77. Milan M. Ćirković, "Space Colonization Remains the Only Long-Term Option for Humanity: A Reply to Torres," *Futures*, no. 105 (2019): 166–173.

78. Ingmar Persson and Julian Savulescu, *Unfit for the Future: The Need for Moral Enhancement* (Oxford: Oxford University Press, 2012).

79. Charles S. Cockell, *Extra-Terrestrial Liberty: An Enquiry into the Nature and Causes of Tyrannical Government beyond the Earth* (London: Shoving Leopard, 2013).

80. Koji Tachibana, "A Hobbesian Qualm with Space Settlement," *Futures* (2019), https://doi.org/10.1016/j.futures.2019.02.011.

81. Neil Levy, *Neuroethics* (Cambridge: Cambridge University Press, 2007).

82. Clark and Chalmers, "The Extended Mind."

83. Jan-Hendrik Heinrichs, "Against Strong Ethical Parity: Situated Cognition Theses and Transcranial Brain Stimulation," *Frontiers in Human Neuroscience*, no. 11 (2017): Article 171: 1–13.

84. Ibid., 11.

85. Agar, *Truly Human Enhancement*, chapter 3.

7. The Virtual Utopia

1. Ana Swanson, "Why Amazing Video Games Could Be Causing a Problem for America," *Washington Post*, September 23, 2016, https://www.washingtonpost.com/news/wonk/wp/2016/09/23/why-amazing-video-games-could-be-causing-a-big-problem-for-america/?utm_term=.68400043e6bd.

2. See Erik Hurst, :Video Killed the Radio Star," 2016, http://review.chicagobooth.edu/economics/2016/article/video-killed-radio-star.

3. Andrew Yang, *The War on Normal People* (New York: Hachette Books, 2018), chapter 14.

4. Nicholas Eberstadt, *Men without Work* (West Conshohocken, PA; Templeton Press, 2016).

5. P. Zimbardo and N. Coulombe, *Man Disconnected* (London: Rider, 2015).

6. A. Przybylski, "Electronic Gaming and Psychosocial Adjustment," *Pediatrics*, no. 134 (2014), http://pediatrics.aappublications.org/content/pediatrics/early/2014/07/29/peds.2013-4021.full.pdf.

7. I am not the first to appeal to Nozick's framework as a response to techno-logical threats. David Runciman makes a similar appeal in his book *How Democracy Ends* (London: Profile Books, 2018). Runciman's discussion is, however, quite brief. I dedicate far more critical attention to the philosophical merits of Nozick's position.

8. These definitions are dotted throughout Jaron Lanier, *Dawn of the New Everything: A Journey through Virtual Reality* (London: Bodley Head, 2017).

9. Neal Stephenson, *Snow Crash* (London: Roc, 1993), 19.

10. For example, Lanier describes Stephenson as the "Apollonian scholar" of the early VR movement. See Lanier, *Dawn of the New Everything*, 246.

11. Jordan Belamire, "My First Virtual Reality Groping," *Athena Talks: Medium*, October 20, 2016.

12. I cannot find the original source for this quote, but it is widely attributed to McKenna.

13. Yuval Noah Harari, *Sapiens: A Brief History of Humankind* (London: Harvill Secker, 2014); and Yuval Noah Harari, *Homo Deus* (London: Harvill Secker, 2016).

14. Yuval Noah Harari, "The Meaning of Life in a World without Work," *The Guardian*, May 8, 2017, https://www.theguardian.com/technology/2017/may/08/virtual-reality-religion-robots-sapiens-book.

15. Ibid.

16. Ibid.

17. Ibid.

18. Ibid.

19. Philip Brey, "The Physical and Social Reality of Virtual Worlds," in *The Oxford Handbook of Virtuality*, ed. M. Grimshaw, 42–54 (Oxford: Oxford University Press, 2014). There are other complex and nuanced accounts of the relationship between virtual reality and reality, for example: Michael Heim, *The Metaphysics of Virtual Reality* (New York: Oxford University Press, 1993); Michael Heim, *Virtual Realism* (New York: Oxford University Press, 1998); Edward Castronova, *Synthetic Worlds: The Business and Culture of Online Games* (Chicago: University of Chicago Press, 2005); and Edward Castronova, "Exodus to the Virtual World: How Online Fun Is Changing Reality" (New York: Palgrave Macmillan, 2007).

20. John Searle, *The Construction of Social Reality* (New York: Free Press, 1995); John Searle, *Making the Social World* (Oxford: Oxford University Press, 2010).

21. The name, obviously, comes from the *Matrix* movies, which imagine a future world in which machines hook humans up to an elaborate simulation of the real world and make them think that it is real.

22. Bernard Suits, *The Grasshopper: Games, Life and Utopia* (Calgary: Broadview Press, 2005; originally published 1978).

23. Mike McNamee, *Sports, Virtues and Vices: Morality Plays* (London: Routledge, 2008).

24. Graham McFee, *Sports, Rules and Values* (London: Routledge, 2003), chapter 8.

25. Thomas Hurka, "Games and the Good," *Proceedings of the Aristotelian Society* 675, no. 106 (2006): 217–235; and Thomas Hurka, *The Best Things in Life* (Oxford: Oxford University Press, 2011).

26. Hurka, "Games and the Good," 233–234.

27. Richard Sennett, *The Craftsman* (London: Penguin, 2008), 20.

28. Ibid., 21.

29. Hubert Dreyfus and Sean Dorrance Kelly, *All Things Shining* (New York: Free Press, 2011), 197.

30. Ibid., 207.

31. Sennett, *The Craftsman,* 38.

32. Andrew Yang in *The War on Normal People* makes a similar point, arguing that the work ethic and the game ethic can be quite similar. The big—and critical—difference between the two is that we do not play games under conditions of economic need.

33. Christopher Yorke, "Endless Summer: What Kinds of Games Will Suits's Utopians Play?" *Journal of the Philosophy of Sport,* no. 44 (2017): 213–228.

34. M. Andrew Holowchak, "Games as Pastimes in Suits's Utopia: Meaningful Living and the Metaphysics of Leisure," *Journal of the Philosophy of Sport,* no. 34 (2007): 88–96.

35. Yorke, "Endless Summer."

36. Ibid., 217.

37. Ibid., 217

38. Ibid., 218.

39. Ibid., 222.

40. Ibid., 224.

41. This is essentially the argument in Steven Pinker, *Enlightenment Now* (London: Penguin, 2018).

42. Robert Nozick, *Anarchy, State and Utopia* (New York: Basic Books, 1974).

43. See for example these two blog posts by Thomas Jesse on Nozick's "framework for utopia": https://polyology.wordpress.com/2011/08/25/robert-nozicks

-framework-for-utopia/ and https://polyology.wordpress.com/2011/09/09/the
-internet-and-the-framework-for-utopia/. See also Runciman, *How Democracy Ends*.

44. Ralf Bader, "The Framework for Utopia," in *The Cambridge Companion to Nozick's Anarchy, State and Utopia*. ed. R. Bader and I. Meadowcroft, 255–288 (Cambridge: Cambridge University Press, 2011). References in text are to the following version: http://users.ox.ac.uk/~sfop0426/Framework%20for%20 utopia%20%28R.%20Bader%29.pdf.

45. Bader, "The Framework for Utopia," 21.

46. This is something for which Chandran Kukathas criticizes Nozick in his discussion of the meta-utopian idea. He argues that Nozick's proposal would require the creation of a rather maximalist state, not a minimal one. See Kukathas, "E Pluribus Plurum, or, How to Fail to Get to Utopia in Spite of Really Trying," in *The Cambridge Companion to Nozick's Anarchy, State, and Utopia*, ed. R. Bader and J. Meadowcroft, 289–302 (Cambridge: Cambridge University Press, 2011).

47. See, for example, https://www.seasteading.org—who, at the time of writing, were pursuing a project to build a floating city off of French Polynesia. This project has, however, recently run into difficulty: https://www .citylab.com/design/2018/04/the-unsinkable-dream-of-the-floating-city /559058/.

48. I mention him because he is a financial backer of the Seasteading Institute.

49. Robert Nozick, *The Examined Life* (New York: Simon and Schuster, 1989), 104.

50. Ben Bramble, "The Experience Machine," *Philosophy Compass*, no. 11 (2016): 136–145.

51. Felipe De Brigard, "If You Like It, Does It Matter If It's Real," *Philosophical Psychology*, no. 23 (2010): 43–57; and Dan Weijers, "Nozick's Experience Machine Is Dead, Long Live the Experience Machine!," *Philosophical Psychology*, no. 27 (2014): 513–535.

52. De Brigard, "If You Like It."

53. Weijers, "Nozick's Experience Machine."

54. Morgan Luck, "The Gamer's Dilemma: An Analysis of the Arguments for the Moral Distinction between Virtual Murder and Virtual Paedophilia," *Ethics and Information Technology*, no. 11 (2009), 31–36; Morgan Luck, "Has Ali Dissolved the Gamer's Dilemma?," *Ethics and Information Technology* (2018), DOI: 10.1007 / s10676-018-9455-7; Morgan Luck and Nathan Ellerby,

"Has Bartel Resolved the Gamer's Dilemma?," *Ethics and Information Technology*, no. 15 (2013): 229–233.

55. The Ring of Gyges is a mythical ring that renders its wearer invisible and allows them to perform immoral actions without being reprimanded or punished for them. It features noticeably in Plato's dialogue *The Republic*.

56. Morgan Luck, "The Gamer's Dilemma"; Stephanie Patridge, "The Incorrigible Social Meaning of Video Game Imagery," *Ethics and Information Technology*, no. 13 (2011): 303–312; S. Ostritsch, "The Amoralist Challenge to Gaming and the Gamer's Moral Obligation," *Ethics and Information Technology*, no. 19 (2017): 117–128; J. Tillson "Is It Distinctively Wrong to Simulate Wrongdoing?" *Ethics and Information Technology* (2018), DOI: 10.1007 / s10676-018-9463-7.

57. John Danaher, "Robotic Rape and Robotic Child Sexual Abuse: Should They Be Criminalised?" *Criminal Law and Philosophy*, no. 11 (2017): 71–95; John Danaher, "The Symbolic-Consequences Argument in the Sex Robot Debate," in *Robot Sex: Social and Ethical Implications*, ed. John Danaher and Neil McArthur, 103–132 (Cambridge, MA: MIT Press, 2017); and John Danaher, "The Law and Ethics of Virtual Assault," in *The Law of Virtual and Augmented Reality*, ed. W. Barfield and M. Blitz, 362–388 (Cheltenham: Edward Elgar Publishing, 2018).

58. Michael Pollan, *How to Change Your Mind* (London: Penguin Random House, 2017), reviews the recent scientific research on the topic.

59. One reason for this that I have not explored in this chapter is that many proponents of psychedelics see virtual reality as a way of recreating the kinds of phenomenological experiences you have whilst on psychedelic drugs. Lanier in *The Dawn of the New Everything* discusses the influence of the psychedelics movement on the early development of VR technology. David Gunkel also explores the connections at some length in "VRx: Media Technology, Drugs, and Codependency," in *Thinking Otherwise* (West Lafayette, IN: Purdue University Press, 2007).

Epilogue

1. In the story, Borges's librarian is explicit in believing that though the library may be infinite, the total number of books is not.

2. Jorge Luis Borges, *Fictions*, trans. Andrew Hurley (New York: Penguin, 1998), 69.

3. Ibid., 70.

Acknowledgments

Books would not be possible without an abundance of tolerance. I would like to thank everyone who has tolerated me over the past few years and allowed this book to become a reality.

I would like to thank Miles Brundage, Eoin Daly, Brian Earp, David Gunkel, Michael Hogan, Rónán Kennedy, Ted Kupper, Matthijs Maas, Sven Nyholm, Charles O'Mahony, Donncha O'Connell, Jon Perry, Evan Selinger, Kaj Sotala, Pip Thornton, Brian Tobin, Christopher Yorke, and anyone else with whom I have discussed the ideas or contents of this book. I'm sure I am forgetting many of you. I would particularly like to thank Kaj Sotala for permitting me to use his poem as both the title for and the epigraph to the first chapter in this book.

The original idea for this book came about as part of a research project that was funded by the Irish Research Council (New Horizons grant 2015–2017). I would like to thank the council for their support.

Ideas I have explored in posts to my blog *Philosophical Disquisitions* are expanded on in parts of this book. The section in Chapter 5 titled "Avoiding Violence and the Negative Utopia" includes text posted on January 2, 2018, as "Popper's Critique of Utopianism and Defence of Negative Utilitarianism." Portions of "The Extended Mind, Ethical Parity and the Replaceability Criterion: A Critical Analysis" posted on March 5, 2018, appear in the section of Chapter 6 titled "Replaceability and the Lightness of Being a Cyborg." Text from "Can We Derive Meaning and Value from Virtual Reality? An Analysis of the Postwork Future," posted on June 11, 2017, is used in "The Troubled Boundary between the Real and the Virtual" in Chapter 7. Lastly, the portion of Chapter 7 titled "Understanding Nozick's Meta-Utopia" incorporates text from "What Is Utopia? The Meta-Utopian Argument," posted on November 13, 2016.

I would like to thank Jeff Dean, Emeralde Jensen-Roberts, and the staff at Harvard University Press for their patience and kind assistance in the preparation of this book. It would not have been possible without them.

I would like to thank my partner, Aoife, and my parents and siblings for their continuing and unwavering support.

Finally, although I have already dedicated this book to her memory, I would also like to acknowledge the influence that my sister Sarah had on the contents of this book. Shortly before she died, Sarah told me that utopian thought needed to be rehabilitated and updated. I am sure she would have disagreed with my attempt to do exactly that, but it would have been nice to have had the opportunity to debate it with her.

Index